First World War
and Army of Occupation
War Diary
France, Belgium and Germany

7 DIVISION
Divisional Troops
Royal Army Medical Corps
23 Field Ambulance
7 October 1914 - 30 November 1917

WO95/1648/1

The Naval & Military Press Ltd
www.nmarchive.com
Published in association with The National Archives

Published by

The Naval & Military Press Ltd

Unit 10 Ridgewood Industrial Park,

Uckfield, East Sussex,

TN22 5QE England

Tel: +44 (0) 1825 749494

www.naval-military-press.com

www.nmarchive.com

This diary has been reprinted in facsimile from the original. Any imperfections are inevitably reproduced and the quality may fall short of modern type and cartographic standards.

© **Crown Copyright**
Images reproduced by permission of The National Archives, London, England, 2015.

Contents

Document type	Place/Title	Date From	Date To
Heading	WO95/1648/1		
Heading	7th Division Troops 23rd Field Ambulance Oct 1914-1917 Nov to Italy Dec 1917		
Heading	23rd Field Ambulance Oct 1914		
War Diary	Zeebrugge	07/10/1914	07/10/1914
War Diary	Burges	08/10/1914	08/10/1914
War Diary	Pteene	09/10/1914	09/10/1914
War Diary	Burges	10/10/1914	10/10/1914
War Diary	Beernem	10/10/1914	10/10/1914
War Diary	Cools Camp	12/10/1914	12/10/1914
War Diary	Roulers	13/10/1914	13/10/1914
War Diary	Ypres	14/10/1914	01/11/1914
Heading	23rd Field Amb Nov 1914		
War Diary		02/11/1914	22/11/1914
Heading	23rd Field Amb Dec 1914		
War Diary	Sailly	31/12/1914	31/12/1914
Heading	23rd Fd Amb Feb Vol XIV		
Heading	Vol II War Diary 23rd Field Ambulance January-February 1915		
War Diary	Sailly Sur La Lys	01/01/1915	28/02/1915
Heading	War Diary 23rd Field Ambulance 7th Division March 1st To March 31st Vol III		
War Diary	Sailly	01/03/1915	02/03/1915
War Diary	Vieux Berquin	03/03/1915	07/03/1915
War Diary	Neuf Berquin	08/03/1915	11/03/1915
War Diary	Estaires	11/03/1915	31/03/1915
Heading	War Diary 23rd Field Ambulance Part IV April 1st-April 30th		
War Diary		01/04/1915	30/04/1915
Heading	7th Division 23rd Field Ambulance Vol V May 1915		
War Diary		01/05/1915	10/05/1915
War Diary	Bethune	11/05/1915	31/05/1915
Miscellaneous	O.C. 23rd Field Ambulance	15/05/1915	15/05/1915
Miscellaneous	O.C. 23rd Field Ambulance	14/05/1915	14/05/1915
Operation(al) Order(s)	7th Division R.A.M.C. Operation Order No. 1 by Colonel W.H. Starr A.M.S Commanding RAM Corps 7th Division	06/05/1915	06/05/1915
Miscellaneous	O.C. 23rd F.A	13/05/1915	13/05/1915
Operation(al) Order(s)	7th Division R.A.M.C. Operation Order No.2 by Colonel W.H. Starr Commanding RAM Corps Y' Division	14/05/1915	14/05/1915
Miscellaneous	Report Of Operations Of Bearer Division 23rd Field Ambulance During Action At Festubert	16/05/1915	16/05/1915
Heading	7th Division 23rd Field Ambulance Vol VI June 1915		
War Diary	Robecq	01/06/1915	05/06/1915
War Diary	Le Plouy Farm	06/06/1915	26/06/1915
Miscellaneous	O.C. 23rd Field Ambulance	24/06/1915	24/06/1915
War Diary	La Plouy Farm	27/06/1915	30/06/1915
Miscellaneous	Report Of Operations Of 23rd Field Ambulance Bearer Division Reference Map (B Series) Bethune		

Miscellaneous	O.C. 23rd Field Ambulance	04/06/1915	04/06/1915
Operation(al) Order(s)	VIIth Division R.A.M. Corps Operation Order No.3 by Colonel W.H Starr Commanding 7th Division	13/06/1915	13/06/1915
Miscellaneous	Report Of Operations Bearer Division 23rd Field Ambulance	14/06/1915	14/06/1915
Heading	7th Division 23rd Field Ambulance Vol VII July 1915		
War Diary	La Plouy Farm	01/07/1915	01/07/1915
War Diary	La Miquellerie	02/07/1915	14/07/1915
War Diary	Paradis	14/07/1915	31/07/1915
Operation(al) Order(s)	7th Division R.A.M.C. Operation Order No.4 by Lieut Colonel E.C. Hayes R.A.M. Corps Commanding R.A.M. Corps 7th Division	10/07/1915	10/07/1915
Heading	7th Division 23rd Field Ambulance Vol VIII From 1st To 31st Aug 1915		
War Diary	Robecq	01/08/1915	17/08/1915
War Diary	Avelette	18/08/1915	31/08/1915
Miscellaneous	O.C.23rd Field Ambulance	02/06/1915	02/06/1915
Heading	7th Division 23rd Field Ambulance Vol IX Sept 1-15		
War Diary	La Miquellerie	01/09/1915	03/09/1915
War Diary	Fouquieres	04/09/1915	29/09/1915
War Diary	Annezin	30/09/1915	30/09/1915
Miscellaneous	O.C. 23 Field Ambulance	15/09/1915	15/09/1915
Operation(al) Order(s)	7th Division R.A.M.C. Operation Order No.5 by Colonel W.H. Starr Commanding R.A.M.C. 7th Division	22/09/1915	22/09/1915
Miscellaneous	O.C. 23rd Field Ambulance	29/09/1915	29/09/1915
Miscellaneous	Report On Beaver Division 23 Field Ambulance	03/10/1915	03/10/1915
Heading	7th Division 23rd Field Amb Vol XI Oct 15		
War Diary	Annezin	01/10/1915	16/10/1915
War Diary	Busnettes	17/10/1915	20/10/1915
War Diary	Bethune	21/10/1915	31/10/1915
Operation(al) Order(s)	R.A.M.C. Operation Order No.6	01/10/1915	01/10/1915
Heading	7th Division 23rd Fd Amb Nov Vol XI		
War Diary	Bethune	01/11/1915	30/11/1915
Heading	7th Div 23rd Fd Amb Dec Vol XII		
War Diary	Bethune	01/12/1915	01/12/1915
War Diary	Cense La Vallee	02/12/1915	08/12/1915
War Diary	Picquigny	09/12/1915	31/12/1915
Heading	7th Division 23rd Fd Amb Jan Vol XIII		
War Diary	Picquigny	01/01/1916	31/01/1916
Miscellaneous	O.C. 23 Field Ambce	03/01/1916	03/01/1916
Heading	7th Division 23rd Field Ambulance		
War Diary	Picquigny	01/02/1916	03/02/1916
War Diary	Mericourt	03/02/1916	29/02/1916
Heading	23 Fd Amb Vol XV		
War Diary	Mericourt	01/03/1916	31/03/1916
Heading	7th Div No.23 F. Amb April 1916		
Heading	23 Fd Amb Vol XVI		
War Diary	Mericourt	01/04/1916	30/04/1916
Heading	7th Div No.23 F Amb May1916		
War Diary	Mericourt	01/05/1916	01/06/1916
Heading	7th Division No. 23 Field Ambulance June 1916		
War Diary	Mericourt	01/06/1916	23/06/1916
War Diary	Morlancourt	24/06/1916	30/06/1916
Miscellaneous	Medical Instructions For Forthcoming Operation No.1	24/06/1916	24/06/1916
Heading	No.23 Field Ambulance July 1916		

War Diary	Morlancourt	01/07/1916	06/07/1916
War Diary	Mericourt	06/07/1916	11/07/1916
War Diary	Morlancourt	12/07/1916	22/07/1916
War Diary	Picquigny	23/07/1916	31/07/1916
Map	Map		
Miscellaneous	Report Of Operations From 1st To 5th July 1916 Of Bearer Division 23rd Field Ambulance		
Map	Map		
Miscellaneous	O.C. 23 Field Amb	11/07/1916	11/07/1916
Miscellaneous	O.C. 23 Field Ambce	11/07/1916	11/07/1916
Miscellaneous	O.C. 21 Field Ambce	12/07/1916	12/07/1916
Miscellaneous	O.C. 23 Field Ambce	12/07/1916	12/07/1916
Heading	7th Division No. 23 Field Ambulance Aug 1916		
War Diary	Picquigny	10/08/1916	12/08/1916
War Diary	Buire	13/08/1916	26/08/1916
War Diary	XVth Corps M.D.S (E19.a)	28/08/1916	31/08/1916
Heading	Cpo. 23 F.A 4th Division Sept 1916 Oct 1916		
Heading	War Diary For September 1916 23 Field Ambulance Part XXI		
War Diary	XVth Corps M.D.S Camp Edge Hill (E19a)	01/09/1916	03/09/1916
War Diary	XV Corps M.D.S (E19a)	03/09/1916	04/09/1916
War Diary	XV Corps M.D.S (F7.a)	05/09/1916	15/09/1916
War Diary	Liercourt	16/09/1916	20/09/1916
War Diary	Pont De Nieppe	21/09/1916	31/10/1916
Heading	7th Div 23rd Field Ambulance Nov 1916		
Heading	War Diary 23 Field Ambulance November 1916		
War Diary	Pont De Nieppe	01/11/1916	02/11/1916
War Diary	Caestre	02/11/1916	11/11/1916
War Diary	Nordausques	14/11/1916	22/11/1916
War Diary	Bertrancourt	22/11/1916	30/11/1916
Heading	7th Div 23rd Field Ambulance Dec 1916		
Heading	23 Field Ambulance War Diary Part XXIV December 1916		
War Diary	Bertrancourt	01/12/1916	31/12/1916
Heading	7th Div No.23 Field Ambulance Jan 1917		
Heading	War Diary Part XXV For Period Ending 31 January 1917		
War Diary	Bertrancourt	02/01/1917	23/01/1917
War Diary	Beauval	23/01/1917	30/01/1917
War Diary	Halloy	31/01/1917	31/01/1917
Heading	7th Div 23rd Field Ambulance Feb 1917		
Heading	War Diary For Period 1/2/17 To 28/2/17 Part XXVI		
War Diary	Halloy	05/02/1917	16/02/1917
War Diary	Beauval	17/02/1917	17/02/1917
War Diary	Rubempre	18/02/1917	22/02/1917
War Diary	Bertrancourt	23/02/1917	28/02/1917
Heading	7th Div No.23 Field Ambulance Mar 1917		
War Diary	Bertrancourt	01/03/1917	18/03/1917
War Diary	Red House	19/03/1917	23/03/1917
War Diary	Bucquoy	24/03/1917	31/03/1917
Heading	7th Div No.23 F.A. April 1917		
War Diary	Bucquoy	01/04/1917	29/04/1917
Heading	7th Div No.23 F.A. May 1917		
War Diary	Mory	01/05/1917	08/05/1917
War Diary	Bucquoy	08/05/1917	11/05/1917
War Diary	V Corps Rest Station (G9.c.2.6)	12/05/1917	17/05/1917

War Diary	G9.c.6.2 T Corps Rest Station	20/05/1917	30/05/1917
Heading	No.23 F.A. June 1917		
War Diary	G.9.c.6.2 V Corps Rest Station	01/06/1917	30/06/1917
Heading	7th Div No.23 F.A. July 1917		
War Diary	G.9.c.6.2 V Corps Rest Station	02/07/1917	07/07/1917
War Diary	VI Crs	09/07/1917	31/07/1917
Heading	No. 23 F.A. Aug 1917		
Heading	War Diary Part XXXII Month Ending August 1917		
War Diary	VI. Crs G9c (57c)	01/08/1917	09/08/1917
War Diary	Bellacourt	10/08/1917	31/08/1917
Heading	No. 23.7.a		
War Diary	G.23.a.7.5 (Sheet 28)	01/09/1917	02/09/1917
War Diary	Steenvoorde Q2a.55. (Sheet 27)	03/09/1917	04/09/1917
War Diary	Hondeghem	04/09/1917	13/09/1917
War Diary	Renescure	13/09/1917	14/09/1917
War Diary	Longuenesse	15/09/1917	27/09/1917
War Diary	Lumbres	28/09/1917	29/09/1917
War Diary	Bavinchove Area	29/09/1917	29/09/1917
War Diary	Meteren	30/09/1917	30/09/1917
Heading	No.23 F.a. Oct 1917		
War Diary	Meteren	01/10/1917	04/10/1917
War Diary	Chippewa Camp	05/10/1917	09/10/1917
War Diary	Hooge Crater	10/10/1917	12/10/1917
War Diary	Conqueror Camp M.2.d.8.2 (Sh 28)	13/10/1917	31/10/1917
Heading	No.23. F.A. Nov 1917		
War Diary	Moulin Fontaine	02/11/1917	02/11/1917
War Diary	Racquinghem	03/11/1917	11/11/1917
War Diary	Ouve Wirquin	12/11/1917	13/11/1917
War Diary	Fruges	14/11/1917	14/11/1917
War Diary	Anvin	15/11/1917	16/11/1917
War Diary	Anvin Ref Map Lens 1/100,000	17/11/1917	20/11/1917
War Diary	In The Train Ref Map	21/11/1917	27/11/1917
War Diary	Legnago Ref Map Ferrara 1/200,000	27/11/1917	27/11/1917
War Diary	Noventa (Ferrara) 1/200,000	28/11/1917	28/11/1917
War Diary	Boscodinanti Ref Map Padova 1/100,000	29/11/1917	29/11/1917
War Diary	Campo Ref Map Padova 1/100,000	30/11/1917	30/11/1917
Diagram etc	Diagram		

WO 95/16481

7TH DIVISION TROOPS

23RD FIELD AMBULANCE

OCT 1914 - ~~DEC 1918~~
1917 NOV

To ITALY DEC 17

23rd Field Ambulance.

Army Form C. 2118.

WAR DIARY
or
INTELLIGENCE SUMMARY
(Erase heading not required.)

Instructions regarding War Diaries and Intelligence Summaries are contained in F. S. Regs, Part II. and the Staff Manual respectively. Title pages will be prepared in manuscript.

Hour, Date, Place	Summary of Events and Information	Remarks and References to Appendices
4.0 p.m. 7 Oct. ZEEBRUGGE 9.30 p.m. 7 Oct.	Desembarked from SS Victorian. Marched to Bruges & billets of 1st Airplane (crew) 2nd Torpedo which had descended upon RS Menmap(?) on 6th Sept.	
8.20 a.m. 8 Oct. Bruges	Marched from Bruges. Beaver Strenson accompanied 3rd Brigade. Lieut. Sq. Compt. to recce surroundings of Ostend... ambulances went out... of Milne who went with Intel. ambulance wagon.(?) Intel... Rcnse town of Zandvoorde & Ghent... Lost car & rode back with Inference Chief & Staff Reps... to enter at Ostend at 8.0 am.	
7.45 a.m. 9 Oct. Steene	Remainder of Sq. stay at Steene. Lost 1 officer 10 men.	
9.0 am 9 Oct Steene 1.0 am 10 Oct. Bruges 8.0 pm 10 Oct. Beerveen	My chiefs from Steene went Ostend to Bruges billeted at Xaverien Brotherhood. 10 Night. Left Bruges at 4 pm & marched here billets at Beerveen.	
4.0 pm 12 Oct. Cols camp	Left Beerveen at 9.10 am and having billets there till 11 October arrived at Cols camp billets at 11am from ... till 12 am 21st on we move from ...	
7.30 pm 13 Oct. Roulers 8.0 am 14 Oct. YPRES	Marched from Cols camp and billets at Rue de Lace arrived from Roulers at 8.30 sent 7 men to hospital & others arrived at YPRES at 2.30 billets in Rue Riche de Claire(?) (rear) Hospital admitted 21 men & 1 German (wounded)	

Hour, Date, Place	Summary of Events and Information	Remarks and References to Appendices
October 13th	Remained at YPRES sent 35 sick to Hospital at Dunkirk	
October 14th	Bearer division under myself with 3 ambulances began 1 days Cart + water cart engaged. By 4th 24th Brigade to ZANDVOORDE were we billeted But 4 men into Hospital by the supply column to YPRES	
October 17th	Remainder of Field Ambulance joined up proceeded to billets at Ypres on YPRES ZANDVOORDE road with 4th Bn ZANDVOORDE	
October 18th	3rd Brigade went into action the morning took some prisoners and 40 Germans when they attacked 6 wounded of the Bedford Regt Bearer Staff Group brought into Hospital at 2pm on Cheluvelt Zandvoorde Road But all wounded into YPRES	
October 19th	Bearer Sub Division commenced in Billets had night at 7am 500 yards West of Camp Park at 9 Rets on YPRES- MENIN surrounded 4 Auto Ambulances marched to CHELUVELT and opened Dressing Station in School West of Church 9 wounded dealt with + despatched to YPRES Billets in Dehat during night Bearers had Bivouac bivouac at 3 from	
October 20th	Moved from Cheluvelt + opened in Chateau on Back side of YPRES-MENIN road about 4.6.12.a Two Bearer Divisions sent forward to evacuate 1 mile South of 8 Rds on YPRES-MENIN road	

Army Form C. 2118.

WAR DIARY
or
INTELLIGENCE SUMMARY
(Erase heading not required.)

Hour, Date, Place	Summary of Events and Information	Remarks and References to Appendices
October 21st	Treated several wounded which were sent into YPRES by Motor Ambulances. Two shells fired over the Chateau 2 were slight, wounded. Chateau again shelled several orders to enter further down the road. Billets etc side of road at HALTE No 7. 2 Ko Store on YPRES-MENIN road sent 1-9 Ambulances forward to KRUSEIK to bring wounded & dying from Brigade called I, wounded in camp from Field Ambulance. No orders to Brigade & no Field Ambulance to go to ZANDVOORDE until 10.30 pm. Use ZILLEBEKE.	
October 22nd	Arrived ZANDVOORDE at 1 am met infantry regiment 19th Brigade shelled from a nearby village. Detrained village to S of our own lines. Cannonade & killing village 20 of our own lines & farm. 3/4 mile south all wounded were loaded on wagons and taken to Brigade respect reported to YPRES B+C. Batteries brought to KRUSEIK & from thence returned to Field Ambulance at farm 3/4 mile south of road junction at 6 Kilo on YPRES-MENIN road. 9 wounded cases sent from YPRES our wagon Brigadier in YPRES as Town of left Staff taken in YPRES as town ambulances at 4 pm to Ambulance wagons to Braiding Station 1/2 mile to left of road to YPRES used horses out of the Ambulance wagons for the journey to station Ambulance	

WAR DIARY
or
INTELLIGENCE SUMMARY
(Erase heading not required.)

Army Form C. 2118.

Hour, Date, Place	Summary of Events and Information	Remarks and References to Appendices

Oct 23rd troop train so latter were exhausted after their long journey. remainder of same place. Sent A Regt. for senior Dressing Station & relieve C.B. & to act 3pm. Regt. left train returned on their packhorses. Very little) they thought. 13th moved 18 men also 8 sick men. Joy Staples all there in two far gone to YPRES. But one brig. on into ZANDVOORDE to collect wounded. (from III Cavalry Division which I believe a few) (were returning and reported that we gun had been sent into YPRES. Sent train, 12 men & A&B Recov. left during date forward to reliev a new duty to presumy? Sketch to all sort of wellarment have their places receiving shelters are required on same place.

Oct 24th About 100 wounded were evacuated during the night of 23-24 only about 30 came altogether) in trenches this morning and these were only evacuated) after the Bearing Station had always all 18 Aid Stations Bearing Station to now under rifle fire to 300 yds to shelter set in a new Bearing Station ½ mile from door Direction South East of Calvaire. At 12.30 became

Army Form C. 2118.

WAR DIARY
or
INTELLIGENCE SUMMARY
(Erase heading not required.)

Instructions regarding War Diaries and Intelligence Summaries are contained in F. S. Regs., Part II. and the Staff Manual respectively. Title pages will be prepared in manuscript.

Hour, Date, Place	Summary of Events and Information	Remarks and References to Appendices
Oct. 31. 9.30 A.M.	Notification from ADMS that 40 wagons are on route & in charge of Capt Phillips 21-3d wounded to be adjusted after 6 p.m. Sent Capt Hugh 1 P Tent Division to take over Dressing station so his my executive were expected to to dressing station at 5.30 p.m. and arrangd for wounded to be evacuated from 1st A.S. Phils & Met Ambulance incapable & conducted them to Dressing Station. Capt Hugh informed me that there was about 30 cases to be evacuated. I advd him to collect all sitting cases at housing 7a horse teams & Ambulances wagons for their purpose and to meet the convoy near cross roads Strumbusts YPRES till 9 p.m. and they had not arrived. Sent 10 p.m.	
7.0 p.m	went to meet wagons informed to above and waited	
10.0 p.m	with clerical for wagons to meet them arrived at left to	
11.0 p.m	returned to Head Quarter of Unit. Orderly from HQ Coy with 4 wagons arrived at Camp instructed him to proceed to Dressing	Col Abbott

(9 26 6) W 257—976 100,000 4/12 H W V 79

WAR DIARY
or
INTELLIGENCE SUMMARY

Army Form C. 2118.

Hour, Date, Place	Summary of Events and Information	Remarks and References to Appendices
12 midnight 24/25th	An officer & 10 wagons arrived unit Kenyro sent to him to precise B dressing station	
Oct 25th 9.0	Visited dressing station. Capt Wright informed me that he had evacuated 119 wounded during the night. That 4th sect of wagon repaired to or about 24th, and had come thro' at 2.80 & 3.20 respects & sent that everyone of his wounded had been sent clear (?) & that by 7.30 dressing station was clear. 12 by my own cars & 10 others. by his cars & has been brought in. I immediately arranged to dispatch 4 gmy & 2 sitting in ambulance wagon with 1 Interpretation and sent to Assnt Head Qrs for extra wagons which were necessary to clear supply to come to dressing station on all ways. 12 sitting cars were chalked down in the wagon & more cars arriving in the meanwhile.	
2·30	Returned to Asnt Head Qrs & found that ambulance wagons had just arrived from R E S. Further fresh roads & sent 4 wagons over	

Army Form C. 2118.

WAR DIARY
or
INTELLIGENCE SUMMARY
(Erase heading not required.)

Instructions regarding War Diaries and Intelligence Summaries are contained in F. S. Regs., Part II, and the Staff Manual respectively. Title pages will be prepared in manuscript.

Hour, Date, Place	Summary of Events and Information	Remarks and References to Appendices
Oct 25th	to clear Dressing Station. Stretchers Major Benson & Tent division carried to relieve B. Tent division with a further supply of dressing, stretchers etc. Relieved A. Tent division by B. 7.30 pm went to H.Q. for instructions & got 15 supply wagons to evacuate wounded or assist at Dressing Station from shrapnel & rifle fire. Found dugs bomb some not killed & rifle fire. Sent Bearer & Transport to Dressing Station & wounded collected. Received heavy attacks at 1 am.	
Oct 26th	25, 26 despatched 76 wounded & supply wagon used 10 hr water on train at 7.30 am 4 wounded Officers sent up by Ambulance. Got away further. Was later transported men receiving during the day at 12 on duty bearing station shelled as Major Benson sent off 7 wagon loads with wounded on their return. Dressing station just to demand men killed 4 men and horses of one road away left the coolies. All entrance Coolie will wounded Chiens also

W 257—976   103,000   4/12   H W V   79 / 3298

WAR DIARY
or
INTELLIGENCE SUMMARY
(Erase heading not required.)

Army Form C. 2118.

Hour, Date, Place	Summary of Events and Information	Remarks and References to Appendices
Oct 27th	Who were badly hit were left behind & later came [in later] in a fine state & easily th CHELUVELT & ANDOORDE rd. Thus were remnants of the entirety of our Brigade. Unit supposed to be about YPRES- MENIN road front 60 wounded Chateau near & the time Sent 60 wounded into YPRES by light wagons at 4 a.m. Received at Chateau all day yd 4 hrs received orders from A.D.M.S to send out bearer Sub division to ZILLEBEKE to collect wounded Sent 1 A.B.S.D under I. Webb	
Oct 28th	remained at Chateau Looking ll. Thr morning Genl Major Brown to reconnoitre from ahead he had left – The l Brady wounded men when we were on the 28th He passed there that it the farm 1 day had obers The remainder were very safe and that there was well attended to by Pte Barns R.A.M.C. who staying with them and of then by wishing the gun coming from trolley the entire area and actively fire whenever he could. The action was very localised. He spent the area which was lying with the enemy lines thir unbur were even wounded & dewind (YPRES)	

WAR DIARY
or
INTELLIGENCE SUMMARY
(Erase heading not required.)

Army Form C. 2118.

Hour, Date, Place	Summary of Events and Information	Remarks and References to Appendices
Oct 29th 1914	Proceed to farm 300 yds east of Kruiseik but thought it Commander of an Infantry Battalion. Obtained A Tent instruments, Only two horses were available, to horses too much so it was found necessary to fetch the remaining Tent as a reserve.	
Oct 30th 1914	Told no more lines about to come to was ordered to proceed to 9 & I boys were relief from Kryles Col came in. They were sent up to take up cover at ZANDVOORDE. Reported to	
Oct 31st 1914	Dealt with 242 cases during the last 24 hours. At 1.30 farm surrounding country heavily shelled Was being packed up and departed off. Ambulance horses wounded, one killed. Left the Brown + the Rear Section behind. This took running near Railway crossing in YPRES MENIN road. Proceeded with Tent Section toward Becheleure, Picked up Ambulance began on YPRES and sent them back to Major Brown. Went with Bibble near Belle Birol.	
Nov. 1st 1914	Returned to railway crossing on YPRES MENIN road. Major Brown reported that killed collected 150 wounded during the night.	

Nov 1914

23rd. Field Amb

Army Form C. 2118.

WAR DIARY
or
INTELLIGENCE SUMMARY
(Erase heading not required.)

Instructions regarding War Diaries and Intelligence Summaries are contained in F. S. Regs., Part II. and the Staff Manual respectively. Title pages will be prepared in manuscript.

Hour, Date, Place	Summary of Events and Information	Remarks and References to Appendices
Nov. 2nd 1914	About 40 cases all with cartwright as far as we were was overcrowded. Alarmed Germans in Ahmid & move to a fresh situation stood at Via mill near YPRES with a hurs fence & Army Station. Put all 3 Peace Pensioners out.	
Nov. 3rd 1914	Peace Pensioners returned at 5.30 having collected 92 wounded wounded in more for all day. Sent out Peace Pensioners at 7 pm.	
Nov. 4th 1914	20 wounded dealt with yesterday. Peace returned at 11 pm. Remained in camp. Have during the day. Peace wounded 9 deaths. Out of 17 horses 12 & 6 ambulance wagons drivers went out at 7 pm with 15 wounded men & all 3 had left. Put 3 Peace drivers out with ambulance wagons at 7 pm from Reeves asked & ambulance came & to be attached to Yorkshire Brigade.	
Nov. 5th 1914	Still in same place only 15 wounded men called.	
Nov. 6th 1914	12 wounded were called & today. 90 wounded were dealt with at the Evening Station down yesterday.	
Nov. 7th 1914 11. am.	Germany on same place again today. Germany all wounded. Note to 3 Field Ambulances to evacuate to YOCE to open in Ypres. Ordered to proceed to YPRES- BAILLEUL road (Belgians on YPRES PH[-----] on arriving 3/4	

WAR DIARY
or
INTELLIGENCE SUMMARY

(Erase heading not required.)

Army Form C. 2118.

Hour, Date, Place	Summary of Events and Information	Remarks and References to Appendices
Nov. 8th 1914	9 a.m. rode from LOCRE. Was ordered to finds wounded who went OUTPRE & MONTNOIR and approached LOCRE from South. Arrived at LOCRE at 10 p.m. Received orders to proceed to METEREN and join 2gr Inf Brigade. Opened a Reception Hospital in School on road running N from METEREN	
Nov. 14th 1914	Remained at METEREN till the morning when we marched at 8 a.m. via BAILLEUL - STEENWERCK - CROIX-DU-BAC to BAC ST MAUR went into close billets. Sent 2 officers & 2 NCOs to accompany bearer section of 19th Field Ambulance to learn position of trenches as 20th [?] Brigade were relieving 19th Brigade.	
Nov. 15th 1914	Still in close billets. Sent out 1 Bearer Subdivision to collect wounded from trenches with instructions to evacuate into 22 Field Ambulance which had opened at SAILLY	
Nov. 17th 1914	Moved to SAILLY and opened a hospital in the Mairie	
Nov. 18th	Establish advanced Bearing Station at cross roads on Rue du Quesnes	

Army Form C. 2118.

WAR DIARY
or
INTELLIGENCE SUMMARY
(Erase heading not required.)

Instructions regarding War Diaries and Intelligence Summaries are contained in F. S. Regs., Part II. and the Staff Manual respectively. Title pages will be prepared in manuscript.

Hour, Date, Place	Summary of Events and Information	Remarks and References to Appendices
Nov 19th	There was a hard frost yesterday and one of Fort Bete was admitted. Heavy snow.	
Nov 21st	Several more of Fort Bete have been admitted all wounded & sick have been evacuated daily to MERVILLE	
Nov 22nd	Two Motor Ambulances had night to evacuate sick & wounded from Advanced Dressing Station to Hospital. 46 cases of Frost bite admitted since last night. Owing to the numbers of such it was found necessary to open another 25 beds in a second hospital.	

23rd FIELD AMB

DEC 1914

Dec 31st
Still

The Ambulance has resumed its daily doing ordinary hospital work all such & wounded not likely to be fit for duty soon being evacuated to MERVILLE.

Since the arrival of the ambulance on Oct 7th have passed through, or have remained, 86 Officers & 2512 men
a large number were collected by the ambulance & sent down to Clearing Hospitals. Besides running a send about to Clearing Hospitals without passing through the Ambulance

[signatures]

7

23 Jd Amb
Feb
Vol XIV

121/4634

Vol. II

War Diary.

23rd Field Ambulance

January & February, 1915

WAR DIARY or INTELLIGENCE SUMMARY

Army Form C. 2118

(Erase heading not required.)

Instructions regarding War Diaries and Intelligence Summaries are contained in F. S. Regs., Part II. and the Staff Manual respectively. Title pages will be prepared in manuscript.

Hour, Date, Place	Summary of Events and Information	Remarks and References to Appendices
Pailly sur L. Llys. January 1st	12 sick men admitted. 14 evacuated to Thieville	
2nd	13 sick & 2 wounded admitted. 5 evacuated.	
3rd	15 sick admitted 20 evacuated.	
4th	16 sick admitted 15 evacuated	
5th	9 sick " 7 "	
6th	20 sick & one wounded admitted 17 sick & 1 wounded evacuated	
7th	22 sick admitted 27 evacuated	
8th	19 sick " 11 "	
9th	31 sick & 3 wounded admitted. 32 sick & 3 wounded evacuated	
10th	34 sick & 1 wounded " 20 sick & 1 wounded evacuated	
11th	27 sick admitted 28 evacuated.	
12th	37 sick & 2 wounded admitted 39 sick & 2 wounded evacuated	
13th	19 sick & 1 wounded admitted 27 sick & 1 wounded evacuated	
	Owing to the large number of men being sent sick with "Itch" & scabies, & two divided to open a special place for the treatment - according to a known reliable cure and every sergeant made by Bottin & Salicylic, and all patients suffering from this complaint are sent there & are detained for	
14th	one or two nights, and today 20 men sick & 2 wounded admitted 19 sick & 1 wounded evacuated	

Army Form C. 2118.

WAR DIARY
or
INTELLIGENCE SUMMARY
(Erase heading not required.)

Instructions regarding War Diaries and Intelligence Summaries are contained in F. S. Regs., Part II. and the Staff Manual respectively. Title pages will be prepared in manuscript.

Hour, Date, Place	Summary of Events and Information	Remarks and References to Appendices
Sailly sur la Lys Jan 15.	16 sick & 1 wounded admitted. 15 sick & 1 wounded evacuated.	
16	21 sick, 1 - - 15 " 1 " "	
17	14 " 4 " - " - " "	
18	11 " admitted. 18 " 4 " "	
19	12 sick & 1 wounded admitted. 20 sick evacuated. C section under orders from A.D.M.S. sent 7 officers (convalescent) to NEUF BERQUIN to establish a convalescent Hospital for the slighter cases of sick from the whole Division.	
20	25 sick & 4 wounded admitted. 10 sick & 1 wounded evacuated.	
21	12 sick admitted. 6 sick & 3 wounded evacuated to Merville. 10 sick evacuated to NEUF BERQUIN.	
22	13 sick, 1 wounded admitted. 14 sick & 1 wounded evacuated to MERVILLE. 8 sick to NEUF BER QUIN.	
23	17 sick admitted. 17 evacuated to MERVILLE. 12 sick to NEUF BER QUIN.	
24	96 sick, 2 wounded admitted. 13 sick (wounded) evacuated to MERVILLE. 7 sick to NEUF BERQUIN.	
25	9 sick, 1 wounded admitted. 12 sick & 1 wounded evacuated to Merville. 6 got to hospitals.	
26	25 sick, 1 wounded admitted. 8 sick, 1 wounded to Merville. 7 to hospitals.	
27	10 " 4 " 11 " 3 " " 14 "	
28	7 " 6 " 1 " 8 " "	
29	6 " 5 " 5 " 1 " none	
30	6 " 3 " " 4 " 3 " 1	
31	10 " 4 " " 3 " 3 " 4	

H W V /10 — 79
3298

Army Form C. 2118.

WAR DIARY
or
INTELLIGENCE SUMMARY
(Erase heading not required.)

Instructions regarding War Diaries and Intelligence Summaries are contained in F. S. Regs., Part II. and the Staff Manual respectively. Title pages will be prepared in manuscript.

Hour, Date, Place	Summary of Events and Information	Remarks and References to Appendices
SAILLY SUR LA LYS, Feb. 1	Back 1 wounded admitted 5 sick 3 wounded evacuated to MERVILLE Band to Hosp/Boyen 7 "	
2	13 " 1 " " 5 " " " " 3 "	
3	3 " 2 " " 1 " " " " 4 "	
4	9 " 2 " " 5 " " " " 8 "	
5	13 " 3 " " 2 " " " " 6 " 10 " 1 wounded to Hosp/Boyen	
6	6 " 9 " " 8 " " " " 5 " to "	
7	12 " 3 " " 3 " " " " 5 " 1 wounded "	
8	8 " 2 " " 1 " " " " 6 " lot Hosp/Boyen	
9	14 " 0 " " 4 " " " " 3 "	
10	8 " 4 " " 6 " " " " 7 " 8 wounded "	
11	11 " 6 " " 4 " " " " 7 " to Hosp/Boyen	
12	12 " 2 " " 3 " " " " 11 "	
13	18 " 0 " " 6 " " " " 6 "	
14	9 " 4 " " 2 0# " " " 7 "	
15	18 " 4 " " 5 " " " " 9 "	
16	16 " 3 " " 7 " " " " 8 "	
17	11 " 9 " " 4 " " " " 5 "	
18	8 " 1 " " 4 2 " " "	
19	11 " 4 " " 3 2 " " "	
20	14 " 3 " " 6 1 " " "	

Army Form C. 2118.

WAR DIARY
or
INTELLIGENCE SUMMARY
(Erase heading not required.)

Instructions regarding War Diaries and Intelligence Summaries are contained in F. S. Regs., Part II. and the Staff Manual respectively. Title pages will be prepared in manuscript.

Hour, Date, Place		Summary of Events and Information	Remarks and References to Appendices
SAILLY	Feb. 21	28 sick, 5 wounded admitted	Back 4 wounded evacuated to MERVILLE 12 and 2 NEUF BERQUIN
	22	14 " 3 " "	2, 3 "	9 "
	23	13 - 2 " "	12 " 2 "	9 "
	24	11 " 4 " "	2 " 4 "	6 "
	25	8 " 2 " "	3 " 1 "	7 "
	26	16 " 4 " "	6 " 4 "	9 "
	27	14 " 7 " "	4 " 4 "	7 "
	28	26 " 2 " "	5 " 3 "	8 "

Arranged with O.C. 22nd Field Ambulance to take in all cases from 22 Inf. Brigade as he was closing to 89th
cases admitted today are from 22nd Inf. Brigade.

[signature]
O.C. 22nd Field Ambulance

WAR DIARY

23rd Field Ambulance

7th Division

March 1st to March 31st

Vol. III

WAR DIARY
or
INTELLIGENCE SUMMARY

Army Form C. 2118.

Hour, Date, Place	Summary of Events and Information	Remarks and References to Appendices
SAILLY March 1st " 2nd	40 sick admitted. 1 evacuated to MERVILLE. 20 to NEUF BERQUIN. Div. Brigade revised, commanding 20th Brigade and arranged with him re 7 Medical arrangements. 20th Brigade during move. 1 [?] into St Omer's Rouen histerain ordered to move on to adjoining Dressing Station RHM evening of 4th together with 8 Horse Ambulance + 2 Motor Ambulances & 1 water cart. All sick from the Brigade to be collected by Motor Ambulance and conveyed to No 22 Field Ambulance in ESTAIRES. The remaining [?] of [?] Rouen bit Divisions ordered to march into SAILLY and arrive at 9 a.m. March 3rd. Closed up Tent Section in Horse mentioned on Nos 22nd and handed over this Horse to No 3 Cavalry Field Ambulance. 6 sick admitted. 11 evacuated to MERVILLE. 17 to NEUFBERQUIN	
VIEUX BERQUIN March 3rd	Handed over buildings in SAILLY to No 3 Field Ambulance Cavalry Division during having admitted 11 sick + evacuated 8 to MERVILLE + 9 to NEUFBERQUIN	

WAR DIARY or INTELLIGENCE SUMMARY

Army Form C. 2118.

Hour, Date, Place	Summary of Events and Information	Remarks and References to Appendices
VIEUX BERQUIN March 3rd	Having finished section of being joined by C Beuvry Sub Division, A Section, B Sub Division & C Beuvry Sub Division marched at 10 am from BOLLIEU to VIEUX BERQUIN arriving at 12.30. Opened 1 Tent Sub Division in Girls School. Everyday accommodation for 50 Beds.	
MARCH 4th	6 cases admitted, no sick evacuated	
5th	10 sick admitted, personnel evacuated to MERVILLE 4 to NEUF BERQUIN	
6th	16 " 7 " " 4 " 5 "	
7th	18 " 9 " " 4 " 4 "	
5. p.m.	Received orders to leave J.A. to NEUF BERQUIN by 5 p.m. 8th inst.	
NEUF BERQUIN 8th 11 am	Read with A.D.M.S. 7 Division to reconnoitre ground for dressing station in the event of an attack	
2.30.	Left VIEUX BERQUIN and march to NEUF BERQUIN arrived there 3.30. wound when 2 Cheu. Evacuated 1 Horse. Hugh Renne had already forced St carry the cert. All such from 28 Brigade three orders to the rear & 22 Suchlinkelnlen	

Army Form C 2118.

WAR DIARY
or
INTELLIGENCE SUMMARY
(Erase heading not required.)

Instructions regarding War Diaries and Intelligence Summaries are contained in F. S. Regs, Part II. and the Staff Manual respectively. Title pages will be prepared in manuscript.

Hour, Date, Place	Summary of Events and Information	Remarks and References to Appendices
Neuf-Berquin. March 9th	Took over buildings ex Boys' & girls' Schools & Convent, to form a main Dressing Station. Arranged for Bearer Division & Stretcher Sqds. R.A.T. to enter Camp under Lt Lionel R.A.M.C. to accompany 25th Inf Brigade.	Copy of orders attached A
5.30 a.m. March 10th	Bearer division with 7 Horse Ambulance wagons & Breton Lightload & Water Cart under command of Lieut. & Machie Rume with Sad medl. Sects. Noch & Sch. Trimeth left NEUF BERQUIN to join 20th Inf Brigade. remainder of field Ambulance remained at NEUF BERQUIN.	
9.0 a.m. "	Went forward to see how Bearer were getting on found them halted at Pte Croix waiting to move on to Cameron Lane. Remained with them.	
1.45 p.m.	Bearer division moved off in rear of grenades Guards to Cameron Lane	

WAR DIARY
or
INTELLIGENCE SUMMARY
(Erase heading not required.)

Army Form C. 2118.

Hour, Date, Place	Summary of Events and Information	Remarks and References to Appendices
3 pm. March 10th	Took over from at NW end of CAMERON LANE as dressing station & established bearer then for the night as 20th Brigade advanced in reserve	
5 pm. " "	Brought up all horse ambulances and parked them in field near dressing station. Left Lieut Mackie in charge & returned to NEUF BERQUIN. Lieut RUSSELL RAMC reported for duty	
9.30 am March 11th	Went up to dressing station. Found Bearers had moved to SE end of Cameron lane and established dressing station there. Lieut. WEDD & A bearer sub division had gone forward with Brigade and were collecting casualties along the RUE TILLELOY. Lieut MACKIE & B bearer subdivision was then proceeding to RUE BACQUEROT to collect casualties of 6 R GORDONS. Arranged for motor ambulances to proceed	

WAR DIARY
or
INTELLIGENCE SUMMARY
(Erase heading not required.)

Army Form C. 2118.

Hour, Date, Place	Summary of Events and Information	Remarks and References to Appendices
9 a.m. March 11th (cont)	from ESTAIRES along ESTAIRES-LABASSÉ road to PONT LOGY to collect wounded collected three by Barin	
12.30 pm March 11th	returned to NEUF BERQUIN detailed Lieut C.D. BUCKLEY to proceed to 2nd GORDONS in relief of Lieut. PRIESTLY R.A.M.C. who was wounded. Lieut-Major G.H. BROWN went to Advanced Dressing Station as the Casualties were heavy.	For report of Barins Station from there time see B
5.15. pm. March 11th	Received orders to close Field Station at NEUF BERQUIN on the area of fifteen hospital men to Colours Station and to proceed with ESTAIRES	
8.30 pm "	marched to ESTAIRES	
ESTAIRES 10.30 " "	Arrived ESTAIRES parked wagons in Square near church in the GRANDE RUE & went into	

Army Form C 2118.

WAR DIARY
or
INTELLIGENCE SUMMARY
(Erase heading not required.)

Instructions regarding War Diaries and Intelligence Summaries are contained in F. S. Regs., Part II. and the Staff Manual respectively. Title pages will be prepared in manuscript.

Hour, Date, Place	Summary of Events and Information	Remarks and References to Appendices
10.30 pm March 11th	Billets —	
8.30 am March 12th	Detailed Tent. Russell RAMC to proceed to 2nd Border Regt in relief of Lt. Crawley RAMC who was wounded.	
9.30 am "	Dispatched Capt. WRIGHT. RAMC & B Tent Sub Division to assist No 6 Casualty Clearing Station, sent 2 N.C.Os & 6 men. C Tent Sub Division to assist No 21. Field Ambulance the remainder of C Tent Sub Division were sent to No 22 Field Ambulance. The remainder of Ambulance remained in Billet in ESTAIRES with wagon packed loaded.	
11.30 am	Arranged for the horses of Horse Ambulance to be changed for those ordered by the G.S. Wagon as former had been working all night. Went to 22 FIELD AMBULANCE to assist	

Army Form C. 2118.

WAR DIARY
or
INTELLIGENCE SUMMARY
(Erase heading not required.)

Instructions regarding War Diaries and Intelligence Summaries are contained in F. S. Regs, Part II. and the Staff Manual respectively. Title pages will be prepared in manuscript.

Hour, Date, Place	Summary of Events and Information	Remarks and References to Appendices
7.15 March 12th p.m.	LIEUT. S. WEBB. H.W & HOWLETT L.W. RAMC reported for duty. (Detached) Lt Webb to work on No 22 & Lt Howlett to work on 21.	
8.30 p.m.		
10.0 p.m.	CAPT WRIGHT & Bearer Tent SubDivision from MERVILLE. head over to No 22 to await & work 9 train till 1.30 am	
8.30 am Sund 13th	Sent Capt Wright & Nurses to No 22 with a detachment of C Tent SubDivision and Lt Wills & detachment of A Tent SubDivision to work on No 21.	
2.0 p.m.	Received orders to open extra Tent Division to in buildings in ESTAIRES	
7.0 p.m.	commenced to receive wounded	
8 am Mond 14th	145 cases admitted during the night. 75 of these were evacuated during the night	

WAR DIARY
or
INTELLIGENCE SUMMARY
(Erase heading not required.)

Army Form C. 2118.

Hour, Date, Place	Summary of Events and Information	Remarks and References to Appendices
11.30 am March 16	LIEUT H.W. POWELL & LIEUT G.B. HORROCKS R.A.M.C. reported for duty.	
4.0 pm " "	The remainder of the wounded admitted last night were evacuated during the afternoon	
9.0 am March 18.	89 sick & wounded & 15 wounded Germans were admitted during the night 36 of the wounded were evacuated at 7 am.	
12. 20 pm " "	The remaining sick & wounded 9 were evacuated by ambulance train & Motor Lorry.	
4.0 pm " "	Major Brown with Sergt Wedd & Sinnett returned & reports that the dressing station was closed and the Rendez-vous house (est-----billets) near LEVANTIE. Lieut Mischen & Sgt. remained with the Reserve	
1.30 pm March 18	received orders to take over the Advanced dressing station in LEVANTIE from No 21 F.A.	

WAR DIARY
or
INTELLIGENCE SUMMARY
(Erase heading not required.)

Army Form C. 2118.

Instructions regarding War Diaries and Intelligence Summaries are contained in F. S. Regs., Part II. and the Staff Manual respectively. Title pages will be prepared in manuscript.

Hour, Date, Place	Summary of Events and Information	Remarks and References to Appendices
2.30 pm March 15th	The Bearer division took over Bearing Station from the 21 field ambulance	
4 pm March 16th	During the preceding 24 hours 47 sick & 5 wounded were admitted and 20 sick & 2 wounded were evacuated to MERVILLE. 5 men discharged to duty	
4 pm March 17th	During the preceding 24 hours 23 sick were admitted and 36 sick & 3 wounded evacuated. 16 discharged to duty. LT. HOWLETT R.A.M.C. was ordered to return to BOULOGNE	
4 pm March 18th	LT WEBB R.A.M.C. proceeded to 2/GORDONS in relief of LT BUCKLEY R.A.M.C. who rejoined the field ambulance. LT WEDD R.A.M.C. proceeded to the 2/SCOTS GUARDS in relief of CAPT HEUSTON R.A.M.C. who was placed on the sick list.	
6 pm March 18th	20th Brigade took over the line of trenches near RUE TILLELOY. The bearer division moved from LEVANTIE and established a dressing	

(9 26 6) W 257—76 100,000 4/12 H W V 79/3298

Army Form 2118.

WAR DIARY
or
INTELLIGENCE SUMMARY
(Erase heading not required.)

Hour, Date, Place	Summary of Events and Information	Remarks and References to Appendices
March 19th 4. p.m.	Station at cross junction at A on square M6d 1-40000 sheet 36 FRANCE. During the day 64 sick + 7 wounded were admitted + 20 sick + 6 wounded were evacuated to No 7 C C Station 2 BROOKE McCORMACK wheeled stretchers were received and sent out to Brewn-Borrou on four ambulances an also sent out to Rue Borron to remain with them to evacuate any old cases that might arise. The Motor Ambulances were allowed to proceed to 1st Aid Posts & Dressing Stations at 11 am & 6.30 pm 10 sick & 1 wounded were admitted 85 sick and 1 wounded were evacuated to MERVILLE	

WAR DIARY
or
INTELLIGENCE SUMMARY

(Erase heading not required.)

Army Form C. 2118.

Hour, Date, Place	Summary of Events and Information	Remarks and References to Appendices
4 pm March 20th	17 sick & 4 wounded were admitted. 13 sick & 1 wounded were evacuated to Merville	
4 pm March 21st	26 sick & 2 wounded were admitted. 20 sick & 5 wounded were evacuated to Merville	
4 pm March 22nd	22 sick & 2 wounded admitted. 18 sick & 1 wounded evacuated to MERVILLE	
4 pm March 23rd	29 sick & 4 wounded admitted. 18 sick & 1 wounded evacuated to MERVILLE	
10 am March 24th	Received orders to take over buildings in LA GORGUE at present occupied by No 26 Field Ambulance by 3 pm 25ᵗʰ. Went to enquire at what time the VIII Division 26 were moving, they replied they were not moving till 28ᵗʰ. Relieved A.D.M.S. Division on the matter. I was finally arranged the move was not to take place till 28 & 29ᵗʰ. 18 sick & 3 wounded were admitted. 7 sick & 5 wounded were evacuated to MERVILLE	

WAR DIARY
or
INTELLIGENCE SUMMARY
(Erase heading not required.)

Army Form C. 2118.

Hour, Date, Place	Summary of Events and Information	Remarks and References to Appendices
2 p.m. March 25th	Received letter that 20th Brigade were being relieved by 21st Brigade the evening & received orders that Leicesters Regiment 1st Division should move to LA GORGUE at once and reinforce the 1st Battalion. The Bean Division the remainder of this Division to remain in Divisional Station and collect. Rec'd orders from Trench till 10 a.m. March 26th when they were to hand over to Bean Division of 21st F.A. and proceed to LA GORGUE	
4 p.m. March 25th	16 sick + 4 wounded admitted. 13 sick + 2 wounded evacuated to MERVILLE. Lt. Powell was ordered to take over hospital charge of Lavender St.	
8.30 a.m. March 26th	proceeded to LA GORGUE and took over Chas. H. Teacur. LECONTE	

Army Form C.2118.

WAR DIARY
or
INTELLIGENCE SUMMARY
(Erase heading not required.)

Instructions regarding War Diaries and Intelligence Summaries are contained in F. S. Regs., Part II. and the Staff Manual respectively. Title pages will be prepared in manuscript.

Hour, Date, Place	Summary of Events and Information	Remarks and References to Appendices
12.30 pm August 26th 4 pm August 26th	As a Hospital all slight cases will require evacuation were transferred to ESTAIRES from Steam convoy at 12.30 pm 18 sick & 2 wounded were admitted. Sent 2 wounded were evacuated to MERVILLE	
4 pm August 27th	38 sick were admitted. 12 sick were evacuated to MERVILLE	
4 pm August 28th	96 sick & 1 wounded admitted 27 sick & 1 wounded evacuated to MERVILLE	
4 pm August 29th	Obtained permission to take over buildings in the field adjoining Chateau LECONTE and prepare them for the reception of wounded in case of an action. 34 sick admitted & 14 evacuated to MERVILLE Sent 60 Havresack of SHELL DRESSINGS containing SHELL DRESSINGS.	
August 30th	Issued 20 Havresack of SHELL Dressings to the Staff Battalion on the bigride in stead of J.S.	

(9 26 6) W 257—076 100,000 4/12 H W V 3298

Army Form C. 2118.

WAR DIARY
or
INTELLIGENCE SUMMARY
(Erase heading not required.)

Instructions regarding War Diaries and Intelligence Summaries are contained in F. S. Regs., Part II. and the Staff Manual respectively. Title pages will be prepared in manuscript.

Hour, Date, Place	Summary of Events and Information	Remarks and References to Appendices
March 30th	Received orders to convert buildings in full into convalescent Rest Station for minor cases.	
4 pm March 25th	96 sick admitted. 24 evacuated to MERVILLE	
March 31st 10 am	Opened hill as convalescent station. 15 patients from 21 & 22. F.A.	
" 2. am.	Dispatched A Bearer Sub Division to take over buildings in RUE BAQUEROT previously occupied by a dressing station of 20th INF BRIGADE now going into the trenches in the evening.	
" 4. pm. 27 sick admitted. 14 evacuated to MERVILLE		

H. Wray Jack
F. W. Ramme
O.C. 23rd Field Ambulance

War Diary

23rd Field Ambulance

PART IV

April. 1st – April. 30th

J Hanford
Lt Col RAMC
OC 23rd Field Ambulance

Army Form C. 2118.

WAR DIARY
or
INTELLIGENCE SUMMARY

(Erase heading not required.)

Instructions regarding War Diaries and Intelligence Summaries are contained in F. S. Regs, Part II. and the Staff Manual respectively. Title pages will be prepared in manuscript.

Hour, Date, Place	Summary of Events and Information	Remarks and References to Appendices
4 pm April 1st	39 sick & 1 wounded admitted. 28 sick & 1 wounded evacuated to MERVILLE. 3 sick admitted to the Convalescent Section. 3 cases evacuated to MERVILLE	
4 pm April 2nd	1 Off 29 OR sick & 8 wounded admitted. 1 Off 20 OR sick & 7 wounded evacuated to MERVILLE. 7 sick admitted to Convalescent Section. 1 evacuated to MERVILLE	
4 pm April 3rd	19 sick & 3 wounded admitted. 19 sick & 3 wounded evacuated to MERVILLE. 4 sick admitted to C. Section. 1 sick evacuated to MERVILLE	
4 pm April 4th	1 Off 23 OR sick 7 wounded admitted to MERVILLE. 1 Off 14 OR sick & 5 wounded evacuated to MERVILLE. 7 sick admitted 2 evacuated to pm Conv. Section	
4 pm April 5th	20 sick & 9 wounded admitted. 13 sick & 9 wounded evacuated to MERVILLE. 14 sick admitted to Conval. Section. 5 evacuated to MERVILLE	

WAR DIARY
or
INTELLIGENCE SUMMARY
(Erase heading not required.)

Army Form C. 2118.

Instructions regarding War Diaries and Intelligence Summaries are contained in F. S. Regs., Part II. and the Staff Manual respectively. Title pages will be prepared in manuscript.

Hour, Date, Place	Summary of Events and Information	Remarks and References to Appendices
4 pm April 6th	24 sick & 9 wounded admitted 19 sick & 7 wounded evacuated to MERVILLE. 7 sick admitted to Convel. Station. 2 evacuated to MERVILLE	
4 pm April 7th	90 sick & 4 wounded admitted 8 sick & 3 wounded evacuated to MERVILLE. 4 sick admitted to Convalescent H. 3 evacuated to MERVILLE	
5.30 pm April 7th	9 Welsh reported two severe with A. Team Ambulances having landed over the evening station on RUE DE BACQUEROT & 22 Inf. Brigade. Advance Dressing & Wounded admitted. 15 sick 6 wounded evacuated to MERVILLE.	
4 pm April 8th	61 sick & 5 wounded admitted. 3 evacuated to MERVILLE. 7 sick admitted to Convel. Sta. 3 evacuated to MERVILLE	
4 pm April 9th	32 sick admitted. 16 evacuated to MERVILLE. 3 sick admitted to Convalescent. 3 evacuated to MERVILLE	
4 pm April 10th	1 Off. 21 O.R. admitted. 1 Off. & 16 O.R. evacuated to MERVILLE. 5 sick admitted to C.S. 2 evacuated to MERVILLE	

WAR DIARY
or
INTELLIGENCE SUMMARY
(Erase heading not required.)

Army Form C. 2118.

Hour, Date, Place	Summary of Events and Information	Remarks and References to Appendices
4 pm. 11th April 1915 -	2 Officers + 16 O.R. admitted - 2 Off + 14 O.R. Evacuated to MERVILLE. 6 sick admitted to C.S. None evacuated today Lieut D. Mackie proceeded to 2/ Gordons for temporary duty	
4 pm 12th April -	32 O.R. admitted - 17 O.R. Evacuated to MERVILLE. 5 sick admitted to C.S. 3 evacuated today to MERVILLE Lieut W.S. Milne R.A.M.C. posted to this Ambulance for duty today - Lieut G.B. Horrocks proceeded 1/5 2/Border Regt for temporary duty.	
4 pm. 13th April -	26 O.R. admitted - 15 O.R. Evacuated to MERVILLE 11 sick admitted to C.S. - 4 Evacuated to MERVILLE	
4 pm 14th April	28 O.R. admitted - 26 O.R. Evacuated to MERVILLE 6 sick admitted to C.S. - 4 Evacuated to MERVILLE	
4 pm 15th April	38 O.R. admitted - 17 evacuated to MERVILLE. 7 sick admitted to C.S. - 3 Evacuated to MERVILLE.	
4 pm 16th April	54 O.R. admitted sick - 32 Evacuated to MERVILLE 6 sick admitted to C.S. - 4 Evacuated to MERVILLE	
4 pm 17th April	1 Off + 40 O.R. sick admitted, + 2 wounded - (accidental bomb wound) 1 Off 23 O.R. Sick + 2 wounded Evacuated to MERVILLE 4 O.R. sick admitted to C.S. 7 Evacuated to MERVILLE. Lieut G.B. Horrocks R.A.M.C transferred to 21st Field Ambulance under orders of A.D.M.S 7th Divn. Lieut W.S. Milne R.A.M.C proceeded to 2/Border Regt in relief of Lieut Horrocks	

Army Form C. 2118.

WAR DIARY
or
INTELLIGENCE SUMMARY
(Erase heading not required.)

Instructions regarding War Diaries and Intelligence Summaries are contained in F. S. Regs., Part II. and the Staff Manual respectively. Title pages will be prepared in manuscript.

Hour, Date, Place	Summary of Events and Information	Remarks and References to Appendices
4PM.18th April	41 OR admitted sick - 43 Evacuated to MERVILLE 2 sick admitted to C.C.S-3 Evacuated to MERVILLE.	
4pm 19th April.	2 Off 25 OR admitted sick 2 Off 15 OR evacuated to MERVILLE 5 OR admitted sick to C.S. 1 wounded man admitted	
9. a.m. 20th April	Lieut. E. M. SMITH. R.A.M.C. reported for recruits duty.	
4. p.m. "	36 sick admitted - 27 evacuated to MERVILLE 7 cases admitted to C.S. 4 evacuated to MERVILLE	
6 p.m. "	Lieut. MILNE returned from temporary duty with 2 BORDER reg¹.	
" "	Lieut. Hart. proceeded to 2/V SCOTS GDS. for temporary duty.	
4 p.m. 21st April.	40 sick admitted. 17 evacuated to MERVILLE 6 cases admitted to C.S. 3 evacuated to MERVILLE	
5 p.m. "	B hence hit. Brown wrote Lt MACKIE proceeded to RUE BAQUEROT M.S.d. Map. 36 LILLE 1-40-000 to open Adv. Dressing Station: a Brigade carrying unit Trench	

Army Form C. 2118.

WAR DIARY
or
INTELLIGENCE SUMMARY
(Erase heading not required.)

Instructions regarding War Diaries and Intelligence Summaries are contained in F. S. Regs., Part II. and the Staff Manual respectively. Title pages will be prepared in manuscript.

Hour, Date, Place	Summary of Events and Information	Remarks and References to Appendices
8.30 am April 22nd	LIEUT C.M. SMITH orders to proceed to 8th ROYAL SCOTTS for duty	
4 pm " "	16 sick & 1 wounded admitted 20 sick & 1 wounded evacuated 2 sick admitted to C.S. Boyenville Capt Admirall R.A.M.C. arrived to try the new Coal/Smoke/Kirchenstoffen	
4 pm April 23rd	9 sick & 4 wounded admitted 18 sick & 2 wounded evacuated 5 sick admitted to C.S. 1 evacuated	
4 pm April 24th	17 sick & 5 wounded admitted 12 sick evacuated 5 sick admitted to C.S. 1 evacuated	
6.0 pm April 24th	Received orders to take all cases from 21 & 22 Field Ambulances	
4 pm April 25th	3 O.R. sick & 1 wounded admitted 3 O.R. 22 other ranks evacuated 46 other ranks admitted to C.S. 13 evacuated	
4 pm April 26th	1 Off. 34 O.R. sick & wounded admitted. 1 Off 22 O.R. sick & wounded evacuated 3 sick admitted to C.S. 4 evacuated	

Army Form C. 2118.

WAR DIARY
or
INTELLIGENCE SUMMARY

(Erase heading not required.)

Instructions regarding War Diaries and Intelligence Summaries are contained in F. S. Regs., Part II. and the Staff Manual respectively. Title pages will be prepared in manuscript.

Hour, Date, Place	Summary of Events and Information	Remarks and References to Appendices

April 27th — 29th Brigade reinforced. Took over new section of trenches. Listed new sit for Advanced Dressing Station on Lompree road M.21.a.sht 36. Orders C Parus hot brincies to & front and to the place at St. Jean Ostens. B sub-section RUE RAQUEROT to remain at Dressing Station on VIII th Division for the evening & toti whind by VIII th Division.

4 pm. April 27th — 28 sick & 3 wounded evacuated, 14 sick & 4 wounded evacuated. 1 sick evacuated from Divalanced Station.

April 28th 1.0pm. Received orders that Ambulance was attached to 8th Division.
2.0pm. Lt. MACKIE & B Section Sub Bearers returned. Lt. HART returned & went out to take over command of C Bearer Sub Division.

April 29th 9 am. 45 sick & 10 wounded admitted. 52 sick & 13 wounded evacuated. 40 sick were transferred from 21 & 22 Field Ambulance yesterday.

Army Form C. 2118.

WAR DIARY
or
INTELLIGENCE SUMMARY

(Erase heading not required.)

Instructions regarding War Diaries and Intelligence Summaries are contained in F. S. Regs., Part II. and the Staff Manual respectively. Title pages will be prepared in manuscript.

Hour, Date, Place	Summary of Events and Information	Remarks and References to Appendices
2am April 30th	25 sick & 7 wounded admitted 19 med & 12 wounded evacuated	

W. Kempton
Lt Col RAMC
O.C. 23rd Field Ambulance

121/5444

121/5444
May 1915   4th Division

23rd Field Ambulance

S

Army Form C.2118.

WAR DIARY
or
INTELLIGENCE SUMMARY

(Erase heading not required.)

Instructions regarding War Diaries and Intelligence Summaries are contained in F. S. Regs., Part II. and the Staff Manual respectively. Title pages will be prepared in manuscript.

Hour, Date, Place	Summary of Events and Information	Remarks and References to Appendices
9 am May 1st	35 sick & 9 wounded admitted 10 sick & 4 wounded evacuated	
4 p.m.	Received orders from ADMS 8' Div that all cases in Convalescent Home were not to be shown as in Hospital	
9 am May 2nd	23 sick & 14 wounded admitted 23 sick & 9 wounded evacuated.	
	All convalescent are now formed into a company, and occupy large room over guard.	
9 am May 3rd	20 sick [struck through] admitted. 15 sick & 17 wounded evacuated.	
10.10 am	Proceeded to Dressing Station in LA BASSÉE ROAD & reconnoitred ground with a view to establishing 1st Aid Post: in the case of an attack	
9 am May 4th	29 sick & 2 wounded admitted 23 sick & 2 wounded evacuated	

WAR DIARY
or
INTELLIGENCE SUMMARY
(*Erase heading not required.*)

Army Form C. 2118.

Instructions regarding War Diaries and Intelligence Summaries are contained in F. S. Regs., Part II. and the Staff Manual respectively. Title pages will be prepared in manuscript.

Hour, Date, Place		Summary of Events and Information	Remarks and References to Appendices
May 4th	2.30 pm	A Bearer Sub Division under Lieut WEBB went out to Advanced Bearing Station between C Bearer Sub Division	
"	4.20 pm	C Bearer Sub Division under Lieut HART returned	
May 5th	9 am	27 sick & 4 wounded admitted 28 sick & 1 wounded evacuated	
" 5 -	4 pm	27 sick & 4 wounded admitted 14 sick & 4 wounded evacuated	
		20th Infantry Brigade is to be relieved from the trenches. Ordered Lieut WEDD to evacuate sick & wounded of the Brigade & to come on to Heral Senaita tomorrow 6th inst	
May 8th	11.9 am	Lieut WEDD & A Bearer Division returned to Heral Senaita	
	4 pm	38 sick & 6 wounded admitted 20 sick & 5 wounded evacuated	

Army Form C. 2118.

WAR DIARY
or
INTELLIGENCE SUMMARY
(Erase heading not required.)

Instructions regarding War Diaries and Intelligence Summaries are contained in F. S. Regs., Part II. and the Staff Manual respectively. Title pages will be prepared in manuscript.

Hour, Date, Place	Summary of Events and Information	Remarks and References to Appendices
May 7th. 10 a.m.	Under orders received from ADMS 7th Div. Lieut. MACKIE R.A.M.C. & 12 men with Medical Store cart & water cart proceeded to open Advanced Dressing Station near Rouge de Bout. at G.36.c Map 36 1-40,000. in view of operations expected. Detailed CAPT WRIGHT to proceed with rest of Bearer Division at 7.30 p.m. to Advanced Dressing Station in connection with expected operation.	Appendix I
4 p.m.	41 cart admitted 34 sick & 2 wounded men	
6.45 p.m.	1 horsed ambulance wagon sent to 14th RHA BDE	
7.0 p.m.	Orders received suspending operation for 24 hours. Marks tooth'd on a solution (Hyposulphide Soda) 1 lb. Glycerine 1 pint water (gallon) were issued to all troops.	
July 8th. 2.0 p.m.	Orders caused that last night's operation is also not to be held good for tonight.	

Army Form C. 2118.

WAR DIARY
or
INTELLIGENCE SUMMARY
(Erase heading not required.)

Instructions regarding War Diaries and Intelligence Summaries are contained in F. S. Regs., Part II. and the Staff Manual respectively. Title pages will be prepared in manuscript.

Hour, Date, Place	Summary of Events and Information	Remarks and References to Appendices
May 8th 4 p.m.	19 off & 36 other ranks admitted sick & 1 wounded 1 off & 34 other ranks sick & 3 wounded evacuated	
7.30 p.m.	CAPT WRIGHT R.A.M.C. & Bearer Division proceeded to Advanced Dressing Station.	
May 9th 5.a.m.	Heavy bombardment commenced	
5.30 am	4 Motor Ambulances sent out 1 to A.D.S. 3 to the wagon pack at NUE MONDE	
6.30 am	Took over billets opposite to accommodation for 86 Over of the Convalescent company	
7.30 am	6 Horsed Ambulances sent to wagon pack at NUE MONDE	
11.30 am	Wounded commenced to arrive	
12-0 noon	15 wounded of 8th Bn & 1 wounded 7th Div. admitted.	
4.0 pm	July Stats - 10 sick & 118 wounded admitted. 9 sick & 16 wounded evacuated.	
8.0 pm.	Sent out great coats & advanced dressing station & Bearers & dressing station	

Army Form C. 2118.

WAR DIARY
or
INTELLIGENCE SUMMARY

(Erase heading not required.)

Instructions regarding War Diaries and Intelligence Summaries are contained in F. S. Regs., Part II. and the Staff Manual respectively. Title pages will be prepared in manuscript.

Hour, Date, Place	Summary of Events and Information	Remarks and References to Appendices
May 9th 9. am.	14 wounded admitted since 12 noon.	
9.15 "	Orderly wagon park road arranged for those to be entrained.	
11.20 "	Asked all Ambulances wagons on the push & return to their respective F.A. at 5 am. 10/5/15.	
May 15th 7.30	Under orders from A.D.M.S. Orders were sent to Capt. I.N.B. WRIGHT to detail one Bearer Subsection in mine of necessary & proceed to 8th Div HdQrs. RUE DUQUESNES to assist in removing wounded	
12.55 pm.	Received orders to be ready to move tonight. All sick & wounded to be evacuated to MERVILLE by W cases to 3/WEST RIDING F.A. All men on Convalescent Coy to be handed over to 3/WEST RIDING F.A.	
8.0. pm.	Marched to BETHUNE via LESTREM LOCON road	
11.0. pm.	Arrived at BETHUNE men were billeted in CASERNE DE MONTMORENCY.	

Army Form C. 2118.

WAR DIARY
or
INTELLIGENCE SUMMARY
(Erase heading not required.)

Instructions regarding War Diaries and Intelligence Summaries are contained in F. S. Regs., Part II. and the Staff Manual respectively. Title pages will be prepared in manuscript.

Hour, Date, Place	Summary of Events and Information	Remarks and References to Appendices
BETHUNE		
May 11th 10 a.m.	Went with A.D.M.S 7th Div to reconnoitre area for Advanced Dressing Station. The following sites were selected map (BETHUNE) FRANCE communiqué. Brewery collecting station X.16.b.d. A.D.S. for Brigade operating to NORTH S 13 b.b. A.D.S for Brigade operating to South X 24 a opposite E of EPINETTE	
2 p.m.	Went to ANNEZIN to choose buildings to open as Rest-Stations found village full of French troops & 2 no stations reported to A.D.M.S.	
8.30 p.m.	Received orders to encamp on BETHUNE till further orders	
May 12th 2. 0 p.m.	Took over ECOLE METERNELLE from 21st F.A. as hospital who handed over 12 cases. The men were billeted in church & school nearby	

WAR DIARY
or
INTELLIGENCE SUMMARY
(Erase heading not required.)

Army Form C. 2118.

Hour, Date, Place	Summary of Events and Information	Remarks and References to Appendices
4 pm. May 13th	11 sick + 1 wounded remaining 22 sick + 15 wounded admitted 6 sick + 5 wounded evacuated sick nil to duty nil.	
7.30 pm. "	Instructions received re opening of additional buildings in the event of Question. Demanded from Advance Stores the following 40 stretch, 250 blankets 250 waters 200 pannikins 40 mugs forks & spoons. 100 suits of pyjamas also not other items as required for cleaning & cooking the cooking.	Appendix II
4 am. May 14" "	18 sick + 34 wounded admitted 13 sick + 20 wounded evacuated 4 sick + 10 wounded discharged to duty	
5.0 pm. " "	Operation order No 2 received	
6.30 pm. " "	Operation order postponed for 24 hours	Appendix III
9 am. May 15th "	4 sick + 12 wounded admitted 13 wounded evacuated	

Army Form C. 2118.

WAR DIARY
or
INTELLIGENCE SUMMARY
(Erase heading not required.)

Instructions regarding War Diaries and Intelligence Summaries are contained in F. S. Regs., Part II. and the Staff Manual respectively. Title pages will be prepared in manuscript.

Hour, Date, Place	Summary of Events and Information	Remarks and References to Appendices
6.30 pm. Aug. 15th	Bearer Division under Lieut MACKIE proceeded to advanced Dressing Station at 8.14 a.m. Preparation for the Operation	Report of action Appendix IV
2.0 a.m. Aug 16th	Dispatched 5 Motor ambulance cars to 22nd Field Ambulance in accordance with divisional order No 4 last para	
6.0 a.m. Aug 16	Wounded admitted 17 evacuated nil. Sent out extra supply of dressings to A.D.S.	
10 am " "	Sent out 3 Horsed ambulance to cover station	
12.0 noon " "	wounded admitted 212 evacuated 103	
7.30 pm " "	sent 40 lying & sick & wounded cases to improvised chapel	
9.0 pm " "	140 wounded admitted. 185 evacuated. a further supply of dressings despatched to A.D.S.	
6.0 am Aug 17th	83 wounded admitted. 33 evacuated	

79 / 3298

WAR DIARY
or
INTELLIGENCE SUMMARY

(Erase heading not required.)

Army Form C. 2118.

Instructions regarding War Diaries and Intelligence Summaries are contained in F. S. Regs., Part II. and the Staff Manual respectively. Title pages will be prepared in manuscript.

Hour, Date, Place	Summary of Events and Information	Remarks and References to Appendices
9.0 am May 17th	Daily state for 24 hours 5 sick 371 wounded admitted 9 sick wounded 350 wounded 2 wounded sick	
10.50 am " "	55 "sitting" cases were evacuated to an improvised ambulance train at BETHUNE	
12.0 noon " "	35 wounded admitted 55 evacuated 4 wounded Germans admitted	
9.0 pm " "	61 wounded British. 15 German wounded admitted. 103 wounded evacuated.	
6.0 am May 18th	3 British & 3 German wounded admitted 10 wounded evacuated	
9.0 am May 18th	Daily State. 11 sick & 147 wounded admitted. 2 sick & 151 wounded evacuated. 1 sick & 16 wounded discharged to duty. 16 sick & 28 wounded discharged to Convalescent Cp. 1 wounded sick	
12.0 noon " "	24 British & 2 German wounded admitted 54 evacuated	

Army Form C. 2118.

WAR DIARY
or
INTELLIGENCE SUMMARY
(Erase heading not required.)

Instructions regarding War Diaries and Intelligence Summaries are contained in F. S. Regs., Part II. and the Staff Manual respectively. Title pages will be prepared in manuscript.

Hour, Date, Place	Summary of Events and Information	Remarks and References to Appendices
10.0 am. Aug. 19ᵗʰ	37 British wounded admitted 49 evacuated	
6.0. am Aug. 19ᵗʰ	LIEUT MACKIE RAMC & Beare division returned from Advanced Dressing Station having been relieved by the Canadian Divisn	
	29 British & 1 German wounded admitted 27 evacuated	
9.0 am " "	Daily State 10 sick & 102 wounded admitted 4 sick & 117 wounded evacuated to charge St duty, 4 sick & 11 wounded to Convalescent Cp. 4 sick & 14 wounded died. 3 men	
12.0 noon Aug. 19ᵗʰ	2 wounded admitted 29 evacuated	
12.30 pm " "	Reconnoitre to clear & proceed to ROBECQ	
1.15 pm " "	Marched to ROBECQ 10 light cases conveyed with Ambulance	

Army Form C. 2118.

WAR DIARY
or
INTELLIGENCE SUMMARY
(Erase heading not required.)

Instructions regarding War Diaries and Intelligence Summaries are contained in F. S. Regs., Part II. and the Staff Manual respectively. Title pages will be prepared in manuscript.

Hour, Date, Place	Summary of Events and Information	Remarks and References to Appendices
6.0 p.m. May 19th	Arrived ROBECQ opened our Tent Hospl. Brown in School	
9.0 am Muy. 20th	9 sick admitted 2 wounded. 2 sick & 27 wounded evacuated. 3 sick & 1 off. + 1 O.R. returned to duty. 8 evacuated by 5 and S.B. evacuated. 2 wounded.	
9.0 am. May. 21st	17 sick admitted 1 wounded. 7 sick + 3 wounded evacuated. 1 sick & 1 wounded discharged to duty	
9.0 am May 22nd	19 sick & 1 wounded admitted 15 sick & 1 wounded evacuated. 6 sick & 1 wounded discharged to duty	
9.0 am May. 23rd	14 sick & 2 wounded admitted evacuated 11 sick 1 wounded discharges today 3 sick.	
9.0 am May. 24th	15 sick O.R. & 1 Off. admitted 1 Off. + 18 O.R. sick evacuated 3 sick & 1 wounded discharged to duty	
9.0 am May. 25th	17 sick admitted 12 sick evacuated 1 to duty	

Army Form C.2118.

WAR DIARY
or
INTELLIGENCE SUMMARY
(Erase heading not required.)

Instructions regarding War Diaries and Intelligence Summaries are contained in F. S. Regs., Part II. and the Staff Manual respectively. Title pages will be prepared in manuscript.

Hour, Date, Place	Summary of Events and Information	Remarks and References to Appendices
Aug. 26th 9.0 a.m.	18 sick admitted 10 sick evacuated 2 sick discharged to duty	
27th 9.0 a.m.	26 sick & wounded admitted 18 sick + 1 wounded evacuated 1 sick discharged to duty	
28th 9.0 a.m.	12 sick admitted 18 sick evacuated 8 discharged to duty	
29th 9.0 a.m.	16 sick admitted 12 sick evacuated 4 discharged to duty	
30th 9.0 a.m.	2 Officers +14 other rank sick admitted 2 Officers 13 o.r. sick evacuated 1 discharged to duty	
31st 9.0 a.m.	17 sick admitted 13 evacuated 4 discharged to duty	
2.0 p.m.	LIEUT HART R.A.M.C. & C Bearer Subdivision with Medical store cart & water cart & 2 Motor Ambulances been sent forward to F.5.a BETHUNE continued sick to open an advanced dressing station as 25th Brigade were taking over the line ahead of this point. The Tent Division remained at ROBECQ flying the selection of a site.	

Secret
Urgent

D.6

23rd Field Ambulance
___

Operations postponed yesterday
will take place 15th/16th

15 5/15   [signature]
             Colonel
           A.D.M.S. 7th Division

Secret

O.C. 23rd Sikh amber

Operations are postponed
for twenty four hours.

P H Hudson

14 5/15   Major
                D A O M S g Dun

Copy No 5

Appendix I

4th Division R.A.M.C. Operation Order No 1.
by
Colonel W.H. Starr A.M.S
Commanding R.A.M Corps 4th Division

6th May 1915

No orders or sketches giving information to the enemy are to be taken into the Field

References are to Maps (Reduction) AUBERS and BAS MAISNIL FROMELLES 1/10000 and to the 1/40,000 map

1. <u>Information</u>

4th Division Operation Order No 6 having been fully explained verbally to Officers Commanding 21st, 22nd, 23rd and 3rd West Riding Field Ambulances. the following will be the medical arrangements for the operations therein referred to:-

2. <u>Position of Field Ambulances and Dressing Stations</u>

The three Field Ambulances of the division and 3rd W. Rdg F.A. will remain in their present positions in ESTAIRES and LA GORGUE

Two advanced Dressing Stations will be formed; one by the 22nd and one by the 23rd Field Ambulance in the two farms on North side of road in G 36.d. The A.D.S of the 22nd Field Ambulance being formed in the farm on the EAST that of the 23rd Field Ambulance in the farm on the WEST

The Officers Commanding 22nd and 23rd Field Ambulances will each despatch an advanced party of the Bearer Division consisting of 1 Officer and 12 other Ranks with Forage Cart and equipment and water Cart to their respective A.D.S by 10 a.m. on the 7th instant for the purpose of cleaning up the buildings and making them suitable for reception of wounded.

The remainder of the Bearer Divisions of 22nd and 23rd Field Ambulances will be despatched in time to reach the A.D.S by 9 pm on the 7th instant and will remain there till the advance of the main body of 7th Division on the 8th instant

3. Collection of wounded

The bearer divisions of 22nd and 23rd Field Ambulances (less personnel required at Advanced Dressing Stations) will advance at a reasonable distance in rear of main body of 7th Division keeping in touch with Regimental Stretcher Bearers

The bearers of the 22nd Field Ambulance will collect wounded from left half and bearers of 23rd Field Ambulance from right half of area covered by advance of 7th Division

4. Ambulance Wagons

One Motor Ambulance Wagon will be kept at each A.D.S but will not proceed there till the 7th Division become engaged

The remainder of Motor and Horsed Ambulance Wagons (less 3 horsed wagons allotted to Artillery units) will be parked at NEU MONDE church, and as a full wagon returns from A D S the N C O in charge will send forward to the A D S an empty wagon.

5. Artillery

One horsed Ambulance wagon from 21st 22nd and 23rd Field Ambulances will be despatched by 9 pm 7th instant to the Headquarters of XXII and XXXV R F A Brigades and XIV R H A Brigade respectively and will remain at disposal of these Brigades during the operations

6. Roads

During the first phase of the 7th Division operations Ambulance wagons will proceed to A.D.S by the first road on West of NEU MONDE returning by FROMELLES-SAILLY and PONT DE LA JUSTICE roads

7. Lunches

O C 21st Field Ambulance will make arrangements

for the evacuation of casualties from Flesselles
in reserve at ESTAIRES and such of 1st RW as
Division as is not required for this purpose.

The O.C. 3rd West Riding Field Ambulance will make
arrangements for the evacuation of casualties from C
Doss E Coys.

8. Orders

O.C. Field Ambulances will keep in touch with the
Brigadier Generals Commanding their respective Brigades
and receive orders from them regarding the movements
of their Brigades.

9. Lights

No lights or smoking will be permitted after the
troops fall in to move to their places of assembly.

10. Headquarters

During the operations the A.D.M.S. of Division HdQrs
will be at NEU MONDE with A and Q branches
Headquarters of Division.

sd W H Starr
Colonel
O.C. R.A.M.C. of Division

Issued at 9.30am to:-
```
A.D.M.S.       Copy No 1
D.A.D.M.S.        "  2
O.C. 21st F.A.    "  3
 "  22nd          "  4
 "  23rd          "  5
 "  3 WR F.A.     "  6
Genl Staff of Divn "  7
```

Appendix II

19

To,
O.C. 23rd F.A.

1. In the event of active operations you will take over the unfinished Chapel near the prison + No 9 Place LaMARTINE + prepare them as overflow buildings for the reception of wounded which your F.A. cannot accommodate.

Please let me have an early estimate of the maximum number of patients your present F.A. buildings + these two extra buildings can accommodate.

2. Before the commencement of operations any slight cases of sickness you may have in your F.A. who could be utilized for cleaning purposes should be used for cleaning up the buildings + any men you can spare from your F.A. should also be utilized to prepare the buildings.

3. It is hoped that extra personnel in the form of Nurses, Medical Officers + other ranks R.A.M.C. will be available to assist you in the event of these buildings having to be used, but this assistance cannot be relied on with certainty.

4. The extra buildings will not be utilized until the 22nd F.A. the 5th and 6th London F.A's are full & this information will be duly notified to you.

5. Should the necessity of using the extra buildings arise, only the most slightly wounded should be sent to them after being first dressed & inoculated against Tetanus at your F.A.

6. Assuming that your F.A. can accommodate 200 & each extra building 100 & that your F.A. is evacuated once in 24 hours reported, it will be seen that you may have to deal with 600 cases in the first 24 hours. You will therefore arrange for a sufficient supply of dressings & other surgical material, rations, cooking utensils ~~...~~ and antitetanic serum, for this number & blankets sufficient for the total numbers the F.A. & extra buildings can accommodate at one time. Straw will also be required for extra build~~ings~~

7. You should also be prepared to billet & feed ~~...~~ the following extra personnel — M.O's 8, nurses 10, R.A.M.C. O.R. 10.

13/5/15   W H Stern Colonel A.D.M.S.

23rd F.A. May 1915.

Copy No 5

7th Division R.A.M.C Operation Order No 2
by
Colonel W.H. Starr
Commanding R.A.M.C 7th Division

14th May 1915

Appendix VII

No orders or sketches giving information to the enemy are to be taken into the field.

References are to Maps ILLIES, VIOLAINES, FESTUBERT 1/10,000 and map 1/40,000.

1. Intention

The 1st Army will during the night 14th/15th May and on morning of 15th break the enemy's line on the front FESTUBERT – RICHEBOURG L'AVOUÉ RUE-FERME DE TOULOTTE – RICHEBOURG L'AVOUÉ.

The 7th Division will break the enemy's front N.1 and P.5. on the morning of May 15th. A further advance will be made after daylight.

2. General Plan

The 7th Division will be formed up during the night 14/15 and will assault the enemy's line on the front N1 P5 at 3-15 A.M. on the 15th May.

The 22nd Infantry Brigade and 54th Field Coy R.E. on the right will attack with its right on N1 on a front of 400 yards.

The 20th Infantry Brigade and 55th Field Coy R.E. on the left will attack with its left at P5 on a front of 350 yards.

The 21st Infantry Brigade will be in reserve in the neighbourhood of the Rue D'EPINETTE, with one battalion as garrison for the trenches.

3. Detail

The 7th Division will form up during the night 14/15th as follows:–
(a) 20th Infantry Brigade and 55th Field Coy R.E. about S.14.c and S.20.a moving to that place by

AVELOTTE – LES CHOQUAX and any roads South of
squares X 7, X 8, X 9, X 10 and X 11 – RUE DE BOIS.

~~The Brigade~~ and close this road junction as rapidly as
possible.

The Head of the Brigade should reach the road junction X 18.c (central) at 9 pm

(c) The 25th Infantry Brigade and 54th Field Coy R.E about
S.20.c moving there by the road junction at X.15.c (Central)
and RUE DE L'EPINETTE.

The head of this Brigade should reach the above mentioned
road junction at 9.45 pm.

4. Medical Arrangements.

O.C 22nd and 23rd Field Ambulances will ascertain from the
Brigadier Generals Commanding their respective Brigades the time
and place the Field Ambulance bearers should form up in rear
of the Brigades.

Position of Medical Units

Field Ambulances.

O.C 21st Field Ambulance will open one tent sub-division
in School and Mairie at ESSARS for reception of all sick of
division during the operations, keeping 2 tent sub-divisions
packed, in readiness for an advance.

O.C 22nd Field Ambulance will open tent Division in
ECOLE JEUNE FILLES, RUE de RETOUR, BETHUNE, using
ECOLE MATERNELLE RUE de l'UNIVERS and PENSIONAIRE
RUE BERTHELOT with Chapel as overflow buildings.

O.C 23rd Field Ambulance will open tent Division
in ECOLE MATERNELLE RUE des ECOLES BETHUNE
using the unfinished Chapel and adjoining house opposite
prison as overflow buildings

The Divisional Collecting Station will be formed at
X.16 b.d by O.C 21st Field Ambulance. For this purpose
he will use such personnel and equipment as he considers
necessary.

A proportion of the ambulance wagons and cars will
rendezvous in the vicinity of the Divisional Collecting station
the remainder being held in reserve at LOCON.

O.C 21st Field Ambulance will arrange a system to ensure
a regular supply of cars from the reserve station at LOCON
to the rendezvous and thence to the Advanced Dressing Station

O.C. 21st Field Ambulance will detail an Officer and N.C.O. to regulate the loaded cars at Divisional Collecting Station as follows:-

Not more than four loaded cars or wagons will proceed to any Field Ambulance at one time. The Field Ambulances available for reception of wounded are the 22nd and 23rd Field Ambulances and 5th and 6th London Field Ambulances, and batches of 4 cars or wagons should be sent to these in rotation commencing with 23rd Field Ambulance.

When any Field Ambulance becomes filled, it will fall out of the series till evacuated, when it will again resume its place in above rotation. All wounded Officers will be sent to No. 4 Field Ambulance Officers' section BOULEVARD VICTOR HUGO.

The 5th and 6th London Field Ambulances are situated in ECOLE de JEUNES FILLES and ECOLE MICHELET respectively and steps should be taken to ensure all drivers being acquainted with the positions of Field Ambulances and the authorized routes for Ambulance Cars.

The motor Ambulance Cars will assemble at 22nd Field Ambulance at 2.45pm 15th May and O.C. 21st Field Ambulance will arrange to have them met and conveyed to their stations.

Advanced Dressing Stations

O.C. 22nd and 23rd Field Ambulances will form Advanced Dressing Stations at X 26.a and S 1b.a respectively and will arrange for collection of wounded from right and left halves respectively of area covered by advance of 7th Division.

Carrying Units

One Ambulance wagon (horsed) will be posted to the Headquarters of each Artillery Brigade and will be provided as follows:-

21st Field Ambulance 14th Bde R.H.A. and 22nd Bde R.F.A.
22nd " " 35th Bde R.F.A. and 3rd Bde R.F.A.
23rd " " 1st Bde R.H.A. and 7th Bde R.G.A

These wagons should be posted on evening of 14th May

5. Orders to Divisions
O.C. Bearer Divisions 22nd and 23rd Field Ambulances will keep in touch with the Brigadier General Commanding their respective Brigades and receive orders from them regarding the movements of their Brigades.

6. Headquarters
During the operations the Headquarters of A.D.M.S. 7th Division will be at A.D.Q. opposite LE HAMEL to which place all reports should be sent.

7. Food
Every man will carry one day's rations besides the remainder of current day's issue. 16 hours rations of preserved meat and biscuits at a house in X.18.c.

8. Dress
Troops will carry Cardigan jackets and waterproof sheets. Greatcoats will not be taken further than the Advanced Dressing Station.

9. Lights
No lights or smoking will be permitted after the troops fall in to move to their place of assembly.

10. Road Traffic
The system of road control shown by boards must be strictly adhered to.

P. K. Hendrson.
Major
for Colonel
O.C. R.A.M. Corps 7th Division

Issued 5 p.m.
A.D.M.S. Copy No. 1
D.A.D.M.S. " " 2
O.C. 21st F.A. " 3
" 22nd " " 4
" 23rd " " 5
G.S. 7th Division " 6
A.A.&Q.M.G. " " 7

Appendix IV

23rd F.A.
May 1915.

Report of Operation of Bearer Division 23rd Field Ambulance during action at FESTUBERT May 16th 1915.
Reference FRANCE (BETHUNE) Combined sheet 40,000.

1/ 6.30 pm May 15th. Left with Bearer Division for Advanced Dressing Station RUE DU BOIS. On arriving at VIIth Divisional Collecting Station X 16 b.d. left A & C Bearer Subdivisions in reserve at this point. Proceeded with B Bearer Subdivision, light cart and water cart to advanced dressing station RUE DU BOIS S.11.a and opened to receive which immediately commenced to arrive from the troops of the 20th Brigade marching past on the road.

2/ Owing to congestion of traffic on road it was found impossible for motor ambulances to come up so far as advanced dressing station. Lying cases were therefore removed on wheeled stretchers to the road junction of RUE DE L'EPINETTE X 18.C. where they were loaded on to the cars.

3/ 5 am. May 16th. A & C Bearer Subdivisions came up. These were sent out to collect wounded from the regimental aid posts. The wounded at aid post DEAD-COW FARM S.11.d were brought by communication trenches direct to dressing station. Those from aid posts in INDIAN VILLAGE S.20.b were carried over baths through the fields to RUE DE L'EPINETTE and thence to ambulances at the road junction X 18.C. Two Bearer Subdivisions worked while one rested.

4/ 20th Infantry Brigade were relieved by 21st Brigade on night of 17th. The bearer division still continued to collect wounded from the new brigade.

5. 4 pm on 18th one bearer subdivision of a Field Ambulance of the 111/th Division.

6. 10 pm according to orders London Bearer Subdivision returned to their Headquarters.

7. 11 am. May 18th 3 Medical Officers and four squads of a Canadian Field Ambulance arrived to take over the Dressing Station.

8. 11.5 am Having handed over the Dressing Station set out for Headquarters BETHUNE and arrived at 2 am Wednesday 19th May 1915

(Sgd) D. Mackie.
Lieut R.A.M.C. SR.
O.C. Bearer Division
23rd Field Ambulance.

Summarized

131/5993

auto.

4th Division

23rd Field Ambulance

Vol VI

121/5993

June 1915

Army Form C. 2118.

WAR DIARY
or
INTELLIGENCE SUMMARY

(Erase heading not required.)

Instructions regarding War Diaries and Intelligence Summaries are contained in F. S. Regs., Part II. and the Staff Manual respectively. Title pages will be prepared in manuscript.

Place	Hour, Date	Summary of Events and Information	Remarks and References to Appendices
ROBECQ	June 1st 9.0 am	30 sick admitted. 22 evacuated. Have discharged	
	1st 2.0 pm	Orders received that all sick & wounded from 26th Infantry Brigade were to be sent to No 1 Field Ambulance Highland Division	
	June 2nd 9.0 am	13 sick admitted. 20 evacuated. 7 discharged to duty	
	June 3rd 9.0 am	No sick admitted. 7 evacuated. No men discharged to duty	
	9.20 am	Marched from ROBECQ via HINGES to LE PLOUY FARM (FRANCE BETHUNE [contoured map 1:40,000]) W. 16.d.	
	11.20 am	Arrived at LE PLOUY FARM. Obtained 24 Pull Tents & 6 Operating tents from 21st 22nd Field Ambulance and tents opened tents. Division walk cases in field to NW of Farm	
	4.0 pm	LIEUT MAR of 21st Field Ambulance & LT. MEAGHER of 22nd Field Ambulance arrived to assist in rest- Division as an action was expected	
	4.0 pm	Dispatched LT LINNELL with A.S.B. Horse Field Division to Advanced Dressing Station	Appendix 1

WAR DIARY

or

INTELLIGENCE SUMMARY

(Erase heading not required.)

Army Form C. 2118.

Hour, Date, Place	Summary of Events and Information	Remarks and References to Appendices
June 3rd 4.0 pm	At MARAIS (F.5.c. BETHUNE 1-40000) with 3 from "C" who stationed to clear wounded during action. (Report of work attached.)	Appendix II
June 4th 6.0 am	153 British wounded & 2 German wounded admitted. 2 Officers admitted.	
4th 9.0 am	Early state 9 sick, 150 wounded & 4 Officers wounded admitted. 1 sick transferred to other Hospitals and discharged to duty	
12 noon	2 Officers & 25 men wounded admitted. 4 evacuated.	
2.0	to Barge & 1 man discharged. CAPT W. G. WRIGHT proceeded to No 1 C.C. Station for duty	
9 pm	18 wounded admitted 4 Officers & 134 Other ranks & 2 German wounded evacuated (20 cars to Barge) removed by Motor Ambulance Convoy to LILLERS	
June 5 1.0 am	Bearer Division returned from A.D.S. and were placed in billets at AVELLETE W.17.d. BETHUNE 1-40000	Appendix III

Army Form C. 2118.

WAR DIARY
or
INTELLIGENCE SUMMARY
(Erase heading not required.)

Instructions regarding War Diaries and Intelligence Summaries are contained in F. S. Regs., Part II. and the Staff Manual respectively. Title pages will be prepared in manuscript.

Hour, Date, Place	Summary of Events and Information	Remarks and References to Appendices
LE PLOUY FARM June 5 — 6.0 a.m.	8 wounded admitted no cases evacuated	
9.0 a.m.	Duty State 17 sick & 24 wounded admitted & 1 German 7 sick & 125 wounded OR & Officer & 2 Germans evacuated. 5 sick discharged to duty. 1 died	
June 6th 9.0 a.m.	23 sick & 16 wounded admitted 15 sick & 32 wounded & 1 German evacuated 11 sick & 32 wounded discharged to duty —	
June 7th 12 noon	Lt. Col V.J. Crawford D.S.O. proceeded, under orders of D.M.S. 1st Army, to No.1 Casualty Clearing Stn at CHOCQUES and Command of 23rd Field Ambulance was handed over to Major G. H. J. BROWN RAMC	
1 P.M.	Capt W. G. WRIGHT. returned from No.1 Cas. Cl. Stn. for duty here	
3 P.M.	Lt. MEAGHER. RAMC. returned to 22nd Field Ambulance on completion of temporary duty	
	The 9AM Daily State shows:—	
	1 Off & 28 OR admitted sick — Wounded 10 OR.	
	Evacuations: 1 Off 2 OR sick	5 Sick } to chargers 8 OR Wounded } 5 Wounds } to out, today	

WAR DIARY
or
INTELLIGENCE SUMMARY
(Erase heading not required.)

Army Form C. 2118.

Hour, Date, Place	Summary of Events and Information	Remarks and References to Appendices
LE PLOUY FARM.		
June 8th 9 a.m.	Daily State - Admitted - 19 OR. Sick - 1 Off + 10 OR. wounded. Evacuated - 21 OR. sick - 11 OR. wounded. Discharged to duty - 2 OR. sick - 3 OR. wounded.	
2 PM.	Lieut MARR. Rame returned to 21st F.Amb. on completion of temporary duty. Verbal instructions issued by ADMS 7th Div. that all light cases of sickness are to be transferred daily to 22nd F.Amb. at ROEBECQ.	
June 9th 9 AM.	2 Off + 9 OR. admitted sick. 1 Off + 14 OR. wounded - 2 Off + 14 OR. evacuated sick, 12 OR. wounded evacuated. 1 diseb. 6 Inf. 6 OR. transferred sick + 4 wounded to 22nd Field Amb at ROEBECQ.	
11 AM.	3 Operating + 12 bell auto which were on loan from 21st F.Amb were returned to that unit.	
12 noon	2 "Ford" Ambulance motors + 4 drivers receiving fourteen on charge of this unit.	
June 10th 9 a.m.	31 OR. sick + 11 OR. wounded admitted - 23 OR. sick + 1 Off + 10 OR. wounded evacuated - 9 OR. sick transferred to 22nd F.Amb.	

Army Form C. 2118.

WAR DIARY
or
INTELLIGENCE SUMMARY
(Erase heading not required.)

Instructions regarding War Diaries and Intelligence Summaries are contained in F. S. Regs., Part II. and the Staff Manual respectively. Title pages will be prepared in manuscript.

Hour, Date, Place		Summary of Events and Information	Remarks and References to Appendices
LE PLOY FARM			
June 11th	9 a.m.	10. OR admitted sick - 1 Off + 4. OR wounded admitted - 7. OR sick + 1 Off + 5. OR wounded evacuated - 3. OR sick transferred to 22nd F. Amb.	
	2 p.m.	4 Horsed Ambulances + 4 drivers returned to 7th Divl Train - under instruction from A.D.M.S. 7th Divn. There are now 7 Motor Ambulances + 2 light + 1 heavy horsed ambulances in charge of the unit.	
June 12.	9 a.m.	20. OR sick + 13. OR admitted. 11. OR sick, 5. OR wounded evacuated 7. OR sick + 1 wounded transferred to 22nd F. Amb. 1 wounded man died.	
June 13th	9 a.m.	1 Off + 21. OR sick, 1 Off + 2. OR wounded admitted - 11. OR sick evacuated. 10. OR wounded evacuated. 11. OR transferred to 22nd F. Amb.	
	6.30 p.m.	Copy Operation Orders R.A.M.C. VIIth Divn No. 3 received -	Appendix IV
June 14th	9 a.m.	13. OR sick + 9. OR wounded admitted. 1 Off + 4. OR sick, 1 Off + 6. OR wounded evacuated. 4. OR sick transferred to 22nd F. Amb.	
	10.30 a.m.	20th Bde Operation Orders No. 12 received	
	2 p.m.	Bearer Division under Lt. WEDD proceeded to A.D.S. at F.5.a.c. (1/40,000 Bethune sheet) with water cart + light cart + 2 wheeled stretcher (re foot-attacks)	Appendix V
	8 p.m.	2 Motor Ambulances sent forward to A.D.S.	

Army Form C. 2118.

WAR DIARY
or
INTELLIGENCE SUMMARY

(Erase heading not required.)

Instructions regarding War Diaries and Intelligence Summaries are contained in F. S. Regs, Part II. and the Staff Manual respectively. Title pages will be prepared in manuscript.

Hour, Date, Place	Summary of Events and Information	Remarks and References to Appendices
LA PLOUY FARM 15th June. 9 a.m.	Daily State:- 1 Off + 12 OR Sick, + 25 OR wounded admitted - 1 Off + 6 OR Sick, 13 OR wounded Evacuated - 6 OR Sick + 1 OR wounded transferred to 22nd F. Amb. at ROBECQ. 1 man died (wounded)	
10 a.m.	Visited the ADv Dr. Stn. and completed arrangements prior to operating	
1 p.m.	4 Motor Ambulances + 3 horsed Ambulances sent forward to the Divisional Collecting Station at CHATEAU GORRE (F.3.b.)	
3.30 p.m.	LIEUT. J. E. ALLAN R.A.M.C. reported for duty with this unit vice taken on the strength.	
9 p.m.	Wounded return since 12 noon shows :- 18. OR admitted - 14 OR remaining - 4 OR Evacuated.	
16th June 6 a.m.	2 Off + 126 OR wounded admitted - 2 Off + 68 OR Evacuated	
9 a.m.	Daily State :- 19 OR Sick, 3 Off + 154 OR wounded admitted. 9 OR Sick, 3 Off + 124 OR wounded Evacuated - 11 Off Sick + 1 OR wounded transferred to 22nd F. Amb. 1 wounded man died	
12 noon.	1 Off + 27 OR wounded admitted - 1 Off + 21 OR wounded Evacuated.	
9 P.M.	2 Off + 50 OR wounded admitted - 2 Off + 48 OR wounded Evacuated	

Army Form C. 2118.

WAR DIARY
or
INTELLIGENCE SUMMARY
(Erase heading not required.)

Instructions regarding War Diaries and Intelligence Summaries are contained in F. S. Regs., Part II. and the Staff Manual respectively. Title pages will be prepared in manuscript.

Hour, Date, Place	Summary of Events and Information	Remarks and References to Appendices
LA PLOUY FARM. June 17th		
6 AM	63. OR wounded admitted	
9 AM	Daily State:- 6 OR sick & 2 Off + 134 OR wounded admitted - 12 OR sick, 2 Off + 79 OR wounded evacuated. 2 OR sick & 34 wounded (slight) transferred to 22nd F. Amb	
11 a.m.	Visited Adv. Dr. Station -	
12 noon	1 wounded man admitted - 1 evacuated -	
9 p.m.	9. OR admitted wounded. 22 OR evacuated. 12 OR discharged to Duty	
10 p.m.	Visited A.D.S. Shs to arrange for further operations during the night. Evacuated NIL -	
June 18th 6 a.m.	3 Off + 69 OR wounded admitted. Evacuated NIL-	
9 a.m.	Daily State :- 1 sick man admitted + 1 evacuated (sick) 3 Off. 79 OR admitted - 25 OR wounded evacuated wounded.	
12 noon	21. OR wounded admitted - 68 wounded Off. & 3 Off Evacuated	
9 p.m.	22 OR wounded admitted - 20 OR evacuated.	
12 midnight	Horsed ambulances & motors returned to their Stationg station on relief at Div. Collecting Station -	
June 19th 6 am	10. OR wounded admitted. Evacuated NIL	

Army Form C. 2118.

WAR DIARY
or
INTELLIGENCE SUMMARY
(Erase heading not required.)

Instructions regarding War Diaries and Intelligence Summaries are contained in F. S. Regs., Part II. and the Staff Manual respectively. Title pages will be prepared in manuscript.

Hour, Date, Place		Summary of Events and Information	Remarks and References to Appendices
LA PLOUY FARM.			
June 19th (Cont)	9 a.m.	Daily State :- 1 man Sick admitted. 5 O.R. wounded admitted. 3 Off + 79 O.R. wounded evacuated. 10 men (lightly wounded) returned to Convalescent Company.	
	11 a.m.	Visited Edge B. Station.	
	12 noon	6. O.R. wounded admitted. 5. O.R. evacuated.	
	3 p.m.	Instructions received that the Div. Col. Stn. would be taken up by Flat units would thereafter collect sick wounded in the affiliated Brigades.	
	4 p.m.	8. O.R. wounded admitted. 35. O.R. evacuated. 18. O.R. discharged to Convalescent Company.	
June 20th	9 a.m.	1 Off + 4 O.R. Sick, 1 Off + 38. O.R. wounded admitted. 2. O.R. sick. 1 Off + 2 + 1. O.R. wounded evacuated. B Cases transferred to No 2 Ambulance flotilla.	
June 21st	9 a.m.	2 Off + 9. O.R. Sick; 4. O.R. wounded admitted. 3. Off + 8. O.R. sick. 18. O.R. wounded evacuated.	
	2.30 p.m.	A + C Bearer Subdivisions withdrawn from A. D. S. to Gillak. B Bearer Sub division under Lieut Linnell Rank resumes at A. D. S.	
	4 p.m.	Orders relating to relief of 20th Bde received	

Army Form C. 2118.

WAR DIARY
or
INTELLIGENCE SUMMARY
(Erase heading not required.)

Instructions regarding War Diaries and Intelligence Summaries are contained in F. S. Regs., Part II. and the Staff Manual respectively. Title pages will be prepared in manuscript.

Hour, Date, Place		Summary of Events and Information	Remarks and References to Appendices
LA PLOUY FARM June 21st	9 a.m.	16 OR sick, 1 man wounded admitted. 5 OR sick, 6 OR wounded evacuated.	
	5.30 pm.	A. D. Sn. handed over to 22nd 2. Aul. + "B" bearer sub-division returned to billets at main Brewing Station.	
June 22nd	9 a.m.	Daily State :- 12 OR sick admitted - 10 OR sick + 3 OR wounded evacuated.	
June 23rd	2.30 p.m.	LIEUT. WEDD R.A.M.C. proceeds to 1/Grenadier Guards for temporary duty.	
June 24th	9 a.m.	Daily State :- 1 Off + 25 OR sick. 2 OR wounded admitted. 1 Off + 14 OR sick. 2 OR wounded evacuated.	
	12 noon.	Notified to no that 20th Brigade will relieve Canadian Division in the GIVENCHY Section tonight - Went out to arrange a suitable A.D. Sn.	Appendix VI
June 25th	9 a.m.	1 Off + 27 OR sick admitted. 1 Off + 14 OR evacuated. Wounded nil.	
	2.30 pm.	"C" Bearer Subdivision under LT. MACKIE R.A.M.C., with water-cart, light cart + 3 wheeled stretcher-carriers proceeded to the A.D.S. at F.17.c.w.9. at the road junction. (100000 Bethune Com Sheet)	
	7 pm.	2 motor ambulances sent forward to A.D.S.	
June 26th	9 a.m.	Daily State :- 10 OR sick + 4 OR wounded (1 self inflicted) admitted. 8 OR sick + 1 OR wounded evacuated.	

Confidential   Appendix VI   10

To,
O.C. 23rd Field Ambulance
———————————

The 20th Infantry Brigade will tonight take over the area of trenches in the GIVENCHY Section at present held by Canadian Division –

Please arrange to take over a suitable advanced dressing station & report to this office when this is done, indicating position of A.D.S. selected.

P. H. Henderson Major
D.A.D.M.S. VII Divn

24/6/15

Army Form C. 2118.

WAR DIARY
or
INTELLIGENCE SUMMARY

(Erase heading not required.)

Instructions regarding War Diaries and Intelligence Summaries are contained in F. S. Regs., Part II. and the Staff Manual respectively. Title pages will be prepared in manuscript.

Hour, Date, Place		Summary of Events and Information	Remarks and References to Appendices
La Plouy Farm.			
June 27th	9 a.m.	Daily State:- 1 Off + 20 O.R sick, 1.O.R wounded admitted - 1 Off + 9 O.R sick, 3.O.R wounded evacuated.	
	12 noon.	Visits A.D.S.	
June 28th	9 a.m.	14.O.R sick, 1 Off + 3.O.R wounded admitted. 11.O.R sick, 1 Off + 10.R wounded evacuated	
June 29.	9 a.m.	15.O.R sick 14.O.R wounded admitted - 13.O.R evacuated	
June 30th	9 a.m.	2.Off + 17.O.R sick, 6.O.R wounded admitted 2 Offices + 18.O.R evacuated.	
	10 p.m.	"C" Bearer Subdivision returned to billets on relief of 2O.L. Inf. Bde from the trenches	

Geo. H. Brown
Maj Rann?
O.C. 23rd F. Amb.

1.

Appendix II

Report of operations of 23rd Field Ambulance Bearer Division

Reference Map. (B Series) BETHUNE.

ROBECQ. P.29.b.35.

May 31st. 2. p.m. C bearer subdivision with light cart, water cart and two wheels rests for stretchers proceeded to advanced dressing station at Marais F5 C 5.10. Four motor ambulances were detailed to convey sick and wounded from advanced dressing station to 1st Highland Field Ambulance at LOCON X.7.

MARAIS.

May 31st. 6. p.m. C bearer sub. div. arrived at allotted advanced dressing stn.

June 1st. 9.30 p.m. C bearers with two pairs of wheels for stretchers evacuated 26 cases almost all lying from 2nd Gordons and 1st Grenadier Guards and one case from 6th Gordons.

June 2nd. 3 a.m. C Bearers returned to advanced dressing station.

June 3rd. During afternoon received intimation of proposed attack by 6th Gordons to take place at 9.45 p.m.

6. p.m. A and B bearer subdivisions with 3 pairs of wheels for stretchers and 6 motor ambulances arrived at advanced dressing station.

8.30 p.m. A and B bearer sub divisions with five pairs of wheels for stretchers proceeded to 6th Gordons aid post. F/8 c 4.7. Seven motor ambulances were detailed to proceed via GORRE along south bank of canal to arrive by 10.30 p.m. at bridge F11 d 7.0.

9.15 p.m. C bearer subdivision proceeded to clear 2 Gordons aid post A2c.06. and Grenadier Guards from Estaminet corner F6 c 4.8. where three motor ambulance were detailed to park to await wounded brought down by C bearers and when loaded to proceed to LE PLOUY FERME. V 16.d.58.

10 p.m. A and B. bearers arrived at 6th Gordons aid post. Evacuation of wounded commenced. Conveyed by bearer and wheeled stretcher squads to motor ambulance park.

P.T.O.

at side of canal. The motors when filled proceeded along north bank of canal, crossed canal again at GORRE and going via BETHUNE proceeded to LE PLOUY FERME where tent division had opened.

Evacuation continued by A and B bearers in this manner till 9 a.m. next morning

June 4th.

2-30 a.m. C bearers returned to advanced dressing station

9. a.m. Wounded had ceased to come down to 6th Gordons aid post. Two stretcher squads with wheels left at aid post. Remainder of bearers proceeded back to advanced dressing station and remainder of motor ambulances, after leaving one at canal bank to work with two squads left behind, returned to park at advanced dressing station.

10. a.m. A and B bearers arrived at advanced dressing Station

4. p.m. Received orders to proceed to billets at W.M.6.3.2.

9. p.m. Proceeded to aid posts and evacuated 20th Brigade sick and wounded.

11-15 p.m. Relieved by 22nd Field ambulance and proceed to allotted billets.

1. p.m arrive at billets. W.17.b.

D. Mackie
Lieut RAMC. S.R.
O.C Bearer Division
23rd Field Ambulance.

Urgent O.C.   **Appendix III**   56
          23rd Field Ambulance

The O C 22nd Field Ambulance will
take over the Advanced Dressing Station
now occupied by the 23rd Field Ambulance
and the O C 29th that now occupied by the 22nd Field Ambulance
on the changing over of their respective
Brigades this evening
2 The OC 22nd Field Ambulance
will detail a Medical Officer to
assist the OC 23rd Field Ambulance
in his Tent Sub Division until
further orders
3. Tent divisions will remain in
their present positions 23rd Field
Ambulance receiving all wounded
from the trenches

W H Stow
Colonel
ADMS / Div
4/6/15

VIIth Division R.A.M Corps Operation Order No. 3. Copy No 5.

by

Colonel W.H. Starr   Commanding 7th Division
13th June 1915

Secret
Appendix IV

No orders or sketches giving information to the enemy are to be taken into the Field

References are to Trench Map ILLIES and LA BASSÉE 1/10,000 and 1/40,000

1. Intention The IVth Corps will on June 15th and following days attack & capture the German positions from the GIVENCHY-CHAPELLE ST. ROCH road to the northern end of the RUE D'OUVERT.
The 7th Division will attack on the front H.3 inclusive
The Infantry assaults will be simultaneous & will take place at 6 pm on June 15th

2. General Plan
The 7th Division will form up during night of June 14/15th & the morning of June 15th. The attack will be carried out by 21st Infantry Brigade to which will be attached Highland Field Coy. & two sections 54th Field Coy R.E.
The 20th Brigade will have three Battalions in and in rear of their trenches & the remainder of the Brigade about GORRE
The 22nd Infantry Brigade will be in reserve about ESSARS.

3. Medical Arrangements
(a) <u>Advanced Dressing Stations</u>:- In conjunction with the movements of the 20th, 21st & 22nd Brigades on 14/15th June the 23rd, 21st & 22nd Field Ambulances will form Advanced Dressing Stations at F5 a.c, A7.D.10.8 & W.30 c. respectively
O.o.b 23rd & 21st Advanced Dressing Stations will each take over three wheeled stretcher carriers, & will be responsible for collection & clearance to Field Ambulance

of the casualties occurring in their respective brigades.
As the troops advance the selection of new ADS will rest
with O.C. Field Ambulances who should notify
A.D.M.S. of any changes in positions of Advanced
Dressing Stations.

(b.) <u>Divisional Collecting Station</u>:-

This will be formed at the CHATEAU GORRE F3B
by O.C. 22nd F.A. who will detail for this purpose
one officer, 1 N.C.O. & two stretcher squads from his
bearer division.

From the commencement of operations all Ambulance
cars & wagons, less two cars & one wagon with 22nd
F.A. will assemble at the D.C.S. & come under the orders
of the O.C. D.C.S. who will be responsible for the regular
supply of ambulance cars to the Advanced Dressing Stations
sending forward two empty cars as a full one
returns from an Advanced Dressing Station.

The horsed wagons & one motor lorry will be used
to convey walking cases from the Divl. Collecting Station
to Field Ambulances.

The cars & wagons of 21st F.A. will convey wounded
to 21st F.A. all other cars & wagons will convey
wounded to 23rd Field Ambulance.

(c) <u>Field Ambulances</u>

    21st Field Ambulance at W.17.A.
    23rd   "   "   LE PLOUY FERME W.16.D
    22nd   "   "   at ECOLE ROBECQ P.29B (for all sick & wounded men only)

(d) <u>Artillery Casualties</u>:-

Artillery units will arrange with O.C. F.A's.
for clearance of their casualties to nearest A.D.S.

4. <u>Road Traffic</u>

O.C. Divisional Collecting Station will be responsible
that Ambulance cars & wagons follow the routes

3.

laid down in road traffic map which will be issued later.

5/ Rations:-

Every man will carry one day's rations besides the remainder of the current day's issue.

6/ Headquarters of A.D.M.S.

A.D.M.S. Headquarters will remain at W 24 D. (formerly called the Halte)

Watton Colonel
O.C. R.A.M. Corps 7th Division

Issued at 6 p.m.
To A.D.M.S. Copy No. 1
 " Col. R.M.A. " 2
 " O.C. 21st Field Amb. " 3
 " " 22nd " " 4
 " " 23rd " " 5
 " General Staff 7th Div. " 6
 " A.D.M.S. G. " 7

Appendix V

Report of Operations. Bearer Division. 23rd Field Ambulance.
June 14 - 19. 1915.
Reference. Map 1/40,000 Bethune Sheet.

June. 14. 2.30 pm. The bearer division 23rd Field Ambulance left LAVELETTE with one light cart and watercart, and proceeded via ESSARS to the dressing station occupied by the 22nd Field Ambulance on Tuning-Fork Road, between GORRE and LE PLANTIN, at a point south of square F.5.a. on map, arriving at 4.30 pm.

The dressing station was taken over, and a tour of the positions and existing aid-posts made with the O.C. Bearer Division 22. F.A. During the night a few wounded from the Border Regiment, Grenadiers, and 2nd Gordons were evacuated.

June 15. 1.30. am. A subdivision went out to remove wounded from the aid post of the 2nd Gordons. This had been established at a point near the road junction LE PLANTIN on south side of square A.2.c. on map. Wounded of the Grenadier Guards and other units were also collected at this spot by regimental bearers during the operations.

3.30. am. A section returned to dressing station having cleared the aid post. During the day one or two wounded were evacuated, and sick from the Brigade Grenade Company, and Border Regiment.

7. pm. Numerous wounded began to arrive on foot at dressing station from NORTH LANCASHIRE and ROYAL SCOTS regiments. Those requiring attention were detained, and the rest directed to the Divisional Collecting Station. GORRE.

Four wounded Grenadiers were also evacuated by motor ambulance from a point known as ESTAMINET CORNER at a bend of GORRE - LE PLANTIN road in square F.6.c. on map. With this exception no wounded from 20th Brigade were received.

9. pm. C. bearer subdivision went up to aid-post. LE PLANTIN. Walking cases continued to arrive at dressing station mainly of HIGHLAND Division.

June. 16. 3. am. C. bearers returned to dressing station, and reported aid post clear. No wounded 20th Brigade remaining out. Numerous wounded had been removed from LE PLANTIN to ESTAMINET CORNER, to which motor ambulances were sent, including men

(2)

of the HIGHLAND Division and Wiltshire Regiment.

During the day a few more cases were evacuated.

9 pm. A bearer subdivision went up to LE PLANTIN and cleared aid post.

11.30 pm. Trenches declared free of wounded. A bearers returned.

June 17. A few wounded evacuated during morning. During the afternoon the road between dressing station and GORRE was heavily shelled. One or two casualties occurred.

9 pm. B bearers went out, but found no wounded.

10 pm. Notice of projected attack 2.45 am received.

June 18. 12.30 am. Notice received that wounded Gordons were at aid post. B bearer section went out, and removed these. Numerous walking cases from 2nd Gordons began to arrive at dressing station.

4 am. Bearers returned as it was reported no more wounded could be brought in until dark.

8 am. Notice received of 5 more wounded at aid post. C. subdivision went out, cleared these, and left two squads at ESTAMINET CORNER.

9 pm. A subdivision went out, and cleared the wounded which had remained out during the day.

June 19. 1.30 am. Medical Officer 2nd Gordons reported all wounded had been cleared, and bearers returned.

Remarks. Throughout the operations, many walking cases were received and attended to at dressing station, mainly from HIGHLAND Division. The evacuation of stretcher cases was much facilitated by the fact that wheeled stretchers could be used between aid post and the point ESTAMINET CORNER to which cars could be brought. The work of the bearers was thereby rendered easy. The supply of cars was throughout satisfactory, the number of wounded requiring evacuation never being very large.

Death at Dressing Station 19.6.15. Pte. G. Anderson, Scots Guards
G.S. Wound. Chest. No. 12605. Infirm.
Buried, corner of GORRE wood.
Point S.W. corner of Square F4 a map.

Signed. O. D. Webb. Lieut. R.A.M.C

121/6250

137/6250

12/6250

Mr. Dinain.

23rd Field Ambulance

Vol VII

July 1915

Army Form C. 2118.

WAR DIARY
or
INTELLIGENCE SUMMARY
(Erase heading not required.)

Instructions regarding War Diaries and Intelligence Summaries are contained in F. S. Regs., Part II. and the Staff Manual respectively. Title pages will be prepared in manuscript.

Hour, Date, Place		Summary of Events and Information	Remarks and references to Appendices
LA PLOUY FARM.		The unit marched into their billet at LA MIQUELLERIE	
July 1st	8:30 a.m.	O 30 d 2.1. (Sheet 36A 1/40,000 map. France)	
	9 a.m.	Daily State - 27. OR sick admitted - 35. OR evacuated	
	11.30 a.m.	Arrived at the new billet at LA MIQUELLERIE. A hospital has established under canvas, the personnel going into bivouac	
	2 P.M.	Lt C H HART RAMC reported that he had been admitted to H.P. in No.7 Stationary Hospital BOULOGNE, having been taken ill while returning from England	
LA MAQUELLERIE.			
July 2nd	9 a.m.	4. OR sick admitted - 10. OR sick evacuated	
	12 noon	Lt WEDD RAMC returned on completion of temporary duty with 1st Grenr. Gds.	
July 3rd	9 a.m.	26. OR sick 1 Off sick admitted - 1 Off - 23. OR sick evacuated	
July 4th	9 a.m.	19. OR sick admitted 11 OR evacuated	
July 5th	9 a.m.	22. OR sick " 19 OR "	
July 6th	9 a.m.	11. OR " 14 " "	
July 7th	10 a.m.	Lt D. MACKIE to 2/Gordons } for temporary duty Lt W.S. MILNE to 2/Scots Guards }	

Army Form C. 2118.

WAR DIARY
or
INTELLIGENCE SUMMARY
(Erase heading not required.)

Instructions regarding War Diaries and Intelligence Summaries are contained in F.S. Regs., Part II. and the Staff Manual respectively. Title pages will be prepared in manuscript.

Hour, Date, Place		Summary of Events and Information	Remarks and references to Appendices
LA MIQUELLERIE			
July 7th	9 a.m.	17. OR sick admitted. 15 OR Sick Evacuated	
" 8th	9 a.m.	20. OR " " 12. OR "	
	3 p.m.	Wire received from D.M.S. 1st Army notifying that Lt. J.W. LINNELL has been transferred to Eastern Command for duty	
July 9th	9 a.m.	19. OR sick admitted — 11. OR sick Evacuated	
July 10th	9 a.m.	26 OR sick admitted — 21. OR " "	
July 11th	9 a.m.	26. OR " " — 19. OR " "	
	10 a.m.	7th Divn. Operation Order No. 4 received. I visited the new area during the course of the day. I learned that the 1.S.O. Ind. F.A. is not moving till noon on 14th July from the buildings occupies at PARADIS (H40000 Béthune Outline Sheet Q.18.C. Q.24.a.)	Appendix I
July 12th	9 a.m.	12 OR sick admitted — 14. OR sick Evacuated	
	11.30 a.m.	LIET J. E. BARNES. R.A.M.C (Temp. Com.) reports himself for duty from No. 12 Gen. HP. ROUEN.	
July 13th	9 a.m.	1 Off + 33. OR Sick admitted. 1 Off + 21. OR Sick evacuated. Received intimation that Lt. C.H. HART. R.A.M.C has been transferred to No. 11 Genl. HP. Boulogne — Struck of the strength accordingly	

Army Form C. 2118.

WAR DIARY
or
INTELLIGENCE SUMMARY

(Erase heading not required.)

Instructions regarding War Diaries and Intelligence Summaries are contained in F. S. Regs., Part II. and the Staff Manual respectively. Title pages will be prepared in manuscript.

Hour, Date, Place		Summary of Events and Information	Remarks and references to Appendices
LA MIQUILLERIE July 13th	6 p.m.	All cases in hospital transferred to "B" Section which is remaining behind, to deal with sick of units in the vicinity	
July 14th	9 a.m.	Daily State :- 1 Off + 29 OR Sick admitted - 1 Off + 28 OR Evacuated Sick. The Unit marched at 9 a.m. - leaving behind "B" tent subdivision under CAPT. W.G. WRIGHT. RAMC. - with the section wagons & 2 Motor Ambulances	
PARADIS July 14th	12 noon	Arrived at PARADIS and established the Main Dressing Station in the Infant School. (1000 Bourbier Sheet Returns Q18 a.2.) LT ALLAN RAMC to 6/Gordons for temporary duty	
July 15th	9 a.m.	8 OR sick admitted - 8 OR Sick Evacuated	
July 16th	9 a.m.	2 Off + 28 OR sick admitted - 2 Off + 23 OR sick Evacuated. LT MACKIE RAMC returned, on completion of temporary duty with 2/London Regt. LT MILNE RAMC returned on completion of temporary duty with 2/Scots Guards	
	12 noon	Received 18 Trench Stretchers - issued 3 to each battalion of 20th Bde - Keeping 3 in reserve with this unit -	
July 17th	9 a.m.	32 OR sick + 1 wounded (self inflicted) admitted. 22 OR Sick + 1 " " Evacuated by No 7 MMC	
	4 p.m.	LT FREEMAN RAMC. reported himself for duty - from 20 (Gen?) CCS	

Army Form C. 2118.

WAR DIARY
or
INTELLIGENCE SUMMARY

(Erase heading not required.)

Instructions regarding War Diaries and Intelligence Summaries are contained in F.S. Regs, Part II. and the Staff Manual respectively. Title pages will be prepared in manuscript.

Hour, Date, Place		Summary of Events and Information	Remarks and references to Appendices
PARADIS. July 18th	9 a.m.	34 O.R. sick admitted – 12 O.R. sick evacuated.	
	6 p.m.	"B" Bearer Subdivision under Lt. D. MACKIE R.A.M.C. with light Cart, water cart, + 2 wheel stretcher carriers proceeded forward to take over the A.D.S. at X.11.6. from 21st F. Amb. on relief of the 21st by the 20th Inf. Bde. This A.D.S. is established in sand-bag shelters alongside the trolly-line. Wounded from the trenches are collected in the vicinity of this line + are brought to the A.D.S. on trucks. The 23rd F.A. on the relief being completed, has been detailed to deal with the sick of the 21st Inf Bde. The sick & wounded of 20th Brigade will be sent to the 21st F.A. Dressing Station at ZELOBES being brought back by the Ambulance cars of 21st F.A.	
July 19th	9 a.m.	3 O.R. Sick admitted – 7 O.R. Sick Evacuated.	
	5 p.m.	Visited A.D.S.	
July 20th	9 a.m.	12 O.R. sick admitted – 6 O.R. sick Evacuated. Instructions received from A.D.M.S. 7th Div. that on the relief of the 22nd Inf Bde by 21st Inf Bde on night 21st/22nd July the sick & wounded of 20th Inf Bde will be dealt with by the 22nd F. Amb, the 23rd F. Amb. to deal with the sick of the 22nd Inf Bde	

WAR DIARY
or
INTELLIGENCE SUMMARY
(Erase heading not required.)

Army Form C. 2118.

Hour, Date, Place	Summary of Events and Information	Remarks and references to Appendices
PARADIS		
July 21st 9 a.m.	12 O.R. sick admitted — 12 O.R. sick evacuated	
July 22nd 9 a.m.	1 Off + 9 O.R. sick admitted — 1 Off + 6 O.R. evacuated	
1 p.m.	LIEUT. J.C. SHELMERDINE Rame (T.Sn) reported for duty	
5 p.m.	LT J.E. ALLAN returned on completion of temp. duty with 6/L.Pools.	
July 23rd 9 a.m.	2 Off + 17 O.R. sick admitted. 2 Off + 6 O.R. evacuated	
July 24th 9 a.m.	6 O.R. sick + 2 O.R. wounded admitted — 6 O.R. evacuated	
July 25th 9 a.m.	1 Off + 20 O.R. sick + 2 wounded admitted — 1 Off + 30 O.R. evacuated	
July 26th 9 a.m.	13 O.R. sick admitted — 11 O.R. evacuated	
	Orders received during the day relating to relief of 20th Inf Bde by 22nd Inf Bde on 26/27th inst.	
July 27th 9 a.m.	2 Off + 15 O.R. sick admitted. 2 Off + 26 O.R. sick evacuated	
10.30 a.m.	A. & S.H. handed over to 2/2nd R. Innis. Fus. "B" leaves div. trenches — reformed the unit — 15 Off. sick admitted. 5 O.R. sick evacuated	
July 28th 9 a.m.	LT J.C. SHELMERDINE - Rame to 2/Border Regt. for temporary duty.	

Army Form C. 2118.

WAR DIARY
or
INTELLIGENCE SUMMARY
(Erase heading not required.)

Instructions regarding War Diaries and Intelligence Summaries are contained in F. S. Regs., Part II. and the Staff Manual respectively. Title pages will be prepared in manuscript.

Hour, Date, Place		Summary of Events and Information	Remarks and references to Appendices
PARADIS.			
July 29th	9 a.m.	11. OR Sick admitted — 15 OR Sick Evacuated	
July 30th	9 a.m.	9 OR " " — 9 OR " "	
		Received instructions to move to ROBECQ with 20th L.F. Bde tomorrow.	
July 31st	9 a.m.	1 Off + 13 OR Sick admitted — 1 Off + 7 OR sick Evacuated.	
	3 p.m.	Unit marched from PARADIS — arriving at ROBECQ at 5 p.m. Dressing Station Established in the School, + in a mill warehouse in the village of ROBECQ (1/40,000 Combined Sheet BETHUNE 2.9.6.) These buildings are capable of accommodating 75 sick.	
	6 p.m.	Bearer Section reported afr. closing up, from LA MIQUELLERIE. During the month of July, flies were very prevalent. All latrines tea were fitted with flyproof seats + covers. All Excreta has been incinerated successfully. Mosquitoes to have been very troublesome — Breeding ponds have been daubed out +destroyed with Kerosene oil	

Geo. H. Dawson
Maj. R.A.M.C.
O.C. 23rd Fd Amb.

Appendix I.   Copy No. 6

7th Division R. of M. C. Operation Order No. 4
by Lieut. Colonel T. C. Hayes R.A.M. Corps
Commanding R.A.M. Corps 7th Division

Reference Map FRANCE BETHUNE (Combined sheet)
1-40,000

July 10th 1915

Medical Arrangements for New Area:-

(A.) A Divisional Advanced Dressing Station will be formed at X 11 B by 21st Field Ambulance from 12 noon 11th July. Previous to that hour all casualties of 21st Brigade will be collected to same A.D.S. under arrangements made by A.D.M.S. MEERUT Division.

(B) The 21st Field Ambulance will open on the 11th instant in ZELOBE taking over the buildings at present used for Ambulance purposes by the MEERUT Division.

(C) The 22nd Field Ambulance will open at VIELLE CHAPELLE on 12th instant in the Brewery and other buildings at present used by the 20th British Field Ambulance of MEERUT Division

On the 22nd Infantry Brigade taking over the trenches from VI to Estaires - LA BASSEE Road on night 13th/14th the O.C. 22nd Field Ambulance will arrange in consultation with O.C. 21st Field Ambulance for the evacuation of sick and wounded of 22nd Brigade from the Divisional A.D.S. to 22nd Field Ambulance.

(D.) On the 13th instant the 23rd Field Ambulance less B Section will open in PARADIS in the Moulin Vapeur and other buildings occupied by by Indian Field Ambulance of MEERUT Division.

(E) For time of march Officers Commanding Field Ambulances will arrange with Brigadier Generals Commanding their respective Brigades.

(F) B Section 23rd Field Ambulance will remain in its present position for the collection of sick of the 4th Division Artillery Units, Divisional Ammunition Column, Divisional Cyclists and Squadron of Northumberland Hussars.

(G) The Office of the A.D.M.S. will open in farm at R15D at present occupied by A.D.M.S. MEERUT Division at 6 am on the 14th instant.

Issued at 8.50 pm.

Copy No. 1 to A.D.M.S.
 "   " 2 " AA & QMG 4 Divn
 "   " 3 " General Staff "
 "   " 4 " 21st F.A.
 "   " 5 " 22nd F.A.
 "   " 6 " 23rd F.A.

P. N. Hudson
Major
for Lieut Colonel
Commanding R.A.M.C.
4th Division

121/6550

7th Division

28th Field Ambulance

Vol VIII

From 1st to 31st Aug. 1915

August 15

Army Form C. 2118.

WAR DIARY
or
INTELLIGENCE SUMMARY

(Erase heading not required.)

Instructions regarding War Diaries and Intelligence Summaries are contained in F. S. Regs., Part II. and the Staff Manual respectively. Title pages will be prepared in manuscript.

Hour, Date, Place		Summary of Events and Information	Remarks and references to Appendices
ROBECQ –			
August 1st	9 a.m.	31 O.R. sick admitted – 16. O.R. evacuated	
August 2nd	9 a.m.	19. O.R. " " – 5. O.R. "	
" 3rd	9 a.m.	16. O.R. " " – 11. O.R. "	
" 4th	9 a.m.	LT. J.E. BARNES. R.A.M.C. proceeds to 22 W F.A.mb. for duty.	
		1. Off. & 14. O.R. sick admitted – 1. Off. & O.R. evacuated.	
" 5th	9 a.m.	1. Off. & 32. O.R. " " – 1. Off. & 12. O.R. "	
" 6th	9 a.m.	14. O.R. sick admitted – 12. O.R. evacuated	
	12 noon	LT. J.C. SHELMERDINE returned on completion of temp. duty.	
" 7th	9 a.m.	14. O.R. sick admitted – 11. O.R. evacuated. 1 Sick off admitted	
" 8th	9 a.m.	8 " " – 4 " "	
" 9th	9 a.m.	8 " " – 5 " "	
" 10th	9 a.m.	19 " " – 10 " "	
" 11th	9 a.m.	17 " " – 6 " "	
" 12th	9 a.m.	17 " " – 8 " "	
" 13th	9 a.m.	13 " " – 5 " "	
" 14th	9 a.m.	6 " " – 7 " "	
		Orders received that on relief of 9th Divn. by the 1st Divn., the 23rd 2nd Amb. will establish at AVELETTE (1/40000 Refinee sheet W117A).	

Army Form C. 2118.

WAR DIARY
or
INTELLIGENCE SUMMARY
(Erase heading not required.)

Instructions regarding War Diaries and Intelligence Summaries are contained in F. S. Regs., Part II. and the Staff Manual respectively. Title pages will be prepared in manuscript.

Hour, Date, Place		Summary of Events and Information	Remarks and references to Appendices
ROBECQ			
August 15th	9 a.m.	1 Off + 10 OR sick admitted — 1 Off + 14 OR sick evacuated	
" 16th	9 a.m.	15 OR sick admitted — 15 OR sick evacuated	
	6.30 p.m.	20th Brigade O.O. No 24 relating to relief of 9th by 7th Div.	
" 17th	9 a.m.	18 OR sick admitted — 12 OR evacuated	
	4.30 p.m.	The unit marched to AVELETTE (W.17.a) arriving there about 6 p.m. — A dressing station established under canvas, capable of accommodating 70 cases.	
AVELETTE			
August 18th	9 a.m.	1 Off + 10 OR sick admitted — 1 Off + 11 OR sick evacuated	
" 19th	9 a.m.	8 OR sick " " 3 OR sick "	
" 20th	9 a.m.	8 OR " " " " "	
" 21st	9 a.m.	12 " " " 7 " "	
" 22nd	9 a.m.	8 " " " 9 " "	
" 23rd	9 a.m.	8 " " " 10 " "	
" 24th	9 a.m.	7 " " " 4 " "	
		" " " 10 " "	
	3.30 p.m.	Medical arrangements for 7th Div. on relieving 2nd Div. received	
" 25th	9 a.m.	8 Off sick admitted — None evacuated	Appointment Cancelled.
		Lieut W.S. MILNE, RAMC to 7th Div. Train for temporary duty.	
" 26th	9 a.m.	6 OR sick admitted — 3 OR sick evacuated	
	3.30 p.m.	Medical arrangements orders of 2nd Div. Cancelled. Orders issued for 15th Bde over ADS from 21st 72 Amb. at F5c MARAIS (Vieux Bethune) by 11 Amb. on 27/8.	

Army Form C. 2118.

WAR DIARY
or
INTELLIGENCE SUMMARY
(Erase heading not required.)

Instructions regarding War Diaries and Intelligence Summaries are contained in F. S. Regs., Part II. and the Staff Manual respectively. Title pages will be prepared in manuscript.

Hour, Date, Place		Summary of Events and Information	Remarks and references to Appendices
AVELETTE. August 27-	9 a.m.	1. Off + 4 O.R. sick admitted - 1 Off + 4 O.R. sick evacuated. "C" Bearer Subdivision under Capt. C.D.M. BUCKLEY-RAINE with Motor-cart, forage Cart + 3 Wheel stretcher Carriages proceeded forward to establish A.D.S. Bn. at MARAIS F5c (troops Relative map)	
	1.30 p.m	Instructions received re Medical Arrangements on withdrawal of 7th Div to area about BUSNES.	
" 28th-	9 a.m.	1 Off + 7 O.R. wounded, 13. O.R. sick admitted - 1 wounded + 11.O.R sick evacuated	
" 29th-	9 a.m.	16.O.R. sick + 5.O.R wounded admitted - 4 sick + 4 wounded Evacuated 1 death in A.P. (L.S.W. Antart penetrating button)	
" 30th-	9 a.m.	20. O.R sick + 2. O.R wounded admitted - 18 sick + 8 wounded Evacuated	
" 31st	1 A.M.	"C" Bearer Subdivision Returned on relief of 20th Lt 18th	
" "	9 a.m.	22. O.R Sick + 5.O.R wounded admitted - 26. O.R sick Evacuated	
" "	10 a.m.	The unit marched from AVELETTE	
" "	1.15 p.m	Arrived at LA MIQUELLERIE - Dressing station established Under Canvas at O30 d.2.1. (1/40,000 Sheet 36A AIRE)	

Geo. M. Browne
Maj. R.A.M.C
O.C. 23rd F. Amb.

Appendix 1

To,
O.C. 23rd Field Ambulance

1. You will draw tomorrow morning 3rd June the tentage of 21st & 22nd Field Ambulances with your own tentage open in the clean grass field on the N.W of the farm in W 16 d South of the A in AVELETTE - The farm buildings will be used for billeting the personnel of the F.A. using any tents that may be necessary as overflow for Officer's billets.

   The D.M.S. 1st Army has been asked to provide more marquees.

   Two men of the Divisional Sanitary Section are holding the farm buildings for you.

2. The 22nd F.A. will take over the buildings & billets at present occupied by you in ROBECQ.

W H Starr
Colonel A.D.M.S.
VII Division

2/6/15

121/7050

7th Division

Summarised

23rd Field Ambulance

Intx

Sept. 15

Sept "15"
S

WAR DIARY
or
INTELLIGENCE SUMMARY

(Erase heading not required.)

Army Form C. 2118.

Hour, Date, Place		Summary of Events and Information	Remarks and references to Appendices
LA MIQUELLERIE.			
September 1st	9 a.m.	1 Off + 7 O.R. sick admitted — 1 Off sick + 5 O.R. wounded evacuated	
	2 p.m.	LT. J.C. SHELMERDINE RAMC to 6/Gordons for temporary duty	
" 2nd	7.30 a.m.	"A" bearer sub division proceeded forward under CAPT. J.E. ALLAN to FOUQUIÈRES-LES-BETHUNE (E20 central) to take over site of Dressing Station — a field at E20 b.6.4.	
	9 a.m.	10 Off + 24 O.R. sick admitted — 1 Off + 27 O.R. evacuated	
	4 p.m.	4 Wheel stretcher carriages received.	
" 3rd	9 a.m.	19 O.R. sick admitted — 24 O.R. sick evacuated	
	4.15 p.m.	The unit marched to FOUQUIÈRES-LES-BETHUNE (E20 central) arriving at 7.30 p.m.	
FOUQUIERES.			
" 4th	9 a.m.	4 O.R. sick admitted — 4 O.R. sick evacuated	
	11 a.m.	Orders received to open A.D. Stn at CHATEAU VERNELLES (G8033). All sick are to be sent on to 21st F.D. Ambulance at GONNEHEM (V18 a central)	
	12.30 a.m.	"C" Bearer sub division, under CAPT C.D.M. BUCKLEY RAMC (SR), with water cart, light cart, 3 wheel stretcher carriages and 2 motor ambulance cars, proceeded forward to establish A.D. Stn at CHATEAU VERNELLES	

Army Form C. 2118.

WAR DIARY
or
INTELLIGENCE SUMMARY

(Erase heading not required.)

Instructions regarding War Diaries and Intelligence Summaries are contained in F. S. Regs., Part II. and the Staff Manual respectively. Title pages will be prepared in manuscript.

Hour, Date, Place		Summary of Events and Information	Remarks and references to Appendices
FOUQUIÈRES September 4th	4 p.m.	The Main Dressing Station has been established in a field, in tents. 6 operation + 20 bell-tents pitched. There was a shed which is available give accommodation for 210 wounded.	
" 5th	9 a.m.	11. OR wounded + 13. OR Sick admitted – 10 sick OR Evacuated	
" 6th	9 a.m.	4. OR " + 1 Oths " – 10 wounded + 2 Sick Evacuated	
"	2 p.m.	Visited Ad. Dr. Stn. – The station is sited in the cellars of the ruined CHATEAU VERMELLES – Sand-bag protection has been put up	
" 7th	9 a.m.	10. OR wounded admitted – 4 wounded + 1 Sick Evacuated	
"	3 p.m.	Under orders from A.D.M.S 7th Divn Capt. W.G. WRIGHT. RAMC proceeded to 21st Field Ambulance to assume command of that unit. "A" bearer sub-division proceeded to Ad. Dr. Stn. to relieve "C" bearer sub-division.	
" 8th	9 a.m.	1. Off + 15. OR wounded admitted – 9. OR evacuated – 2 wounded died – both of penetrating abdominal wounds. Capt. G.W. LLOYD RAMC(TC) from 24th 3d Amb. } reported for duty. Lieut. J.T. HURST " (T.C) " 21st " " }	
"	11 a.m.	26th 3d Amb. reported for duty. Lieut. F.W. HARLOW " (T.C) "	
"	3 p.m.	Lieut. J.T. HURST. RAMC posted to 7th Dn Train – in relief of Lieut W.S. MILNE RAMC who rejoins 23rd 3d Amb.	

1247 W 3299 200,000 (E) 8/14 J.B.C. & A. Forms/C. 2118/11.

WAR DIARY
or
INTELLIGENCE SUMMARY

(Erase heading not required.)

Army Form C. 2118.

Hour, Date, Place		Summary of Events and Information	Remarks and references to Appendices
FOUQUIERES September 8th	6 p.m.	LIEUT. J.C. SHELMERDINE. RAMC returned on completion of temporary duty with 6/ Gordon Highlanders.	
" 9 "	9 a.m.	1 wounded + 1 sick (accident) admitted — 1 Off + 12 O.R. wounded), 1 sick evacuated	
	11 a.m.	LIEUT. J.C. SHELMERDINE. RAMC proceeded to 22nd Fd. Amb. transferred for duty with that unit under instruction from A.D.M.S. 7th Div. the A.D.S at CHATEAU VERMELLES was handed over to 22nd Fd. Amb. during the afternoon. The bearer subdivision remaining in there to carry out work on dug-outs &c — 23rd F.A. to collect sick of 21st + 18th.	
" 10th "	9 a.m.	2 O.R. wounded admitted. 3 wounded evacuated	
	3 p.m.	"B" Bearer Subdivision proceeded to CHATEAU VERMELLES under CAPT. F.P. FREEMAN. RAMC. to relieve "A" bearer Sub-division. The latter rejoined the unit, bringing in the sectional equipment	
" 11th "	9 a.m.	1 O.R. wounded admitted — 2 wounded evacuated	
	1 p.m.	CAPT. B.W. ARMSTRONG RAMC (T/C) joined for duty from No 6 Gen. Hp ROUEN.	
" 12th "	9 a.m.	Admissions — NIL — 1 wounded + 1 sick Evacuated	
" 13th "	9 a.m.	" " NIL. Evacuations NIL	
	2 p.m.	"C" Bearer Subdivision under CAPT. G.W. LLOYD RAMC proceeded to VERMELLES to relieve B bearer on digging &c	

Army Form C. 2118.

WAR DIARY
or
INTELLIGENCE SUMMARY
(Erase heading not required.)

Instructions regarding War Diaries and Intelligence Summaries are contained in F. S. Regs., Part II. and the Staff Manual respectively. Title pages will be prepared in manuscript.

Hour, Date, Place		Summary of Events and Information	Remarks and references to Appendices
FOUQUIÈRES			
Sept. 14th	9 a.m.	Daily State. Evacuations & admissions NIL.	
" 15th	9 a.m.	Nil daily state -	Appendix I
	6 p.m.	Medical Arrangements for VIIth Division received	
" 16th	2 p.m.	"A" bearer sub division proceeded to VERMELLES in relief of "C" bearer sub division to provide working parties	
" 17th	9 a.m.	Morning State - NIL.	
" 18th	9 a.m.	" " NIL	
	2 p.m.	"A" bearer sub division returned on completion of duty.	
" 19th	9 a.m.	1 O.R. sick admitted - (G.S.W. accidental).	
	10 a.m.	20th F. Bde O.O. No. 29 received.	
" 20th	9 a.m.	1 O.R. Sick - Evacuated. No admission.	
" 21st	9 a.m.	Morning State - NIL	
	7 p.m.	20 I.B.de O.O. No. 30 received	
" 22nd	9 a.m.	Morning State - NIL	
	10.15 a.m.	R.A.M.C. Operation Order No 5 received.	Appendix II
	12 noon.	The following have been brought to notice for "Mention" in order of merit for consistent & continuous good work. 18678 Q.M.Sgt. ELLIS - LEWIS SPENCER - 18933 S/Sergt. ABBOTT - JOHN JOSEPH 1491 Pte. HARDING - GEORGE 12676 S/Sergt YOUNG - ERNEST ARTHUR.	

Army Form C. 2118.

WAR DIARY
or
INTELLIGENCE SUMMARY

(Erase heading not required.)

Instructions regarding War Diaries and Intelligence Summaries are contained in F. S. Regs., Part II. and the Staff Manual respectively. Title pages will be prepared in manuscript.

Hour, Date, Place		Summary of Events and Information	Remarks and references to Appendices
FOUGUIÈRES			
Sept 23rd	9 a.m.	Morning state – NIL	
"	2 p.m.	3 Brooke-McCormic wheel stretcher Carriages received making a total of 13 "B.McC" + 1 "Miller-James" = 14	
"	5 p.m.	3 Brooke-McCormic stretcher Carriages issued to Artillery units – leaving 11.	
- 24th -	9 a.m.	1 O.R. sick admitted.	
"	5.40 p.m.	The Bearer Division under CAPT. F. P. FREEMAN. R.A.M.C. (SR) proceeded forward in small parties at intervals of 20 minutes taking Medical Store Cart and 10 wheel stretcher carriages. The last party left at 5.40 p.m. They will take up their positions tonight – distributed as follows:-	Report of operations of Bearer Division Appendix A
		① Forward Advanced Dress. Stn. – 16 bearers 8 stretchers	
		1 M.O. + 2 dressers.	
		② No. 1 Relay Post – 16 bearers + 8 stretchers } Bearers + stretchers	
		③ No. 2 " – 16 " 8 " } in each post	
		④ A.D.S. (G.q.a.2.6) 1 M.O.	
		20 bearers with 10 wheel stretcher carriages	
		2 " in reserve	
		3 dressers	
		1 Cook	
		1 M.O. on duty between ① + ④ to supervise evacuation	
		A small Oxygen cylinder + materials for gas poisoning burns placed in the forward A.D.S. + in the A.D.S.	

Army Form C. 2118.

WAR DIARY
or
INTELLIGENCE SUMMARY
(Erase heading not required.)

Hour, Date, Place	Summary of Events and Information	Remarks and references to Appendices
FOUQUIERES — Operations Commence — Sept 25th		
7.30 a.m.	The 3 horsed ambulances left to report at Wagon Rendezvous at SAILLY-LABOURSE. (L3d9.4)	
8.30 a.m.	An urgent message from D.C.S. asking for 2 motor ambulances which were sent at once.	
9 a.m.	Message from A.D.M.S. to send all ambulances to Wagon Rendezvous at SAILLY-LABOURSE at once —	
"	Morning State :- 22. O.R Sick and 3. O.R wounded admitted — 4 sick + 1 wounded evacuated	
"	First wounded arrived, among them being several men suffering from mild gas poisoning.	
12. noon.	5. Off + 105. O.R wounded admitted. Evacuated - Nil.	
3 p.m.	Orders from A.D.M.S. 7th Divn to draw 100 stretchers from Cav. Cl. Shn. On applying, I was informed that no stretchers were available till an Ambulance train arrived	
4 p.m.	Orders from A.D.M.S to cease admitting cases from 4 p.m.; to evacuate all cases by M.A.C by 4.30 p.m.; then pack up & move the unit forward to LABOURSE (L2a)	
4.30 p.m.	Only 28 cases had been removed by M.A.C. so the unit could not move. One section packing up to go forward.	
5 p.m.	Orders from A.D.M.S. cancelling the order to move. One section only to go forward, the other two sections remaining open.	
6.30 p.m.	"B" tent-subdivision under Capt. MACKIE - RAMC(SR) moved forward to LABOURSE (L2.a) Parked there in a field, & revisited wounded again being admitted	21st Fd Amb.

Army Form C. 2118.

WAR DIARY
or
INTELLIGENCE SUMMARY

(Erase heading not required.)

Instructions regarding War Diaries and Intelligence Summaries are contained in F. S. Regs., Part II. and the Staff Manual respectively. Title pages will be prepared in manuscript.

Hour, Date, Place		Summary of Events and Information	Remarks and references to Appendices
FOUQUIÈRES Sept 25th (Cont'd)	9 p.m.	Since 12 noon. 12. Off + 252. OR wounded admitted - Evacuated 4 Off + 20 OR. Reported to ADMS 7th Div. that Evacuation was very slow, + that Congestion of wounded was occurring here.	
	10.30 p.m.	Capt. B.W. ARMSTRONG (RAMC.(TC) left to join the 9th Devon. Regt. in Compliance with ADMS. orders	
Sept 26th	12.45 a.m.	Numbers of wounded coming in - Again reports the Congestion to ADMS.	
	2 a.m.	So many cases had collected, that there was no room in the Camp + barns. School at FOUQUIÈRES situated about E20c8.5 taken over, + opened as an annexe to the Camp. This building accommodates 20 stretcher + 40 sitting cases.	
	6 a.m.	12. Off. 205 OR wounded admitted - 12. Off + 120 OR. evacuated	
	9 a.m.	DAILY STATE :- 29. Off - 574. OR wounded admitted - 21 Off. 229 OR evacuated Died - 1 Off + 2 OR - During the afternoon a report was received that a motor ambulance wagon had been damaged by rifle fire while picking up wounded. No M2/076770 Pte J. HOLMES - A.S.C.(MT) the driver of this car did a very brave + fine piece of work in getting the car away under fire - During the afternoon about 75 stretchers were sent up from Cas. Cl. Stn by M.A.C. - These were sent forward to D. C. Stn	

Army Form C. 2118.

WAR DIARY
or
INTELLIGENCE SUMMARY
(Erase heading not required.)

Instructions regarding War Diaries and Intelligence Summaries are contained in F. S. Regs., Part II. and the Staff Manual respectively. Title pages will be prepared in manuscript.

Hour, Date, Place	Summary of Events and Information	Remarks and references to Appendices
FOUQUIERES Sept 26th Cont	9 a.m. 1 Off + 111 OR wounded admitted - 1 Off + 63 OR evacuated -	
	12 noon	
	9 p.m. 95 OR wounded admitted - 127 OR evacuated) Drew about 25 stretchers from Ambulance train at CHOCQUES. Making a total of about 100 in all. These were sent up. During the night of 26th. N° 20201 Pte E. WHITE RAMC. "A"bearer sub division 23rd F.A. was killed while collecting wounded. G.S.W. through the neck. N° 1796 Pte J. McCLURE RAMC. "C" bearer sub division was wounded - G.S.W. buttock.	
Sept. 27th -	6 a.m. 8 Off 112 OR wounded admitted - also 3 German prisoners wounded) 5 Off 240 OR evacuated	
	9 a.m. DAILY STATE :- 10 Off 291 OR wounded admitted - 10 Off 506 OR evacuated) (On the state, 97 units were represented.) Died :- 3. OR.	
	12 noon 1 Off - 32 OR wounded admitted - 4 Off + 80 OR + 3 German evacuated.	
	4 p.m. "B" Sub-division reformed	
	9 p.m. 1 Off 30 OR wounded admitted - 29 OR evacuated	

Army Form C. 2118.

WAR DIARY
or
INTELLIGENCE SUMMARY
(Erase heading not required.)

Hour, Date, Place		Summary of Events and Information	Remarks and references to Appendices
Sept 28th	6. a.m.	32.OR admitted wounded — 37.OR evacuated) (66.OR remaining. These are light cases).	
	9 a.m.	DAILY STATE:— 1.Off, 87.OR wounded, 8 OR sick admitted — 1.Off 128 OR wounded evacuated — 24.OR sent to Conv. Camp + Duty Died :— 1.OR.	
	12 noon	1.Off + 28 OR wounded admitted — 1.Off + 32.OR evacuated	
	9 p.m.	13.OR wounded admitted — 8.OR wounded evacuated	
Sept 29th	6 a.m.	27.OR " " — 38.OR "	
	9 a.m.	Daily State :— 1.Off + 55.OR wounded + 7 Sick admitted. — 1.Off, 80.OR wounded + 6 Sick evacuated. 2.OR died —	
	12 noon	Orders from ADMS to withdraw all ambulance wagons — less two motor ambulances — to main dressing Station — The 2 motors to be left at the D.C.S at CHATEAU VERMELLES. Also that 2 bearer sub-divisions might be withdrawn, if the military situation permits. In consultation with 2b th Bde HqQrs it was decided that the 2 Sub-divisions might be withdrawn at night	
	2.30 p.m. 4 pm	Orders from ADMS to move the ambulance to ECOLE ANNEZIN. 36.OR sick (wounded) transferred to ECOLE JULES FERRY.	Appendix III

Army Form C. 2118.

WAR DIARY
or
INTELLIGENCE SUMMARY

(Erase heading not required.)

Instructions regarding War Diaries and Intelligence Summaries are contained in F. S. Regs, Part II. and the Staff Manual respectively. Title pages will be prepared in manuscript.

Hour, Date, Place		Summary of Events and Information	Remarks and references to Appendices
FOUQUIÈRES Sept 29th (Con.d)	4.45pm	"B" Tent Subdivision under Capt. D. Mackie proceeds to ANNEZIN and by 6 p.m. this section was established ready to receive wounded —	
	7.50pm	The remainder of the Ambulance marched out, arriving at ANNEZIN at 8.45 p.m. and establishes the main dressing station at ECOLE GARÇONS — (E 9.4.3.6) by 10 P.M. with accommodation for 90 wounded	
	9 p.m.	11. OR wounded admits — 31. OR evacuated. No 12175 Pte Campbell (Sh.R.Thyh.) & 10685 Pte Beardsley W.H. (Sh.Ht.Abs.mal. Superficie) of the A unit reports as being wounded.	
ANNEZIN. September 30—	8 a.m.	"A" & "C" bearer Subdivisions returnes to billets at ANNEZIN leaving "B" bearer Subdivision under Capt. FREEMAN at CHATEAU VERMELLES Sun.Gl. Sta. with 2 motor ambulances.	
	6 a.m.	wounded — NIL —	
	9 a.m.	Daily Stat: — 1 Off + 18. OR wounded + 3 OR sick admittes — 10 Off + 45. OR evacuates	
	12 noon	wounded — NIL —	
	9 p.m.	2. OR wounded admites. "B" bearer Subdivision returnes to billets at ANNEZIN.	

Geo H Brown
Rame
Maj. RAMC
OC 23rd Fd Amb

Appendix I

O.C.
No 23 Field Ambulance
───────────────────

Medical Arrangements for VII<u>th</u> Division

1. O.C. 21<u>st</u> Field Ambulance will take over the A.D.S. at the Chateau VERMELLES at 11 a.m. on 18<u>th</u> instant from O.C. 23<u>rd</u> Field Ambulance and clear all sick and wounded from the 7<u>th</u> Division trenches to the A.D.S.

He will keep two ambulance cars at the A.D.S. for the evacuation of all urgent cases of sick and wounded, which occur between the usual hours of clearance, to the Field Ambulances.

As at present all sick of the Division will go to 21<u>st</u> Field Ambulance, all wounded to 22<u>nd</u> and 23<u>rd</u> Field Ambulances.

2. O.C. 22<u>nd</u> Field Ambulance will continue to collect sick and wounded of units billeted in Lumbres area, clearing the A.D.S. at the usual collecting hours.

3. O.C. 23<u>rd</u> and 21<u>st</u> Field Ambulances will continue to collect sick and wounded from units in Sercat and BONNEHEM billeting areas respectively.

4. From 18th inst. Captain Gunless R.A.M.C. will be in sole command of all R.A.M.C. working parties in the Trench area.

15/9/15   P.H. Hudson Major for Colonel
                                A.D.M.S. 7<u>th</u> Division

Secret   Appendix II   Copy No. 5.

7th Division R.A.M.C. Operation Order No. 5
by
Colonel W.T. Starr, Commanding R.A.M.C. 7th Divn

Reference Maps: Trench Sheets 36^c N.W. 1 and 3   1/10,000
               BETHUNE Combined Sheet 1/40,000
               N.W. EUROPE, VALENCIENNES 1/100,000

No orders or sketches giving information to the enemy will be taken into the field.

22nd September 1915.

---

1. **Information**

7th Division front will be held as follows:—
20th Brigade Column on right from VERMELLES–HULLUCH Road to a point immediately NORTH of FOSSE WAY.
22nd Brigade Column on left from point immediately NORTH of FOSSE WAY to a point "K" in G4D.
21st Brigade Column will be in reserve about NOYELLES and LABOURSE
Divisional Cavalry + Cyclists at LABOURSE
The 1st Division is on our right the 9th Division on our left.

2. **Intention**

(a) In conjunction with the French the 1st Army will assume the offensive on September 25th and advance between LENS + the LA BASSEE Canal towards the line HENIN–LIETARD–CARVIN.
(b) The task of VII Division is to clear the trenches in front of them, occupy the NORTH EASTERN end of HULLUCH, BENIFONTAINE (H8D), PUITS N°13, and CITE ST ELIE, and from these places continue the advance

on PONT-A-VENDIN and MEURCHIN, seizing the canal crossings about these places.

3. The movements necessary to give effect to the following Medical Arrangements, less those for the Ambulance Cars & Waggon rendezvous, will be completed by 10.30 p.m. on 24th September. They should be so timed that the Bearer Divisions of the F.As. do not reach NOYELLES-LES-VERMELLES before 4 p.m.

The N.C.O. and two men with Ambulance Cars & Waggons detailed to assemble at the rendezvous SAILLY-LABOURSE will arrive there at 10 a.m. on 25th September.

4. Medical Arrangements

A. ADVANCED DRESSING STATIONS —

At the commencement of operations there will be three A.D.S? situated as follows:—

Two on the north side of STANSFELD ROAD at its junction with CURLY CRESCENT.

One on the west of the Railway line at G 9 A 2.6.

The one near the Railway ~~line at G 9 A 2.6~~, will be a combined station for 22nd and 23rd F.A? and will be under command of the senior R.A.M.C. Officer present.

The one nearest CURLY CRESCENT is allotted to 22nd F.A. and the remaining one to 23rd F.A.

In the event of an advance O's. C. F.A? will select suitable A.D.S.s as required, reporting their positions to the A.D.M.S.

B. RELAY POSTS — Two stretcher bearer relay posts are formed as follows:— No 1 on south side of STANSFELD ROAD a few yards east of its junction with HULLUCH ALLEY.

No 2 on the south side of HULLUCH ALLEY a few yards west of HULLUCH KEEP.

Both relay posts are to be used conjointly by 22nd and 23rd F.As

C. <u>DIVISIONAL COLLECTING STATION</u>—

This will be opened in the CHATEAU VERMELLES G 8 c 3.3. by the 21st F.A.

Not more than four Ambulance Cars & the motor LORRY will be kept at the D.C.S. at one time and every care will be taken to protect these from shell fire.

D. <u>AMBULANCE CAR AND WAGGON RENDEZVOUS.</u>

This will be formed by 21st F.A. at SAILLY-LABOURSE on the road leading from L 3 D 9.4. northwards into the main BETHUNE-LENS ROAD.

One N.C.O. and two men will be constantly employed at this post in regulating the supply of cars to the D.C.S.

The system will be as follows:—

Four Ambulance Cars and the motor lorry will assemble at the D.C.S. on the night of 24th September. Sixteen Ambulance Cars and eight Ambulance waggons will rendezvous at SAILLY-LABOURSE on 25th September.

O.C. 21st F.A. will retain at GONNEHEM one Ambulance car and one Ambulance Waggon

Three Ambulance Cars & one Ambulance Waggon of 21st F.A. will be allotted to 22nd F.A. & the same number to 23rd F.A.

The Ambulance Cars and Waggons of the 22nd and 23rd F.As. will convey casualties to their respective F.As. only.

The motor lorry will convey sitting cases from the D.C.S to car rendezvous where the cases will be transferred to Ambulance waggons for conveyance to Main Dressing Stations at FOUQUIERES.

When a loaded car passes the rendezvous an

empty one will be immediately sent forward to D.C.S. & the N.C.O will be responsible that cars from 22nd & 23rd F.As are sent alternately & he will similarly regulate the departure of waggons with sitting cases.

Should there be large numbers of sitting cases & the lorry & waggons do not prove sufficient for their clearance, Ambulance Cars will also be used when available.

All Ambulance Cars & Waggons will proceed only on the routes laid down in traffic maps.

E. MAIN DRESSING STATIONS.

21st F.A. at GONNEHEM for reception of all sick of Division which will be collected by the Ambulance Car and Waggon retained by that F.A. During the operations no sick will be shown on the A & D books of 22nd and 23rd F.As. - all will be direct admissions to 21st F.A.

22nd F.A. at French Infectious Hospital FOUQUIERES E.21 A 8.8.

23rd F.A. under canvas at FOUQUIERES E 20 B.33.

5 Dress & Equipment -

A waterproof sheet & cardigan jacket will be carried in the pack.

6. Drinking Water & Rations

A sufficient supply of Drinking water will be stored in A.D.Ss & in Relay posts. 60 petrol tins are available for this purpose at D.C.S.

A complete days ration will be carried in addition to the iron ration.

7. Fires & lights:-

Fires will not be permitted in the open in places not usually occupied by troops.

Lights will not be used at night in the open.

One electric lamp is available for each A.D.S. & for the D.C.S. These should not be burned continuously but only when cases are being dressed at night. Should they get out of order they will be at once returned to 23rd F.A. for repair.

8. Trench Control—

(a) CHAPEL ALLEY and FOSSE WAY on the right, and GORDON ALLEY, and HULLUCH ALLEY (east of its junction with GORDON ALLEY) are reserved for forward traffic only.

(b) STANSFELD ROAD, and HULLUCH ALLEY west of its junction with STANSFELD ROAD is reserved for backward traffic only, but special arrangements have been made for the forward passage of stretcher bearers ~~only~~ along the last named route.

9. Reports

Reports to A.D.M.S. ECOLE FOUGUIERES E.21.A.4.6

W A Stares Lt Colonel
O.C. R.A.M.C. 7th Division

Issued at 10 a.m.
To — A.D.M.S. Copy No. 1
    D.A.D.M.S.   "   " 2
    O.C. 21st F.A. " " 3
    " 22nd F.A. " " 4
    " 23rd F.A. " " 5
    G.S. 7th Divn " " 6
    A. & Q.M.G. 7 Div. " " 7
    D.D.M.S. 1st Corps " " 8

Appendix III

O.C.
23rd Field Ambulance

(1) You will move your Field Ambulance less the Bearer Division as early as possible today and open at the ECOLE ANNEZIN. The Bearer Division will stand fast for the present until the 20th Brigade is relieved from the trenches when it will rejoin the Field Ambulance.

(2) Any cases remaining in your Field Ambulance will be transferred to the ECOLE JULES FERRY by order of the DDMS 1st Corps.

(3) Arrangements for the billeting of the personnel should be made through the Mairie.

P. H. Hudson
Major
DADMS 7 Divn

29/9/15

Appendix A

Report on [Br]ass Division
28 Field Ambulance
during the operations between 24th – 29th
September 1915.

Reference Maps:

French Map Sht. 36c N.W. 1/10000
BETHUNE combined Sht. 1/40000

___

24th Sept.

I arrived at VERMELLES at 6.30 p.m. on the evening of the 24th Sept. with the Brass Division. By 9 p.m. we had taken up our allotted positions at the Forward Advanced Dressing Station STANSFIELD ROAD, the 1st Relay Post STANSFIELD ROAD, the 2nd Relay Post HULLUCH ALLEY at the Advanced Dressing Station by the railway at HULLUCH ALLEY. We remained there during the night.

25th Sept.

The attack commenced about 6 a.m. and we started work about 6 a.m. I continued to dress cases at the Forward Advanced Dressing Station STANSFIELD ROAD in the dug out up to 12 noon.

Owing to the great number of wounded both walking & stretcher cases the one track was absolutely insufficient to accomodate the up-down stream of traffic. Fortunately as the result of the advance made by our troops my Bearers were enabled to take stretchers into the open and carry wounded along side the trench. About 12 noon my Bearers commenced to clear the area over which our troops had advanced.

The Advanced Dressing Station was now moved forward to the position where the Forward Advanced Dressing Station had been

25th Sept.

During the afternoon there was a great deal of hostile shelling which rendered the clearing of the field to a considerable extent [illegible].

About 5 p.m. we started using the Trolley line which ran from the Cité de Madagascar Road to the BREWERY, VERMELLES, where the wounded were transferred to Motor Ambulance cars and conveyed to the Divisional Collecting Station at the CHATEAU VERMELLES (S.P. of BETHUNE). This manner of clearing continued during the remainder of operations. At 8 p.m. Motor Ambulances and wheel stretchers were brought up HULLUCH ROAD to the old Br. Line German Trench and cleared cases through the night.

26th Sept.

The cars continued taking cases during the morning up to about 11.30 a.m. when the heavy shelling was made further use of the road impossible owing to direct rifle and shell fire.

During daylight we continued clearing by the Trolley Line. On the night of the 26th we again used HULLUCH ROAD and cleared large numbers of wounded by Motor Ambulances, Wheel Stretchers, carriers, Motor Waggons and any other mode of conveyance we could find.

No. 16 Pte. 3020 — Pte White E. was killed on HULLUCH ROAD during the night and 1796 — Pte McClure J. was wounded while working on the Trolley Line.

27th Sept.

We continued using the Trolley Line by day and night and HULLUCH ROAD by night and during the day when possible.

27th Sept.

At times clearing in the open was quite impossible owing to heavy sniping & Shell fire by the enemy, but during the entire day there was a continuous stream of wounded through the trenches to our Advanced Dressing Station at STANSFIELD ROAD, the majority being from units other than those of our Division.

28th Sept.

We continued collecting until our Brigade wounded were brought in and the field cleared as far as we could ascertain.

29th Sept.

18175 Pte Cross R.A.M.C. and 10655 Pte Priestley R.A.M.C. were wounded.

I received orders from OC 23 Field Ambulance to send back two (2) Bearer Sections.

30th Sept.

I received orders from ADMS to take in remaining Bearer Section to the Ambulance at ANNEZIN.

─────────

I should like to point out the following:-
(1) That we were greatly handicapped by want of stretchers and in my opinion a large reserve should be kept at the Advanced Dressing Station.

(2) The Trolley Line and Wheel Stretcher Carriers saved an enormous amount of labour. The Trolley Line was in constant use despite continuous shell fire.

(3) The excellent work done by all the Bearers who worked continuously altho greatly fatigued

and having no sleep for 47 hours. During the whole of the time they were exposed to heavy fire and rifle fire.

(4) The health conditions rendered carrying very difficult indeed, as even the rain started the whole country over which we were carrying was turned into a veritable quagmire.

3/10/15.

(Sd.) Frank Freeman
Capt R.A.M.C

121/7449

7ᵏ Kanoun

23 Wakel Amb:
Vol: XI
Oct 15

Army Form C. 2118.

WAR DIARY
or
INTELLIGENCE SUMMARY

(Erase heading not required.)

Instructions regarding War Diaries and Intelligence Summaries are contained in F. S. Regs., Part II. and the Staff Manual respectively. Title pages will be prepared in manuscript.

Hour, Date, Place	Summary of Events and Information	Remarks and references to Appendices
ANNEZIN. October 1st		
9 a.m.	Daily State:- 2 O.R. wounded admitted - Evacuated Nil.	
12 noon	Sent in the following "recommendation" for despatches (ADMS 7th Div)	
	Capt. FRANK PERCY FREEMAN RAMC (SR) — M.C.	
	" JOHN EDWARD ALLAN " — mention.	
	M2/076770 Pte JOSEPH HOLMES. ASC (MT) — D.S.M	
	478 Pte ROBERT WALKER SYMES RAMC — D.C.M.	
	9007 Pte RICHARD TREGLOWN - RAMC ⎱ mention	
	2245 Sergt. ARTHUR GEORGE CRIPPS " ⎰	
	Wounded State:- Since 6 a.m.- 2 O.R. admitted. Evacuated Nil.	
5 p.m.	20th Infty Bde. O.O. No. 31 received.	
9 p.m.	Wounded State - Nil	
10 pm	Ramc O.O. No 6 received -	Appendix I
6 a.m.	State - Nil	
Oct. 2nd 8.30 a.m.	Capt. J.E. ALLAN Ramc with 20 men, medical store cart, water cart & 3 wheel stretcher carriages proceeded forward to take over A.D.S at HARLEY STREET (A20.d.2.8.) 1 N.C.O. + 2 men with 2 horse ambulance wagons proceeded to the collecting station at BEUVRY, taken over from No 6 F. Amb.	

Army Form C. 2118.

WAR DIARY
or
INTELLIGENCE SUMMARY

(Erase heading not required.)

Instructions regarding War Diaries and Intelligence Summaries are contained in F. S. Regs., Part II. and the Staff Manual respectively. Title pages will be prepared in manuscript.

Hour, Date, Place		Summary of Events and Information	Remarks and references to Appendices
ANNEZIN –			
Oct 2nd (Cont.)	9 a.m.	Daily State :– 1 Off 4 O.R. sick + 1 O.R. wounded admitted	
		1 " 3 " + 2 " " Evacuated	
	12. noon	State – NIL	
	5 p.m.	Visited A.D.S. Stencils of 2 large dugouts off the communication trench – one for wounded + one for personnel. The trench is a wide one, + a stretcher can be carried along it. 2 Motor ambulances are kept further back at HARLEY STREET.	
	9 p.m.	6. O.R. wounded admitted –	
Oct 3rd	6 a.m.	1 O.R. " "	
	9 a.m.	Daily State :–	
		29. O.R. sick, 22 O.R. wounded admitted	
		5 " " , 4 " " Evacuated	
	12. noon	Nil admitted – 14 O.R. Evacuated.	
	9 p.m.	1 Off 15 O.R. wounded admitted – 1 Off 11. O.R. Evacuated.	
Oct 4th	6 a.m.	NIL	
	9 a.m.	Daily State :– 16. O.R. wounded + 18 Off sick admitted	
		30. O.R. " + 31. O.R. " Evacuated.	
	12 noon	NIL	
	9 p.m.	NIL	

WAR DIARY
or
INTELLIGENCE SUMMARY

(Erase heading not required.)

Army Form C. 2118.

Hour, Date, Place	Summary of Events and Information	Remarks and references to Appendices
ANNEZIN		
Oct 5th 6 a.m.	8 O.R. admitted - None Evacuated	
9 a.m.	Daily State:- 1 Off. 9 O.R. sick, 11 O.R. wounded. admitted 1 O.R. wounded Evacuated 1 O.R. Died.	
12 noon	Admitted nil -	
3 p.m.	5 O.R. admitted - 9 O.R. Evacuated	
9 p.m.	- 4 O.R. Evacuated	
Oct 6th 9 a.m.	Daily State:-	
	21 O.R. sick, 5 O.R. wounded admitted -	
	10 " " 8 " " Evacuated	
	1 O.R. wounded died.	
Oct 7th 9 a.m.	3 O.R. wounded + 2 5 O.R. sick admitted	
	3 " " 14 " " Evacuated.	
4.30 p.m.	In accordance with A.D.M.S. orders received at 3 p.m. "C" tent sub division under Capt HARLOW proceed to ECOLE JULES FERRY in BETHUNE (E16 b 5.8) - to hold the place. The Section is not to open till further instructions are received. This School will accommodate 255 cases, under ordinary hospital conditions - In necessity another 50 could be taken in.	
Oct 8th 9 a.m.	1 Off. 17 O.R. sick, 4 O.R. wounded admitted	
	1 " 20 " " 6 " " Evacuated.	

Army Form C. 2118.

WAR DIARY
or
INTELLIGENCE SUMMARY
(Erase heading not required.)

Instructions regarding War Diaries and Intelligence Summaries are contained in F. S. Regs., Part II. and the Staff Manual respectively. Title pages will be prepared in manuscript.

Hour, Date, Place		Summary of Events and Information	Remarks and references to Appendices
ANNEZIN.			
Oct 9th	9 a.m.	4. O.R. sick, 7. O.R. wounded admitted — 10. O.R. sick, 4. O.R. wounded evacuated	
Oct 10th	9 a.m.	4. O.R. — 7. O.R. " — 4 " " 4 " "	
	3 p.m.	20th Inf Bde O.O. No 34 received — Medical arrangements:- On the brigade being relieved, the aid posts held by 23rd F.A. to be handed over to 21st F.A. The Dressing Station at BEUVRY to be handed over to No 5. F.A. All bearers & personnel to be withdrawn to the unit.	
	7 p.m.	"A" bearer subdivision returned to the unit	
Oct 11th	9 a.m.	9. O.R. sick + 4. O.R. wounded admitted — 6. O.R. sick, 4. O.R. wounded evacuated	
Oct 12th	9 a.m.	8 " " 1 " " — 11 " " evacuated	
	10 a.m.	Capt. J.E. ALLEN to 6/Gordons for temporary duty " F.W. HARLOW to XXXV to Bde R.F.A. "	
Oct 13th	9 a.m.	11. O.R. sick 3. O.R. wounded admitted — 10. O.R. sick. 3. O.R. wd. evacuated. During the afternoon, under ADMS instructions, the unit packs to move into JULES FERRY School — "C" tent subdivision has opened there about mid-day. At 3 p.m the cases were sent over; but at 4.30 p.m. the enemy began to shell the town of BETHUNE. Two very large shells fell some 500 yards from the school, & fragments fell about the roof & yard. I reported to the ADMS that the place was not safe for sick, & the move was cancelled by him.	

WAR DIARY or INTELLIGENCE SUMMARY

Army Form C. 2118.

(Erase heading not required.)

Hour, Date, Place		Summary of Events and Information	Remarks and references to Appendices
ANNEZIN - Oct 13th (cont.)	6.30 p.m.	The Sick were brought back, & the Main Dressing Station re-established in ANNEZIN. 3 Officers & 32 OR sick & wounded arrived from the 22nd Fd Amb - to be "detained" for the night - the 22nd Fd Amb having been hit during the shelling of the town.	
	10.50 p.m.	Late Rgt O.O. No 35 received.	
Oct 14th	9 a.m.	12 OR sick admitted - 13 OR evacuated	
	9.30 a.m.	The sick and wounded from 22nd Fd Amb were collected and taken back by that unit.	
	2 p.m.	20 men of "B" bearer subdivision to under CAPT FREEMAN proceeded forward with M.S. Cart water-cart to MDS at MAISON ROUGE (opposite CAMBRIN) taking over all dug-outs &c from 2/1st F.A. on relief of 21st Inf Bde by 20th Inf Bde.	
	4 p.m.	LIEUT J.S. CHISHOLM Rawe (T.C) reports for duty -	
Oct 15th	9 a.m.	29 OR sick, 3 OR wounded admitted - 10 OR sick evacuated	
" 16 -	9 a.m.	1 Off + 6 OR wounded, 14 OR sick admitted - 5 OR wounded, 15 OR sick evacuated	
	3 p.m.	In accordance with orders, the MDS was handed over to 19 th Fd Amb.	
	7 p.m.	"B" bearers returned to ANNEZIN	
	11 p.m.	20 th Bde O.O. No 37 received. CAPT G.W. LLOYD Rawe was evacuated to No 1 C.C.S during the day - sick with P.U.O.	

Army Form C. 2118.

WAR DIARY
or
INTELLIGENCE SUMMARY
(Erase heading not required.)

Instructions regarding War Diaries and Intelligence Summaries are contained in F.S. Regs., Part II. and the Staff Manual respectively. Title pages will be prepared in manuscript.

Hour, Date, Place		Summary of Events and Information	Remarks and references to Appendices
BUSNETTES			
Oct 17th	8.a.m.	The unit marched to BUSNETTES (V15), arriving there at 10.30 a.m. and established the Main D.S. under canvas in a field at V.15.C.2.B. with accommodation for 100 sick (wounded)	
	9 a.m.	Daily State:- 2.Off, 5.OR sick admitted - 2.Off + 10.OR sick evacuated. 1.Off + 3.OR wounded	
Oct 18th	9 a.m.	10.OR sick admitted - 4.OR sick evacuated. LIEUT W.G. MILNE - RAMC (T.C.) left for England on completion of his one year's contract.	
Oct 19th	9 a.m.	7.OR sick admitted. 11.OR sick evacuated.	
	9 p.m.	Orders received from ADMS 7th Divn. that the AD.St's at LONE FARM (A.14 a 2.7.) to be taken over from 86th Fd Amb. on 20th inst. Tent Division to remain at BUSNETTES till further orders - Casualties to be evacuated to 86 Fd Amb. at ECOLE LIBRE, BETHUNE.	
Oct 20th	9 a.m.	1.Off + 30.OR sick admitted. 1.Off 7.OR sick evacuated.	
	11.30 a.m.	"C" bearer subdivision under CAPT. FREEMAN proceeded forward with water cart, medical store cart + 3 wheel stretcher carriages to take over LONE FARM ADS -	

Army Form C. 2118.

WAR DIARY
or
INTELLIGENCE SUMMARY
(Erase heading not required.)

Instructions regarding War Diaries and Intelligence Summaries are contained in F.S. Regs., Part II. and the Staff Manual respectively. Title pages will be prepared in manuscript.

Hour, Date, Place		Summary of Events and Information	Remarks and references to Appendices
BUSNETTES. Oct 20th (Cont)	12 noon	Under verbal instructions from A.D.M.S. to take over the ECOLE LIBRE in RUE DU TIR, BETHUNE (from 86th D? Mt. Sent forward) "C" tent subdivision under CAPT BUCKLEY to take over this school.	
	1.30 p.m.	The subdivision marched at 1.30 p.m. & opened in the School	
	3 p.m.	Under telegraphic instructions from D.D.T.S 3 Wolseley Motor ambulances (Nos A9170, M1078, M1094H.) were transferred to N°86 F? Amb., 28th Div in exchange for 3 Daimler ambulances	
	6 p.m.	26 light cases sick transferred to "C" tent subdivision at ECOLE LIBRE -	
BETHUNE. Oct 21st	9 a.m.	12. OR sick admitted - 20. OR sick evacuated	
	10 a.m.	The unit having packed up marched to BETHUNE On arrival there, the ECOLE LIBRE was opened as the main dressing station - with accommodation for 80 wounded.	
	4 p.m.	Visited M.D.S at LONE FARM.	
Oct 22nd	9 a.m.	35. OR sick admitted - 24. OR sick evacuated	
	12 noon	CAPT. F.W. HARLOW. RAMC (T.C) sent to Labour Ammunition Column in exchange with CAPT D.M. PAILTHORPE RAMC(TC) under instructions of D.M.S 1st Army. CAPT PAILTHORPE to XXXV & BSRA?, vice CAPT HARLOW - for temporary duty.	

Army Form C. 2118.

WAR DIARY
or
INTELLIGENCE SUMMARY
(Erase heading not required.)

Instructions regarding War Diaries and Intelligence Summaries are contained in F. S. Regs., Part II. and the Staff Manual respectively. Title pages will be prepared in manuscript.

Hour, Date, Place	Summary of Events and Information	Remarks and references to Appendices
BETHUNE.		
Oct 23rd 9 a.m.	30 OR sick, 4 OR wounded admitted - 20 OR sick & 1 wounded Evacuated	
10 p.m.	Received instructions that ADS is to be handed over to 21st Inf.Bde on relief of 20th Inf Bde by 21st Inf.Bde.	
Oct 24th 9 a.m.	7 OR sick, 8 OR wounded admitted. 16 OR sick 7 OR wounded Evacuated	
1.30 p.m.	ADS handed over to 21st Fd Amb. "C" bearer Subdivision returned at 4 p.m.	
Oct 25th 9 a.m.	7 OR sick, 1 OR wounded admitted. 4 OR sick & 5 wounded Evacuated	
Oct 26th 9 a.m.	12 OR sick admitted - 3 OR sick Evacuated.	
11 a.m.	The town was shelled by the enemy. One very heavy shell burst in the CHAMPS DE MARS about 50 yards from the Dressing station, shattering all the glass of the building. One man was slightly cut by falling glass. No other casualty.	
Oct 27th 9 a.m.	25 OR sick admitted. 13 OR sick Evacuated.	
	CAPTS. PAILTHORPE and ALLEN. Raine reported the unit on completion of temporary duty with xxxv Bde. R.F.A + 1/6 Gordons respectively	

Army Form C. 2118.

WAR DIARY
or
INTELLIGENCE SUMMARY
(Erase heading not required.)

Instructions regarding War Diaries and Intelligence Summaries are contained in F. S. Regs., Part II. and the Staff Manual respectively. Title pages will be prepared in manuscript.

Hour, Date, Place		Summary of Events and Information	Remarks and references to Appendices
BETHUNE.			
Oct 28th	9 a.m.	24. O.R. sick admitted – 12. O.R. sick evacuated	
Oct 29th	9 a.m.	19 " " – 11 " "	
Oct 30th	9 a.m.	31 " " – 26 " "	
Oct 31st	9 a.m.	16 " " – 14 " "	
	4 p.m.	Orders received from A.D.M.S. 7th Div. that on relief of 22nd Inf. Bde. by 20th Inf. Bde. the A.D.S. will be taken over by 23rd F.Amb.	
	9 p.m.	20th Inf. Bde. O.O. No. 41 received.	

Geo. N. Brown
Maj. Rawe
O.C. 23rd F. Amb.

R.A.M.C. Divisional Order No 6   Copy No 4
Secret
Appendix 1   Reference BETHUNE 1" Squared Sheet 1/40,000
                                    1st October 1915

The A.D.M.S. 19th Division will detail a Bearer Sub division for the collection of casualties of 55th Infy Brigade which takes over the line from GUN STREET A.21.b.30 to the Canal on night 1st/2nd October. Casualties will be taken to the A.D.S. at HARLEY STREET A.20.d.2.5 from whence they will be evacuated in 7th Division Ambulances and Cars to F.A's of 7th Division. The O.C. of the Bearer Sub Division detailed from 19th Division should be present at HARLEY St A.D.S. on the night 1st/2nd Octr at 8 p.m. to take over the duties from O.C. Bearer Division No 6 F.A. and acquaint himself with the location of all Aid Posts and method of clearance of casualties to A.D.S.

(2) The Bearer Sub Divn from 19th Division will be attached for rations to 22nd Field Ambulance from 3rd instant.

(3) The 22nd Infantry Brigade takes over line from N.E. inclusive to the Road A.27.b.2.7 exclusive on the night 1st/2nd October. O.C. 22nd F.A. will arrange in consultation with O.C. 19th F.A. to take over the collection and evacuation of casualties from this area when the Infantry relief is completed.

(4) The 20th Infantry Brigade takes over line from Road A.27.b.2.7 to GUN STREET exclusive on night 1st-2nd Octr. O.C. 23rd Field Ambulance will arrange in consultation with O.C. No 19 F.A. to take over the collection and evacuation of casualties from this area.

when the Infantry relief is completed it will also take over from No 6 F.A. the collecting station at BEUVRY and hold it with 1 N.C.O and 2 men.

(5) Not more than four Ambulance Cars will be kept at the A.D.S at HARLEY STREET. The O.Cs 22nd and 23rd F.As will each provide 2 —

(6) The A.D.S at HARLEY STREET will be used conjointly by the 3 F.As concerned in the above evacuation and will be under the command of the Senior Officer present. As the accommodation is limited O.C 6 F.A will limit as far as possible the number of bearers detailed.

A. Sutton
Colonel
A.D.M.S. ——

1 October 1915
8.5 pm
No 1 — A.D.M.S
  2 — " — 19 Divn
  3 — O.C 22nd F. Amb
  4 — " — 23rd "

7th Brigade

Nov 1915.

23rd F. Amb.
Nov / vol XI

12/7694

Army Form C. 2118.

23rd F. Amb.

WAR DIARY
or
INTELLIGENCE SUMMARY

(Erase heading not required.)

Instructions regarding War Diaries and Intelligence Summaries are contained in F. S. Regs, Part II. and the Staff Manual respectively. Title pages will be prepared in manuscript.

Hour, Date, Place	Summary of Events and Information	Remarks and references to Appendices
BETHUNE.		
Nov 1st 9 a.m.	17. O.R. admitted – 8. O.R. sick Evacuated	
10 a.m.	"A" bearer subdivision under CAPT ALLAN RAWE, with water cart, medical store cart, 3 wheel stretcher-carriages, & 2 Motor Ambulance cars proceeded forward to take over the A.D.S. at LONE FARM from 22nd F. Amb.	
12 noon	CAPT H. SMITH RAWE (TC) joined for duty from 22nd F. Amb. under instructions from A.D.M.S. 7th Div.	
Nov 2nd 9 a.m.	17. O.R. sick admitted – 16. O.R. sick Evacuated	
Nov 3rd 9 a.m.	3. O.R. wounded, 27. O.R. sick admitted. 3. O.R. wd. & 78. O.R. sick Evacuated. 2nd ll Bde. O.O. No. 42 received. Under instructions of A.D.M.S. 7th Div. Each F. Amb. of the Div. will, in turn, do duty at the A.D.S. for 4 complete days. O.C's to arrange with each other to carry out reliefs on that day.	
11.40 p.m.	2nd ll Bde O.O. Nos. 43 & 44 received	
Nov 4th 9 a.m.	1 Off + 24. O.R. sick, & 3. O.R. wounded admitted. 1 " + 34 " " 3 " " Evacuated	

Army Form C. 2118.

WAR DIARY
or
INTELLIGENCE SUMMARY

(Erase heading not required.)

Instructions regarding War Diaries and Intelligence Summaries are contained in F. S. Regs., Part II. and the Staff Manual respectively. Title pages will be prepared in manuscript.

Hour, Date, Place		Summary of Events and Information	Remarks and references to Appendices
BETHUNE			
Nov. 5th	9 a.m.	27 O.R. sick, 6 wounded admitted – 17 sick + 5 wounded evacuated	
	11 a.m.	Capt H. Smith Rame to 2nd Border Regt. on temp duty	
	2 p.m.	A heavy ambulance returned on relief at MDS by 21st FA.	
Nov 6th	9 a.m.	86 O.R. sick + 1 wounded admitted – 52 sick + 5 wounded evacuated. Of the sick admitted 35 were cases of Trench Foot. The weather has been very wet & cold lately, & the men have been up to the waist in mud in places.	
Nov 7th	9 a.m.	25 O.R. sick admitted – 5 O.R. sick evacuated	
Nov 8th	9 a.m.	12 " " – 12 " "	
		Capt C.D.M. Buckley Rame of the unit was admitted to the ambulance in the afternoon suffering from a fractured femur & clavicle, the result of an accident. He was sent straight on to No 1 C.C.S. at Chocques	
Nov 9th	9 a.m.	2 Off + 21 O.R. sick admitted – 2 Off + 6 O.R. sick evacuated	
	11.20 p.m.	20th Bde O.O. No. 47 received	
Nov 10th	9 a.m.	29 O.R. sick admitted { 12 O.R. sick evacuated. 1 O.R. wounded } 1 O.R. wounded	

WAR DIARY
or
INTELLIGENCE SUMMARY

(Erase heading not required.)

Army Form C. 2118.

Hour, Date, Place		Summary of Events and Information	Remarks and references to Appendices
BETHUNE. Nov. 11th	9 a.m.	OR 22 sick and 12 wounded admitted - 14 OR evacuated sick. 1 OR wounded evacuated. 1 OR wounded died.	
	2 p.m.	Lieutenant C.J. Stephen RAMC ( ) joined for temporary duty from No. 14 general hospital, Boulogne, under instructions from ADMS. 7th Division.	
	4.30 a.m.	20th Brigade O.O's No 47 received.	
Nov. 12th	9 a.m.	25 OR sick and 9 wounded Admitted. 11 OR sick and 6 wounded evacuated. 1 OR brought in dead to hospital.	
	11 a.m.	CAPT. F. P. FREEMAN with 'B' bearer subdivision, water cart, medical store cart, 3 wheel stretcher carriages and two motor ambulance cars proceeded forward to take over the A.D.S. at LONE FARM from 22 Field Ambulance.	
Nov. 13.	9 a.m.	33 OR sick and 1 wounded admitted. - 15 OR sick and eleven wounded evacuated.	
	4 p.m.	20th Brigade O.O's No. 48 received.	
Nov. 14.	9 a.m.	19 OR sick admitted - 22 OR sick and two wounded evacuated.	
	10.40 p.m.	20th Brigade O.O's No. 49 received.	
Nov. 15	9 a.m.	7 OR sick and 3 wounded admitted - 9 OR sick evacuated.	
	10.30 a.m.	LIEUT. C. J. Stephen to VII divisional ammunition column to proceed in relief of CAPTAIN. A. L. CHRISTIE	

Army Form C. 2118.

WAR DIARY
or
INTELLIGENCE SUMMARY

(Erase heading not required.)

Instructions regarding War Diaries and Intelligence Summaries are contained in F.S. Regs., Part II. and the Staff Manual respectively. Title pages will be prepared in manuscript.

Hour, Date, Place			Summary of Events and Information	Remarks and references to Appendices
BETHUNE.				
Nov.	15th	10.40 a.m.	20th Brigade O.O.s. No 50. received.	
Nov	16th	8.45 a.m	20th Brigade O.O.s. No 51 received.	
		9 a.m.	25 OR. Sick and 2 wounded admitted. 7 OR sick and 4 wounded evacuated.	
		2 p.m.	B.Coy Sub division under Capt Freeman arrived from A.D.S. 2nd FA having taken over.	
Nov	17	9 a.m	14 OR Sick and 2 wounded admitted. 17 OR Sick and 1 wounded evacuated.	
		12 a.m	CAPT. SMITH. R.A.M.C. rejoined from temporary duty with 2nd Batt. Border Regt	
		4 p.m.	CAPT. C.D.M. BUCKLEY R.A.M.C. rejoined for duty from No 1 C.C.S. at CHOCQUES	
Nov	18.	9 a.m.	25 OR Sick and 2 wounded admitted. 13 OR sick and 3 wounded evacuated.	
Nov	19.	9 a.m	10 OR Sick admitted. 7 OR Sick evacuated.	
Nov	20.	9 a.m	9 OR Sick admitted. 13 OR Sick evacuated.	
Nov	21	9 a.m	21 OR Sick admitted. 12 OR Sick evacuated.	
		10.30 a.m	CAPT. D.M. PALTHORPE. R.A.M.C. to 22nd Brigade R.F.A. for temporary duty.	
		1 p.m	20th Brigade O.O. No 52 received.	
Nov	22	9 a.m.	13 OR Sick admitted. 12 OR sick evacuated	

Army Form C. 2118.

WAR DIARY
or
INTELLIGENCE SUMMARY

(Erase heading not required.)

Hour, Date, Place		Summary of Events and Information	Remarks and references to Appendices
BETHUNE			
Nov 23rd	9 a.m.	23. OR sick admitted. 13. OR sick evacuated.	
	1 p.m.	"C" bearer subdivision proceeded forward to take over A.D.S. on TUNING FORK ROAD - with the usual equipment &waggons.	
	2 p.m.	Visited the A.D.S. + arranged for a signal to be posted in FESTUBERT near the line of Aid Posts	
Nov 24th	9 a.m.	24. OR Sick + 9 wounded admitted - 9. OR sick evacuated	
	2 p.m.	Visited A.D.S. - Owing to the large number of men employed as working parties near FESTUBERT increased the post there to 8 men with 3 wheel stretcher carriages	
" 25th	9 a.m.	17 sick + 5 wounded admitted.	
		12 " + 2 " evacuated	
" 26th	8 a.m.	Lieut CHISHOLM RAMC to 6/Gordons for temporary duty	
	9 a.m.	9 sick + 21 wounded admitted - 4 sick + 8 wounded evacuated	
" 27th	9 a.m.	29. OR sick + 14 wounded admitted - 12 sick + 15 wounded evacuated	
	10 a.m.	Capt. H. SMITH RAMC to 2/Gordons temporary duty	

Army Form C. 2118.

WAR DIARY
or
INTELLIGENCE SUMMARY
(Erase heading not required.)

Hour, Date, Place		Summary of Events and Information	Remarks and references to Appendices
BETHUNE			
Nov 28th	9 a.m.	46 sick & 11 wounded admitted - 38 sick & 7 wounded evacuated	
	4 p.m.	1 wounded died. Orders received from H.Q. 1st re handing over to 99th F.A. Revd KERR C of E chaplain reports himself vice Revd ABBOT - transferred to BOULOGNE.	
Nov 29th	9 a.m.	49 sick admitted - 42 sick & 8 wounded evacuated. 31 cases of "trench foot" admitted - these were from 2nd Gordons & 8/Devons, who held the wettest part of the line, & to the result of the intense frost during the past 36 hours.	
Nov 30th	9 a.m.	29 sick & 4 wounded admitted - 42 sick & 8 wounded evacuated.	
	11 a.m.	Orders to hand over main Dressing Station to 99th F.A. The ADS is to be handed over to 99th at noon on 1st Dec. The 101st F.A. will take over Ecole LIBRE.	
	11 p.m.	20th Bde O.O. No 53 received	

G. A. H. Brown
Maj. Ramc
O.C. 23rd F. Amb.

23rd P. Ann.
Dec
Vol. XII

131/7930

Dec. 5

Army Form C. 2118.

WAR DIARY
or
INTELLIGENCE SUMMARY

(Erase heading not required.)

Instructions regarding War Diaries and Intelligence Summaries are contained in F. S. Regs, Part II. and the Staff Manual respectively. Title pages will be prepared in manuscript.

Hour, Date, Place		Summary of Events and Information	Remarks and references to Appendices
BETHUNE Dec 1st	9 a.m.	37. O.R. sick + 9 wounded admitted – 32 Sick + 8 wounded Evacuated	
	12 noon.	Handed over A.D.S. to 99th F.A. One Officer + 2 Squads remain on till 20th Bde is clear of the trenches.	
	9 p.m.	"C" bearer sub-division, all reported from the A.D.S. after clearing wounded on relief of 20th Bde. Horse-ambulance wagons were sent out to march in rear of units in accordance with orders –	
CENSE LA VALLÉE Dec 2nd	9 a.m.	17 Sick + 2 wounded admitted. 21 Sick + 4 wounded Evacuated.	
		The unit closed at 4 p.m. yesterday – After that hour all cases were sent to 99th F.A. – Under instructions of A.D.M.S 7th Div. the unit marches at	
	9.30 a.m.	to billet at BLACK WATER FARM. (VII.C.1.7) CENSE LA VALLÉE – Until further orders the unit will remain "closed", but will collect all sick of 22nd Inf Bde after 5 pm on 2/12/15, + send them to 22nd F. Amb. at ANNEZIN for treatment –	
Dec 3rd	9 a.m.	Daily State :- NIL	
	4 p.m.	Lt CHISHOLM returned from 6/Gordons on completion of temporary duty.	

1247 W 3299 200,000 (E) 8/14 J.B.C. & A. Forms/C. 2118/11.

WAR DIARY
or
INTELLIGENCE SUMMARY

(Erase heading not required.)

Army Form C. 2118.

Hour, Date, Place	Summary of Events and Information	Remarks and references to Appendices
CENSE LA VALLÉE Dec 3rd (Cont'd)	7th Divl. O.O. received last night relating to the coming transfer of 7th Div. to III Army. The 23rd F.A. will entrain at BERGUETTE at 13.21 on 7th inst.	
Dec 4th	A.D.M.S. 7th Div. instructions:- On detraining at PONT REMY the unit will march to PICQUIGNY and establish a train Dressing station there. A billetting party will proceed by motor on 4th inst to PICQUIGNY.	
6 a.m.	CAPT B.H WEDD, with 3 motor ambulances + party proceed to PICQUIGNY	
Dec 5th 9 a.m.	Daily State:— NIL	
Dec 6th 9 a.m.	" " :— NIL	
9 a.m.	" " :— NIL	
2.30 p.m.	Orders received from H.Q. 7th Div. postponing time of Entraining to 4.21 p.m. on 7th	
Dec 7th 3.20 a.m.	Orders from H.Q. 7th Div cancelling postponement of Entraining time — The original order to hold good.	
8 a.m.	The unit marched for BERGUETTE arriving there at 10.20 a.m. Loading commenced at 10.53 a.m Trucks completed at 11.30 a.m. — The wagons were loaded on flat trucks & men & horses in covered Vans.	
1.21 p.m.	Train left BERGUETTE — There was a good deal	

WAR DIARY or INTELLIGENCE SUMMARY

Army Form C. 2118.

Hour, Date, Place	Summary of Events and Information	Remarks and references to Appendices
Dec 7th (Cont.)	of delay on the journey, the train not reaching PONT REMY till 11.p.m. Offloading commenced at once. The siding was small & the ramps so steep that it took 1¼ hours to unload.	
Dec 8th 1 A.M.	After being held up for ½ hour at a railway crossing the unit marched from PONT REMY at 1 A.M. The distance to PICQUIGNY (23½ Kilomet.) was covered in 6 hours (15 min halt in each hour being allowed) the unit arrived at PICQUIGNY at 7 a.m. The men were sent to billets to rest.	
PICQUIGNY Dec 9th 9 a.m. 4 p.m.	1 Off. 11. OR sick admitted - 1 Off + 11 sick evacuated. CAPT PAILTHORPE rejoined on completion of temporary duty.	
Dec 9th 9 a.m.	8 sick admitted - 1 sick evacuated. The Main Dressing Station was opened this morning in a Chateau with accommodation for 200 Cases including 6 beds for Officers. Arrangements were made to bath all patients & to clothe them in Pyjamas. Also for washing & disinfecting all clothing. Also for numerous dieting of the sick.	
Dec 10th 9 a.m. 10 a.m.	21. OR sick admitted - 3. OR sick evacuated. CAPT FREEMAN to XIII Corps H.Q. for duty.	

WAR DIARY
or
INTELLIGENCE SUMMARY

(Erase heading not required.)

Army Form C. 2118.

Hour, Date, Place	Summary of Events and Information	Remarks and references to Appendices
PICQUIGNY. Dec 10th	Medical Arrangements :- All skin disease cases to be sent to 21st F.A. Amb at LE MESGE for treatment - All other cases requiring admission to F.A. to be treated in 23rd F.A. Amb at PICQUIGNY - including Officers -	
12 Noon	CAPT. H. SMITH RAMC rejoins on completion of temporary duty with 2/ Gordons -	
Dec 11th 12 noon	Admitted :- 1. Off + 12. OR sick - Evacuated 1 Off + 5.OR sick. Transfers from other F.A. - 29.OR sick " " 21st F.A. - Nil	
Dec 12th 12 noon	Admitted 1. Off + 8. OR sick Evacuated 1 " + 8 " " | Transfers from F.A. - 10. OR sick " " 21st F.A. - 2. OR.	
Dec 13th 12 noon	Admitted 2. OR sick 1 wounded (acc) Evacuated - 5 OR "	
Dec 14th 12 noon	Admitted 13.OR sick admitted.	2 Off 4.OR sick Transf. from Other F. 8 sick 1 wd Evacuated " " " "	
	LIEUT. HUTTON-ATTENBOROUGH. RAMC reports for duty.	
Dec 15th 12 noon	Admitted - 1.Off 9.OR sick	Transfers from Other H.P. 1.Off 14.OR sick Evacuated 17. OR sick " " " " 1 OR.	
Dec 16th 12 noon	A. 10.OR sick	Tr. from other H.P. 18.OR sick E. 17.OR " " " " Nil	
	LIEUT ATTENBOROUGH to 8th Devons temp duty.	

Army Form C. 2118.

WAR DIARY
or
INTELLIGENCE SUMMARY
(Erase heading not required.)

Instructions regarding War Diaries and Intelligence Summaries are contained in F. S. Regs., Part II. and the Staff Manual respectively. Title pages will be prepared in manuscript.

Hour, Date, Place		Summary of Events and Information	Remarks and references to Appendices
PICQUIGNY Dec. 17th	12 noon	A. 21.OR arrvd | Tr. from Show Up. 7. OR sick E. 8.OR " | " to 6 " 1.OR "	
" 18th	12 noon	A. 11.OR sick | Tr. from — 10.OR sick E. 9 " " | " to 6 — NIL.	
" 19th	12 noon	A. 19.OR " | Tr. from — 8.OR. sick E. 5.OR " | Tr to 6 — 1 " "	
" 20th	12 noon	A. 16.OR Sick 1 W^d (acc) | Tr. from — 7. OR. sick E. 16 " " — | " to 6 — 3 " "	
" 21st	12 noon	A. 1.Off. 10.OR. Sick | Tr. from — 8 " " E. 1 " 12 " " | To 6 — 2 " "	
" 22nd	12 noon	A. 10.OR died | Tr. from — 15 " " E. 16 " " +2 Off. | Tr. to 6 — 1 " "	
" 23rd	12 noon	A. 5 " " | Tr from — 9 " " E. 10 " " | " to 6 — NIL.	
" 24th	12 noon	A. 3 " " | Tr. from — 1. " E. 3 " " +1W^d | " to 6 — nil.	

WAR DIARY
or
INTELLIGENCE SUMMARY

(Erase heading not required.)

Army Form C. 2118.

Hour, Date, Place		Summary of Events and Information	Remarks and references to Appendices
PICQUIGNY			
Dec 25th	12 noon	A 9. OR sick E 5.OR sick - T⁰ from - 11. OR sick	
Dec 26th	12 noon	A 8 " " E 2 " " T⁰ " NIL	
Dec 27th	12 noon	A 9 " " E 8 " " T⁰ " 5. - T⁰ to - 1.	
" 28th	12 "	A 13 " " E 10 " " T⁰ " nil	
" 29th	12 noon	A 30 " " E 2 " " T⁰ " 3. -	
" 30th	12 noon	A 10 " " E 21 " " T⁰ " 14 T⁰ to - 1.	
		LIEUT. ATTENBOROUGH ROWE returned on completion	
		of temporary duty.	
" 31st	9 am.	LIEUT ATTEBOROUGH to 9/Devons on temporary duty	
	12 noon	A 10ff. 7.OR sick E 10ff.12.OR - Transfers - nil	
		Since opening at Picquigny -	
		Admissions 266. 3 + 43	
		Transfers from - 177. 3	
		Evacuated 196 = 44.2 % of Admissions & transfers	
		D. to D. 172. = 36.6 % " "	

73 J'd Aul
Jan
Vol XIII

Mr Dawson
F 1122/1

Jan 1916

Army Form C. 2118.

WAR DIARY
or
INTELLIGENCE SUMMARY

(Erase heading not required.)

Instructions regarding War Diaries and Intelligence Summaries are contained in F. S. Regs, Part II. and the Staff Manual respectively. Title pages will be prepared in manuscript.

Hour, Date, Place	Summary of Events and Information	Remarks and references to Appendices
1916. PICQUIGNY		
Jan 1st	LIEUT. T.J.J. CURRAN. R.A.M.C. (T.c.) reported for duty last evening from 24th Manchester Regt.	
12 noon.	A. 6. OR sick Tr. from 12. OR sick E. 8 " " " to " " "	
Jan 2nd	A. 16 " " Tr. from nil E. 13 " " " to " nil	
Jan 3rd	A. 13 " " Tr. from 8 " " E. 12 " " " to " nil	
6.15 p.m.	22 Bde. O.O. 54 received - Also R.A.M.C. 7 Div. Order. T. 2.	Appendix I
Jan 4th 7.45 a.m.	B Section under Capt MACKIE R.A.M.C. will be attached wagons complete marched to AILLY-LE-HAUT-CLOCHER establishing a dressing station (20 beds) in the HOTEL DE-VILLE there.	
12 noon	A. 1 off 20. OR sick Tr. from 5. OR sick E. 12 OR " to " nil	
Jan 5th 9 a.m.	Under instruction O.O. No 3 13th Corps Lieut T.J.J. CURRAN proceeded to No. 14 Adv. Base Med. Stores at CORBIE for duty	

Army Form C. 2118.

WAR DIARY
or
INTELLIGENCE SUMMARY

(Erase heading not required.)

Instructions regarding War Diaries and Intelligence Summaries are contained in F. S. Regs, Part II. and the Staff Manual respectively. Title pages will be prepared in manuscript.

Hour, Date, Place		Summary of Events and Information	Remarks and references to Appendices
PLOEGSTEERT			
Jan'y 5th	12 noon	A. 25 - O.R sick / To from 3 M.L	
		E. 14 " " / " to	
Jan'y 6th	12 noon	A. 7. O.R / To from — 10. O.R sick	
		E. 10 " " / " to — nil	
" 7th	12 noon	A. 5 " " / 1 Off-D.o.D. — 1 " — nil	
		E. 19 " " / — from — 4 "	
" 8th	12 noon	A. 3 " " / " to — nil	
		E. 8 " " / from — 5 "	
			" to — nil
" 9th	12 noon	A. 1 " " / from — 6 "	
		E. 2 " " / 6 to — nil	
" 10th	12 noon	A. 4 " " / from — 16	
		E. 7 " " / 6 to — nil	
" 11th	12 noon	A. 2 " " / from — 18	
		E. 5 " " + 1 Off / " to — nil	
	8pm	Rev'd F.D. LANGLANDS - C.F. (Pres) reports his arrival in relief of Rev'd W.S. JAFFRAY. C.F. (Pres)	
12th	9 a.m.	Rev'd W.S. JAFFRAY left to join 9th Div. no return of the strength	

Army Form C. 2118.

WAR DIARY
or
INTELLIGENCE SUMMARY

(Erase heading not required.)

Instructions regarding War Diaries and Intelligence Summaries are contained in F. S. Regs., Part II. and the Staff Manual respectively. Title pages will be prepared in manuscript.

Hour, Date, Place		Summary of Events and Information	Remarks and references to Appendices
12th. May (Cont.)	12 noon.	A. 7 O.R. Sick E. 19 " "	T. from 12 O.R. sick " to " nil.
13th. "	12 noon	A. 3 " " E. 14 " + 1 Off sick	" from 10 " " " to 1 " "
14th. "	12 noon	A. 8 " " E. 13 " "	" from 5 " " " to 1 " "
15th. "	12 noon	A. 7 " " E. 7 " "	" from 4 " nil " to " nil
16th. "	12 noon	A. 7 " " E. 6 " "	" from 5 " " " to " nil
17th. "	12 noon	A. 3 " " E. 4 " "	" from 8 " " " to " nil.
18th. "	12 noon	A. 5 " " E. 4 " "	" from 10 " " " to — nil —
19th. "	12 noon	A. 3 " " E. 7 " "	" from — 11 " " " to — nil.

Army Form C. 2118.

WAR DIARY
or
INTELLIGENCE SUMMARY

(Erase heading not required.)

Instructions regarding War Diaries and Intelligence Summaries are contained in F. S. Regs., Part II. and the Staff Manual respectively. Title pages will be prepared in manuscript.

Hour, Date, Place	Summary of Events and Information	Remarks and references to Appendices
PICQUIGNY		
20th/Jan - 12 noon	A. 8. OR Sick To: from - 4. OR Sick E. 8. " " " to - nil	
Jany 21st - 12 noon	Lt. A.F. READDIE R.A.M.C.(T.C.) attached to the unit for instructⁿ from 21st C.C.S. - A. 5. OR Sick To: from - 4. OR Sick E. 10. OR " " to - nil	
" 22nd - 12 noon	A. 6 " " + 1 Off. To: from - 6 " " E. 2 " " " to - nil	
" 23rd - 12 noon	A. 4 " " " " " from - 2 " " E. 7 " " + 1 Off. " to - nil 1 Death in H. from Pyæmia. (P.M.E.)	
" 24th - 12 noon	A. 2. OR Sick To: from - 4 " " E. 6 " " " to - nil	
" 24th - 2 p.m.	LIEUT A. DAVIDSON. R.A.M.C. joined for duty from No 2 C.C.S.	
" 25th - 12 noon	A. 2. OR Sick + 2 Officers To: from - 4. OR Sick E. 2 " " " to - 1 " "	

Army Form C. 2118.

WAR DIARY
or
INTELLIGENCE SUMMARY

(Erase heading not required.)

Instructions regarding War Diaries and Intelligence Summaries are contained in F. S. Regs., Part II. and the Staff Manual respectively. Title pages will be prepared in manuscript.

Place	Hour, Date	Summary of Events and Information	Remarks and references to Appendices
PICQUIGNY	10 a.m. 26th Jany	Capt. D.W. PAILTHORPE- RAMC (T.C.) to RE for duty	
	12 noon	A. 3. OR Sick — To from — 1.OR Sick	
		A/E 2 " " — to — nil	
	12 noon Jany 27th	A. 2 " " — from — 12 " "	
		A/E 7 " " — to — nil	
	10 a.m. 28th	Capt J.E. ALLAN RAMC to 9th Devons temp'y duty	
	12 noon	A. 12. OR — from — 25. OR Sick	
		A/E nil — to — nil	
	4 p.m.	20th Bde O.O. No 55 received at 10 a.m.	
		"B" Section rejoined, on return of 20th Inf. Bde.	
	12 noon 29th	A. 2 Off + 7.OR Sick — To from — 20. OR sick	
		A/E 2 " + 40. OR " — to — nil	
	12 noon 30th	A. 18. OR sick — from — 3 "	
		A/E 1 Off + 3 " OR. — to — nil	
	12 noon 31st	A. 13. OR Sick — from — nil	
		A/E 2 " " — to — 3 "	
	12.15 pm	20th Bde O.O. No 56 received.	

Geo H Browne
Major RAMC
O.C. 23rd F.A.

SECRET. Appendix I

To
O.C.
23 Field Ambce.

Re 7th Divn. No 2663/A. attached.

(1) Will you please detail one Section of your Field Ambulance to march to AILLY LE HAUT CLOCHER tomorrow and open in the Town Hall there.

Ascertain from 20th Bde. the hours that Battalions are marching and move your unit so as to leave the roads clear for the Infantry.

(2) Please arrange for a horse Ambulance Wagon to march in rear of each Battalion. O.C. 21st Field Ambce has been requested to send you two horse Ambulance wagons to assist in this duty.

H S Roch
D.D.M.S. 7 Dn.

Jan. 3. 1916.

76th Division

23rd Field Ambulance.

Tel. S
Mar 1916 S 1

Army Form C. 2118.

WAR DIARY
or
INTELLIGENCE SUMMARY

(Erase heading not required.)

Instructions regarding War Diaries and Intelligence Summaries are contained in F.S. Regs., Part II. and the Staff Manual respectively. Title pages will be prepared in manuscript.

Hour, Date, Place		Summary of Events and Information	Remarks and references to Appendices
PICQUIGNY			
FEB. 1st 1916	9.a.m.	Under instructions of M.O.u.8, Capt D. MACKIE, with part of 114 OR + 3 Motor Ambulance Cars proceeded forward to BRAY (ALBERT Coubres Sheet 1/40000) L.15 to take over A.D.S. from	
		During the day A & B sections packed up, C section taking over the Dressing Station at PICQUIGNY — C section to march with the Artillery later.	
	12 noon	28. OR sick admitted — 3. OR evacuated.	
Feby 2nd	10 a.m.	A & B Sections under Capt B.H. WEDD marches with the remainder of 20th Inf Bde to COISY, where they went into billets for the night.	
	12 noon	17 sick & 7 wounded admitted. (wounded by acc. bomb expl.) 34 " + 7 " evacuated. — 39 sick left with C. section. In the afternoon, Ambulance Cars were sent out to clear the sick of 20th Inf Bde. These were brought back to PICQUIGNY.	
Feby 3rd	10 A.M.	A & B Sections marched from COISY to PONT NOYELLES to billets. — At 10.30am I proceeded with 3 Ambulance Cars from PICQUIGNY, arriving at 12.30 p.m.	

Army Form C. 2118.

WAR DIARY
or
INTELLIGENCE SUMMARY

(Erase heading not required.)

Hour, Date, Place	Summary of Events and Information	Remarks and references to Appendices
MERICOURT.		Ref. 1/40,000 map ALBERT Combines Sheet.
Feby 3rd (Cont)	On arrival, the O.C. 54th Fd Amb informed me that he had orders to hand over the ADS & M.D.S on the 4th. I sent orders to A+B Sections to march forthwith to MERICOURT, where they arrived at 6.30 pm. An advance party under Capt GREENLEES D.S.O was sent forward to the A.D.S. in MÉAULTE at E.16.d.5.5. During the day 13 O.R sick were collected on the march & were evacuated to C.C.S at CORBIE.	
Feby 4th 9.30 a.m.	A.D.S taken over from 54 to 9 Amb. One bearer Sub-division proceeded there, accompanied by light Cart & 6 wheel Stretcher carriages.	
12 noon.	Capt MACKIE & his party returned from BRAY, having been relieved by 21st Fd Amb. One of the Motors was damaged by shell fire in BRAY. O.C. 54th Fd Amb informed me that he was not to move till 5th morning. I arranged that he should take in the Div. Sick & wounded during the day & night.	
Daily Statis-	1 Off + 12 O.R sick, + 1 wounded admitted. 1 Off 17 O.R sick, 1 W. Evac.	
Feby 5th 9. a.m.	Took over Main Dressing Station at MERICOURT (J3.d.6.2) from 54th Fd Amb. Accommodation for 60 wounded in 2 huts, etc. If necessary 500 wounded can be housed in barns had as recreation rooms at present.	

WAR DIARY or INTELLIGENCE SUMMARY

(Erase heading not required.)

Army Form C. 2118.

Hour, Date, Place		Summary of Events and Information	Remarks and references to Appendices
MERICOURT			
Feby 5th (Cont.)	12 noon	20 sick & 1 wounded admits - 4 Sick evacuated). "C" Section marched with the Artillery from PICQUIGNY, (under Capt BUCKLEY) to ST GRATIEN where they went into billets for the night -	
Feby 6th	12 noon	14 Sick & 1 W⁴ admits - Evacuated) 8 sick & 1 wounded. Visited ADS & the front lines - The evacuation is as follows :- Aid Posts at F.2.a.10. & F.8.a.7.2. ADS in a house in MÉAULTE (E.16.d.5.5) with an Advanced post in BÉCORDEL-BÉCOURT (F.7.c.8.5). The latter is staffed by 1 Sergt & 16 men with 3 wheeled Stretcher-Carriages, from there 1 Squad with a Stretcher-Carriage is furnished to do duty for 24 hours at each Reg¹ Aid post. The MEAULTE-BÉCORDEL road is visible to the enemy hourly Ford Cars are allowed up by day - Anything larger is visible over the screen which has been erected. Cases are brought from Aid post at F8.a.72 by hand along SOUTH AVENUE Communication trench to the Advanced Post in BÉCORDEL. From Aid post F2.a.10. they are brought by wheel stretcher Carriage to the Adv. Post. A message is sent by telephone from Aid Post to Brigade H.Q. in MÉAULTE, who warn the ADS. (? Post) Car goes up & meets the cases at BÉCORDEL. At night all heads are available	

Army Form C. 2118.

WAR DIARY
or
INTELLIGENCE SUMMARY
(Erase heading not required.)

Instructions regarding War Diaries and Intelligence Summaries are contained in F. S. Regs., Part II. and the Staff Manual respectively. Title pages will be prepared in manuscript.

Hour, Date, Place		Summary of Events and Information	Remarks and references to Appendices
MERICOURT			
Feby 6th (contd)	5 p.m.	C. Section rejoined.	
Feby 7th	10 a.m.	Visited A.D.S. & arranged for splinter proof shelter to be built, to hold 4 stretchers – Existing cellars to be improved to take 8 stretchers & 15 sitting cases.	
	12 noon	29 Sick & 3 wounded admitted – 5 Sick & 3 W. evacuated. 34 Sick sent to Divl. Rest Station at CORBIE, 9 penes by 22nd Fd Amb.	
	5 p.m.	Capt. C. H. HART (RAMC) T.C. reported for duty in exchange with Capt. H. SMITH RAMC SR. who is to proceed to No 11 Gen. Hp BOULOGNE.	
Feby 8th	12 noon		
	5 p.m.	Capt. H. SMITH left for BOULOGNE. The roads in the district are in a very bad state of repair, & the strain on the Motor Ambulances is causing numerous break downs. This I reported to the A.D.M.S.	
Feby 9th	12 noon		
	2 p.m.	Visited A.D.S. The village was shelled in the afternoon – A French woman was brought to the A.D.S. (Shell wound left arm) wounded in MÉAULTE – brought to M.D.S., & sent on to Civilian Hp in AMIENS (on 10th)	

1247 W 3299 200,000 (E) 8/14 J.B.C. & A. Forms/C. 2118/11.

Army Form C. 2118.

WAR DIARY
or
INTELLIGENCE SUMMARY

(Erase heading not required.)

Instructions regarding War Diaries and Intelligence Summaries are contained in F.S. Regs., Part II. and the Staff Manual respectively. Title pages will be prepared in manuscript.

Hour, Date, Place		Summary of Events and Information	Remarks and references to Appendices
MERICOURT			
Feby 10th	12 noon	Visited the Regimental Aid Posts, with A.D.M.S. 7th Divn.	
	9 p.m.	1 Off (accid.) + W.d. & 28. O.R. sick admitted — 20. O.R. sick & 1 W.d. to D.Rest.Sh. — evacuated —	
Feby 11th	12 noon	1. 12 O.R. sick & 4 W.d. —	
		Capt. ALLAN RAMC rejoined on Completion of temporary duty with 9th Devons, & proceeded to A.D.S. for duty	
Feby 12th	12 noon	34. O.R. sick admitted — 23. O.R. sick to D.R.Sh.	
		10 " " evacuated	
Feby 13th	12 noon	19. O.R. " admitted 12 " " "	
		4 " " evacuated	
" 14th	10.30 a.m.	Lt. DAVIDSON with 36. O.R. proceeded to A.D.S in relief of the personnel there.	
		Capt. C.H. HART to 37th Bde R.F.A. for temporary duty.	
	12 noon	1 Off. 21. O.R. sick + 6 wounded admitted. 14. O.R. sick to D.R.S.	
		1 " 8 " " + 5 " evacuated	
		1. O.R. died — Severe shell injuries — L. leg torn off below knee.	
" 15th	12 noon	41. O.R. sick + 4 wounded admitted — 4. O.R sick to D.R.Sh.	
		16 " " + 2 " " evacuated	
" 16th	12 noon	29 " " admitted — 19 sick + 1 W.d. to D.R.S.	
		9 " " + 1 " " evacuated	

Army Form C. 2118.

WAR DIARY
or
INTELLIGENCE SUMMARY
(Erase heading not required.)

Instructions regarding War Diaries and Intelligence Summaries are contained in F. S. Regs., Part II. and the Staff Manual respectively. Title pages will be prepared in manuscript.

Hour, Date, Place		Summary of Events and Information	Remarks and references to Appendices
MERICOURT			
Feby 17th	12 noon	2 Off. 28 OR Sick admitted + 2 wounded. - 1 Off + 20 Off Sick to D.R.S	
		1 " 19 " " Evacuated	
" 18th	12 noon	- 42 OR Sick admitted - 11 Off Sick to D.R.S	
		20 " " 3 wounded Evacuated	
" 19th	12 noon	- 51 " " admitted 21 " " "	
		- 12 " " 4 " Evacuated	
		The Advanced Dressing Station has been improved by the addition of a dugout. This station was hit by shell-fire a few days ago, but no casualties occurred.	
" 20th	12 noon	2 Off. 30 OR Sick admitted. 3 wounded admitted. 19 OR Sick to D.R.S	
		19 "	2 Off evacuated wounded
			16 OR Sick to D.R.S
			(C. Beaver Substance)
" 21st	10 a.m.	Lt. CHISHOLM RAMC & 36 OR rank & file	
		proceeded to M.D.S as a relief	
" 22nd	12 noon	42 OR Sick admitted 1 wounded Off. 1 wounded OR admitted	15 OR Sick to D.R.S
		24 OR Sick evacuated 1 wounded Off. 2 wounded OR evacuated	
	12 noon	34 OR Sick and 15 OR wounded admitted	15 OR sic to D.R.S
		4 OR Sick and 14 OR wounded evacuated	
	8 pm.	Information has received that an Enemy attack might be expected. 24 OR with Extra stretchers, dressings & Amb. cars sent to A.D.S. immediately.	

1247 W 3299 200,000 (E) 8/14 J.B.C. & A. Forms/C. 2118/11.

Army Form C. 2118.

WAR DIARY
or
INTELLIGENCE SUMMARY

(Erase heading not required.)

Hour, Date, Place	Summary of Events and Information	Remarks and references to Appendices
MERICOURT.		
Feby 23rd 12 noon	1 off and 19 OR sick admitted	
	4 off and 64 OR wounded "	
	1 off Sick 5 OR sick evacuated.	31 OR sick transferred to FA's
	4 off and 3 OR wounded "	
24th 12 noon	36 OR sick admitted.	
	— 7 OR wounded —	
	— 6 OR sick evacuated	32 OR sick. FA8
	— 53 OR wounded	3 " wounded FA8
26th 12 noon	36 OR sick admitted	
	1 off and 2 OR wounded	20 OR sick. to FA8
	1 off and 9 OR sick evacuated	1 OR. wounded to FA2 }
	1 off and 4 OR wounded "	
26th 12 noon	31 OR sick admitted	
	1 off and — wounded "	
	1 off 10 OR sick evacuated.	25 OR sick to FA8
27th 12 noon	1 off and 2 OR wounded "	
	33 OR sick admitted	
	7 OR sick evacuated.	21 OR sick to FA8

WAR DIARY
or
INTELLIGENCE SUMMARY

(Erase heading not required.)

Army Form C. 2118.

Hour, Date, Place	Summary of Events and Information	Remarks and references to Appendices
MERICOURT 28th February. 10.a.m.	"A" bearer Subdivision with G.S. waggon, under Lieut DAVIDSON proceeded to A.D.S. at MEAULTE to relieve C. Subdivision bearers.	
12 noon.	25 OR sick admitted 1 OR wounded " 3 OR sick evacuated 1 OR wounded "	
	4 OR sick OR to R.R.B.	
5.30.p.m.	"C" bearer Subdivision with Blanket waggon under Capt ALLAN returned to the field ambulance	
29th 12 noon	26 OR sick admitted 2 OR wounded " 13 OR sick evacuated 1 OR wounded "	
	20 OR sick transferred to RfS	

T Mackie
W Mackie S.R
Capt Rwie ..
for O.C. 2 [?] Field Ambulance

23 7d Amb
Vol XV

Army Form C. 2118.

WAR DIARY
or
INTELLIGENCE SUMMARY

(Erase heading not required.)

Instructions regarding War Diaries and Intelligence Summaries are contained in F. S. Regs., Part II. and the Staff Manual respectively. Title pages will be prepared in manuscript.

Hour, Date, Place		Summary of Events and Information	Remarks and references to Appendices
MERICOURT			
1st March	12 noon	37 OR Sick admitted	
		18 OR Wounded "	
		6 OR Sick evacuated "	
		4 OR Wounded "	23 OR Sick Transferred to PH3
			1 OR Wounded "
2nd "	12 noon	28 OR Sick admitted	
		5 OR Wounded "	
		7 OR Sick evacuated "	24 OR Sick "
		14 OR Wounded "	1 OR Wounded "
3rd "	12 noon	38 OR Sick admitted	
		3 OR Wounded "	
		9 OR Sick evacuated "	26 OR Sick "
		1 OR Wounded "	1 OR Wounded "
4th "	12 noon	3 off 35 OR Sick admitted	
		1 OR Wounded "	
		2 off 5 OR Sick evacuated	
		1 OR Wounded "	1 off 14 OR Sick "
5th "	12 noon	37 OR Sick admitted	
		Wounded	

Army Form C. 2118.

WAR DIARY
or
INTELLIGENCE SUMMARY
(Erase heading not required.)

Instructions regarding War Diaries and Intelligence Summaries are contained in F. S. Regs., Part II. and the Staff Manual respectively. Title pages will be prepared in manuscript.

Hour, Date, Place		Summary of Events and Information	Remarks and references to Appendices
MERICOURT			
5th (cont) March	12 noon	15 OR. Sick evacuated. 27 OR Sick transferred to Rfd S.	
6th March	10 a.m.	B bearer Subdivision under Capt Allan proceed to ADS at MERULTE to relieve Lieut Chisholm and A Section.	
	12 noon	37 OR. Sick admitted	
		5 OR. wounded "	
		9 OR. Sick evacuated	16 OR Sick trans. to FR1
		4 OR wounded "	1 OR wounded "
	5·30 p.m.	A bearer Subdivision under Lieut Chisholm returned to 2/3 Field Ambulance at MERICOURT.	
7th	12 noon	60 OR sick admitted	
		9 OR wounded	
		20 OR Sick evacuated	28 OR Sick trans to FR1
		4 OR wounded "	1 OR wounded " "
	6·30 p.m.	Capt W.W. REID RAMC joined the Field Ambulance for duty from No. 9 Stationary Hospital.	
8th	12 noon	54 OR Sick admitted	
		5 OR wounded "	

Army Form C. 2118.

WAR DIARY
or
INTELLIGENCE SUMMARY

(Erase heading not required.)

Instructions regarding War Diaries and Intelligence Summaries are contained in F. S. Regs., Part II. and the Staff Manual respectively. Title pages will be prepared in manuscript.

Hour, Date, Place	Summary of Events and Information	Remarks and references to Appendices
MERICOURT		
8th March (aux) 12 noon	19 OR sick evacuated. 35 OR sick transferred to R.R.S.	
	6 OR wounded " 1 OR wounded " "	
9th 12 noon	52 OR sick admitted	
	9 OR wounded "	
	17 OR sick evacuated 33 OR sick " "	
	5 OR wounded "	
10th 12 noon	1 Off, 37 OR sick, 3 OR wounded admitted – 33 OR, 6 Offs sick	
	1 " 22 " " 11 " " evacuated	
11th 12 noon	1 Off, 49 OR sick, 1 Off + 2 OR wounded admitted	
	- 7 " " 1 " 7 " " evacuated	
	1 Off + 28 " sick to R.R.S.	
12th 12 noon	47 Off sick, 1 Off + 2 OR wounded admitted 26 OR sick to DRS	
	1st 19 OR " 1 " +19 " " evacuated	
	Orders from ADMS to take over the Div. Officers Rest Station at CORBIE from 22nd Jt Amb.	

Army Form C. 2118.

WAR DIARY
or
INTELLIGENCE SUMMARY
(Erase heading not required.)

Instructions regarding War Diaries and Intelligence Summaries are contained in F. S. Regs., Part II. and the Staff Manual respectively. Title pages will be prepared in manuscript.

Hour, Date, Place		Summary of Events and Information	Remarks and references to Appendices
MERICOURT			
March 13th	9.30 a.m.	Capt WEDD R.A.M.C with 14 OR & Medical Store Wagon proceeded to CORBIE to take over the Divisional Offrs Rest Station	
	12 noon	1 Off 18 OR sick, 5 (wounded) admitted. 1 Off 15 OR sick to D.R.S. 13 OR " 5 " " evacuated	
	2 p.m.	Lieut CHISHOLM to A.D.S in relief of Lieut DAVIDSON.	
	6 p.m.	Capt C.H. HART returned on completion of temporary duty.	
14th	12 noon	37 OR sick, 1 Off 2 OR w² admitted 17 OR sick to D.R.S. 22 " " 1 " 3 " " evacuated	
	2 p.m.	Visited A.D.S. The splinter proof shelter for stretcher cases has been completed.	
	4 p.m.	Revd SMITH. R.C. Chaplain returned to duty from hospital	
15th	12 noon	1 Off 7 OR w², 41 OR sick admitted 22 OR sick + 1 w² to D.R.S. 1 " 4 " " 5 " " evacuated	
	2 p.m.	Visited Officers Rest Station CORBIE.	
16th	12 noon	10 OR w² - 28 OR sick admitted 22 OR sick to D.R.S. 10 " " 8 " " evacuated	

Army Form C. 2118.

WAR DIARY
or
INTELLIGENCE SUMMARY

(Erase heading not required.)

Instructions regarding War Diaries and Intelligence Summaries are contained in F. S. Regs., Part II. and the Staff Manual respectively. Title pages will be prepared in manuscript.

Hour, Date, Place		Summary of Events and Information	Remarks and references to Appendices
MERICOURT			
March 17th	12 noon.	29 OR sick 3 wounded admitted 22 OR sick to D.R.S.	
		7 " " 6 " evacuated	
" 18th	12 noon.	1 Off 28 OR sick, 1 Off 12 OR wounded admitted 21 March + 1 OR S	
		— " 10 " " 1 " 3 " evacuated 1 OR wd died	
" 19th	12 "	— " 23 " " — " 13 " admitted 16 sick + 1 wd to D.R.S.	
		— " 6 " " 1 " 11 " evacuated	
" 20th	12 "	1 Off 20 " " 1 " 11 " admitted 13 sick, 3 wd to D.R.S.	
		1 " 3 " " — " 9 " evacuated 1 OR wd died	
	2 pm.	Capt A Hart to H.D.S in relief of Capt Allan.	
" 21st	12 noon.	26 OR sick, 4 wounded admitted 25 OR sick to D.R.S.	
		4 " " 8 " evacuated	
	2 pm.	Capt W.W. REID Ranne proceeded to 2/R Welsh Fusiliers	
		for instruction - on completion of which he to to join	
		21st Manchester Regt. for duty.	
" 22nd	12 noon.	1 Off 19 OR sick, 3 wounded admitted 12 OR sick to D.R.S.	
		1 " 4 " " 2 " evacuated	

Army Form C. 2118.

WAR DIARY
or
INTELLIGENCE SUMMARY
(Erase heading not required.)

Instructions regarding War Diaries and Intelligence Summaries are contained in F. S. Regs., Part II. and the Staff Manual respectively. Title pages will be prepared in manuscript.

Hour, Date, Place		Summary of Events and Information	Remarks and references to Appendices
MERICOURT			
March 22nd	5 p.m.	Under ADMS instructions Capt ALLAN proceeds to BRAY for attachment to and duty with 21st F.A.	
" 23rd	12 noon	19 O.R. sick, 6 wounded admitted 11 O.R. sick 6 D.R.S.	
		6 " " 2 " " evacuated	
" 24th	12 noon	15 " " 4 " " admitted 18 O.R. sick, 5 wounded 6 D.R.S.	
		— " " 3 " " evacuated	
" 25th	12 noon	2 3 " " — " " admitted 19 " " 2 " 6 D.R.S.	
		2 " " 3 " " evacuated	
" 26th	12 noon	14 " " 1 " " admitted 7 " " — 6 D.R.S.	
		— Nil " " evacuated	
" 27th	12 noon	21 " " 3 " " admitted 16 " " — 6 D.R.S.	
		1 " " 3 " " evacuated	
" 28th	12 noon	32 " " 5 " " admitted 18 " " 1 " 6 D.R.S.	
		5 " " 3 " " evacuated	
" 29th	12 noon	30 " " 2 " " admitted 21 " " — 6 D.R.S.	
		5 " " 4 " " evacuated	
	6 p.m.	Lieut DAVIDSON Rowe to 2/Border Regt for temporary duty.	
" 30th	9 a.m.	Under instructions from ADMS, all sick & wounded from the front line are to be received by 23rd F.A., as the 21st F.A. is moving	

Army Form C. 2118.

WAR DIARY
or
INTELLIGENCE SUMMARY
(Erase heading not required.)

Hour, Date, Place		Summary of Events and Information	Remarks and references to Appendices
MERICOURT			
March 30th	12 noon	19 sick & 2 wounded admitted. 12 sick & wounded to DRS. 4 " & 1 " evacuated	
" 31st	12 noon	33 " & 18 " admitted. 17 sick & wounded to DRS. 6 " & 5 " evacuated (P.M. Sr. chronic Intestinal nephritis form) 1 case died of Uraemia. To increase the existing accommodation a canvas hut has been built near the present huts during the last two days. This hut has accommodation for 40 stretchers —	

Geo. M. Brown
Lt Col RAMC
O.C. 23rd Fd Amb.

April 1916.

No. 23 F. Amb.

COMMITTEE FOR THE
MEDICAL HISTORY OF THE WAR
Date 9 - JUN. 1915

7

23 Ja Aul
Vol XVI

Army Form C. 2118.

WAR DIARY
or
INTELLIGENCE SUMMARY

(Erase heading not required.)

Instructions regarding War Diaries and Intelligence Summaries are contained in F. S. Regs., Part II. and the Staff Manual respectively. Title pages will be prepared in manuscript.

Hour, Date, Place		Summary of Events and Information	Remarks and references to Appendices
MERICOURT			
April 1st	12 noon.	44. OR sick, 17 wounded admitted. 30 sick + 4 wounded to DRS	
		12 " " 17 " evacuated	
	10 p.m.	Capt. J.E. ALLAN reported on completion of temporary duty with 21st Fd. Ambulance	
" 2nd	12 noon	1 Off. 37 OR sick, 5 wounded admitted. 46 sick to DRS.	
		1 " 3 " " 9 " " evacuated	
" 3rd	12 noon	1 " 34 " " 4 " " admitted. 26 sick to DRS.	
		1 " 2 " " 4 " " evacuated	
" 4th	12 noon	2 Off sick, 1 Off wd, 26 OR sick, 7 wd admitted. 22 sick + 1 wd. to DRS.	
		2 " " 1 " " 9 " 3 " evacuated	
"	7 p.m.	2olt Bde O.O. 59 received also instructions from ADMS 7th Divn. to hand over the ADS at MÉAULTE to 65th Fd Amb. (21st Divn.) on the 6th	
" 5th	12 noon	2 Off sick, 1 Off wd -, 31. OR sick 10 wd admitted. 17 sick to DRS.	
		2 " 1 " 7 " " 7 " evacuated	
" 6th	10.30 a.m.	ADS at MÉAULTE handed over to 65th Fd Amb.	

Army Form C. 2118.

WAR DIARY
or
INTELLIGENCE SUMMARY
(Erase heading not required.)

Instructions regarding War Diaries and Intelligence Summaries are contained in F. S. Regs., Part II. and the Staff Manual respectively. Title pages will be prepared in manuscript.

Hour, Date, Place		Summary of Events and Information	Remarks and references to Appendices
MERICOURT			
April 6th	12 noon	40. OR sick, 7 wounded admitted 25 sick to D.R.S	
		3 " 10 " evacuated	
" 7th	12 noon	Bearer Subdivision rejoined from MÉAULTE —	
" 8th	12 noon	34 OR sick, 4 wounded admitted 34 sick to D.R.S	
		6 " 4 " evacuated	
		1 Off sick, 1 Off wounded, 15.OR sick 3 w. admitted 15 sick to D.R.S	
		1 " 1 " 2 " 3 " evacuated	
	2.30 pm.	Under instructions of A.D.M.S 7th Div., the Officers Rest Station at CORBIE was handed over to 21st Fd. Amb. Personnel rejoined at H.Qrs of the Ambulance.	
" 9th	12 noon	1, Off + 22.OR sick, 2.OR wounded admitted 19 sick to D.R.S	
		1 " 3 " 6 " evacuated	
" 10th	12 noon	1 " 29 " 6 " admitted 14 " to D.R.S.	
		1 " 8 " — evacuated	
	7 pm	Lieut CHISHOLM. Renue to 8/ Devons for temporary duty.	
" 11th	12 noon	1.Off 16. OR sick, 11 wounded admitted 11 sick to D.R.S.	
		1 " 3 " 5 " evacuated	
	8 pm	Rsvd W. SANDIFORD C.F (R.C) joins for duty with 2/6 A.& S.H.

Army Form C. 2118.

WAR DIARY
or
INTELLIGENCE SUMMARY

(Erase heading not required.)

Instructions regarding War Diaries and Intelligence Summaries are contained in F. S. Regs., Part II. and the Staff Manual respectively. Title pages will be prepared in manuscript.

Hour, Date, Place		Summary of Events and Information	Remarks and references to Appendices
MERICOURT			
April 12th	12 noon	1. Off 29. O.R sick, 5 wounded & 9 unfit as 24 sick + 1 W. to D.R.S.	
		1 " 5 " " 11 " " evacuated	
" 13th	12 noon	1 " 29 " " 6 " " admitted 1 Off + 20 sick to D.R.S.	
		— " 1 " " 3 " " evacuated	
		Lieut Davidson Rawe reported on completion of temporary duty with 1/Border Regt.	
		Instructions received from A.D.M.S. 7. Div. directing that the 23rd F.A. should take over collection of wounded & sick in the front line from 21st F.A. — Relief to be completed by 19th inst.	
	9 p.m.	Instructions received to cancel all further leave to recall all officers known on leave at present — This to be done by letter.	
" 14th	12 noon	1. Off. 24 O.R sick, 3. O.R wounded admitted 1. Off 18. O.R sick to D.R.S	
		— " 5 " " 7 " " evacuated	
	12.30 p.m	Capt B.H WEDD Rawe to Royal Engineers 7th Div. for permanent duty.	
	3 p.m.	Lieut G COOPER RAMC(TC) from 2/Gordons reported for duty with the ambulance.	

Army Form C. 2118.

WAR DIARY
or
INTELLIGENCE SUMMARY

(Erase heading not required.)

Instructions regarding War Diaries and Intelligence Summaries are contained in F.S. Regs., Part II. and the Staff Manual respectively. Title pages will be prepared in manuscript.

Hour, Date, Place		Summary of Events and Information	Remarks and references to Appendices
MERICOURT			
April 14th	5.30 p.m.	Advance party of 1 NCO + 15 men under Capt. R. Meache with one motor ambulance proceeded forward to BRAY to relieve a similar party of 21st F.A. at the "CITADEL" A.D.S.	
" 15th	8 a.m.	Rev'd G.L. SMITH (C.F.) left for H.Q. Gen'l H.P. at ETAPLES	
	11 a.m.	Capt. Allan with 23.O.R., 1 N.C.O., 1 G.S. Store cart, 1 water cart, 2 wheeled stretcher carriages, 1 motor cyclist proceeded forward to take over the A.D.S. at BRAY from 21st F.A.	
	12 noon	2.Off. 29.O.R sick + 6 wounded admitted. 1.Off. 29.O.R. sick to D.R.S.	
		1 " 9 " " 2 " " evacuated	
" 16th	3 p.m.	Via. to A.D.S. at BRAY	
	12 noon	1.Off. 22.O.R. sick; 1.Off. 7.O.R. wounded admitted. 17.O.R. sick to D.R.S.	
		6 " 1 " 6 " " evacuated	
	2 p.m.	Capt. C.H. Hart Rawe with 24.O.R., 1 light cart, 1 wheeled stretcher carriages + 1 Motor Ambulance proceeded forward to complete the relief of 21st F.A. at the CITADEL A.D.S.	
" 17th	12 noon	19.O.R sick + 9 wounded admitted 1.Off. + 18.O.R. sick + 1 man slightly from to D.R.S.	
		4 " 7 " " evacuated	
" 18th	12 noon	1.Off. 19 " + 16.Off. 13.O.R. " admitted. 1.Off. 12.O.R. sick + 1 W. to D.R.S.	
		" 11 " " evacuated	

WAR DIARY
or
INTELLIGENCE SUMMARY

(Erase heading not required.)

Army Form C. 2118.

Hour, Date, Place		Summary of Events and Information	Remarks and references to Appendices
MERICOURT			
April 19th	12 noon	1 Off, 14 OR sick admitted + 3 OR wounded. 16 Sick to D.D.S. 1 Off, 3 " (sick) evacuated (10 Off W-)	
" 20th	12 noon	LIEUT DOWZER RAMC (T.C) reports for duty. 1 Off 30 OR sick, 3 Off + 59 OR wounded admitted) 13 Sick to D.D.S. 1 " 8 " " 1 " " - " (Evacuated) The large number of wounded was the result of an enemy raid on our trenches about MANSEL COPSE. On information from A.D.Ss being received, all the motor ambulances were sent up to the CITADEL + BRAY A.D.Ss. The bearers of the working parties were called in at once to remove the wounded. There was no total in the evacuation of wounded. Some of the walking cases arrived at the M.D.S. at MERICOURT within two hours of the time they were wounded.	
	8 pm	Visited the BRAY + CITADEL A.D.Ss. also Reg+ Aid Post of BORDER REGT- A considerable amount of shelling by the enemy was going on in the neighbourhood of the Aid Post.	
" 21st	12 noon	33 OR sick + 21 OR wounded admitted) 15 OR sick + 1 still sick 20 Off 7 " 57 " " (Evacuated) to D.D.S.	

WAR DIARY or INTELLIGENCE SUMMARY

Army Form C. 2118.

Hour, Date, Place		Summary of Events and Information	Remarks and references to Appendices
April 22nd NERICOURT	9 a.m.	20 W/ Off to O.O. No 60 Reserve). Two ambulances to accompany us to on the march, details) -	
	12 noon	1. Off. 21 O.R. sick + 12 O.R. wounded admitted 21 sick to D.R.S.	
		1 " 8 " 19 " " evacuated	
		Reserve dressings for the 3 Regimental Aid Posts were sent up to the CITADEL A.D.S. today. There are being two sacks each containing 3 lbs cotton wool, 30 rollers bandages, 12 triangular bandages, 1 pint Iodo Carbolic lotion & 6 jars of meat & butter. These two will be kept at the A.D.S. & issues only during the emergency of an action - If the Regimental Medical Officer seems short of dressings.	
23rd	12 noon	2. Off., 4. O.R. sick, 1. Off + 7. O.R. wounded admitted. (1 Off 25 O.R. Sick + 1 w.d. to D.R.S.) evacuated	
		- 11 " " , 1 " + 7 " " "	
24th	12 noon	1 " 25 " " , - " " " admitted 10 Off + 21 Sick to C.R.S.	
		- " 9 " " , - " " " evacuated	
		1 " 7 " " , - " " " admitted	
25th	12 noon	1 " 22 " " , 1 " 6 " " admitted 1 Off + 17 sick to D.R.S.	
		- " 5 " " , - " 4 " " evacuated	
		Instructions received that leave will reopen from 26th inst.	

Army Form C. 2118.

WAR DIARY
or
INTELLIGENCE SUMMARY
(Erase heading not required.)

Hour, Date, Place		Summary of Events and Information	Remarks and references to Appendices
MERICOURT			
26th April	10 a.m.	2 O/C Inf. Bde O.O. no. 61 received	
	12 noon	2 Off 26 OR sick + 3 wounded admitted 15 OR sick to DRS	
27th "	"	— " — 1 Off 19 " " Evacuated	
	12 noon	— " 9 " — 13 " admitted 14 OR sick to DRS	
		2 " 30 " — 5 " Evacuated	
28th "	12 noon	4 " 9 " — 25 " admitted 22 Sick Ind to 6 DRS	
		1 " 28 " — 1 " 10 " Evacuated	
		1 " 3 " — 1 "	
		Capt. BUCKLEY to Citadel in relief of Capt MACKIE	
		Capt HART from Citadel MDS to MDS at Mericourt	
29th "	12 noon	3 Off 36 OR sick, 8 OR wounded admitted 18 OR Sept D.R.S	
		2 " 10 " 23 " " Evacuated	
		Lieut Cooper to Citadel MDS vice Capt Hart — Capt Mackie	
		returned to M.D.S. at Mericourt	
30th "	12 noon	1 Off 32 OR sick, 9 OR wounded admitted 20 OR sick to DRS	
		1 " 15 " " 8 " " Evacuated	

Army Form C. 2118.

WAR DIARY
or
INTELLIGENCE SUMMARY

(Erase heading not required.)

Instructions regarding War Diaries and Intelligence Summaries are contained in F. S. Regs., Part II. and the Staff Manual respectively. Title pages will be prepared in manuscript.

Hour, Date, Place	Summary of Events and Information	Remarks and references to Appendices
MERICOURT	During the latter half of the month, the men have been employed on various duties besides that of collecting wounded. A party with G.S. wagons has been employed daily on Divisional fatigues at the Quarry (for road-metal) or cutting pit-sawing timber. Two other parties have been engaged in shielding dug-outs for wounded behind the front lines. The Citadel A.D.S has been greatly improved by the addition of a large Cook-house, Stew(ard)-baggage, latrine — A XIIth Corps fatigue too has been undertaken, ie the making of a large 2nd Amb: Encampment in the N.W quadrant of the cross roads in K 15.d. (1/40,000 ALBERT Sheet. 1st Edn) This entails the planting of a number of hospital marquees, tramping of the banks of the field, widening of the hoa S corner, metalling of roads All the N.CO's + men have worked in a very willing + praiseworthy manner at these various fatigues.	Geo H Brown Lt Col RAMC O.C. 23rd - 2nd Amb.

May 1916.

No. 23 4 Amb

COMMITTEE FOR THE
MEDICAL HISTORY OF THE WAR
Date 26 JUN '25

WAR DIARY or INTELLIGENCE SUMMARY

Army Form C. 2118.

23rd Aust

Hour, Date, Place	Summary of Events and Information	Remarks and references to Appendices
1916 MERICOURT May 1st.	Last night, about 8.40 p.m. a wave of "lacrymatory" gas swept over the village, causing discomfort to every-body. The symptoms were burning + lacrymation of the Eyes with burning dryness of the throat. The down draughts Replyed Bromide - (Lauats) for fully half an hour - There was a heavy bombard-ment from 7.40 to 8 p.m. + the fire probably came from the shells fires by the Enemy - It apparently drifted down the valley from MEAULTE - VILLE - MERICOURT - the winds being Easterly at the time.	
12 noon	1 Off 25 OR Sick, 34 OR Wounded) admitted 14 OR Sick + 1 W. Off DTS. 1 " 9 " 10 " " Evacuated. The wounded included 6 men suffering from "lacrymatory gas" - None of them were very Serious Cases.	
12 noon	1 Off 39 OR Sick + 44 Wounded) admitted 20 OR Sick + 2 W.(Shell shock) 2 " 6 " + 24 " " Evacuated to D.R.S. Instructions from A.D.M.S. 7th Div. that the Div. Rest Station at DAOURS will close from today. Arrangements were accordingly made, 6 treat slight cases at the M.D.S. Six beds were to hung extra accommodation for 48 sick were fitted - this gave accommodation for a total of about 120 Sick + wounded.	

Army Form C. 2118.

WAR DIARY
or
INTELLIGENCE SUMMARY

(Erase heading not required.)

Hour, Date, Place		Summary of Events and Information	Remarks and references to Appendices
MERICOURT			
May 3rd	12 noon	32. OR sick + 10 wounded admitted	
		17 " 4 " evacuated.	
		4 out of the 6 cases admitted on 1st as "cases" returned to duty today. Headache and nausea were the symptoms that prevailed longest. The remaining two will be fit for duty tomorrow. S.O.S. Bizaut pro XV in Avy 3; every 2 hours appeared to afford much relief.	
" 4th	12 noon	2. Off 28. OR sick; 1. Off 8. OR wounded admitted	
		2 " 15 " — " 9 " evacuated	
" 5th	12 noon	Visited BRAY & CITADEL ADS. to Stations in the evening -	
		2. Off 36. OR sick, 7 wounded admitted	
		1 " 7 " " 7 " evacuated.	
" 6th	12 noon	— " 30 " " 5 " admitted	
		1 " 22 " " 7 " evacuated	
" 7th	12 noon	— " 23 " " 11 " admitted	
		— " 23 " " 9 " evacuated.	
" 8th	12 noon	2 " 27 " " 8 " admitted. 20 sick to 21st DRS	
		1 " 11 " " 7 " evacuated at ALLONVILLE.	

Army Form C. 2118.

WAR DIARY
or
INTELLIGENCE SUMMARY

(Erase heading not required.)

Instructions regarding War Diaries and Intelligence Summaries are contained in F. S. Regs., Part II. and the Staff Manual respectively. Title pages will be prepared in manuscript.

Hour, Date, Place		Summary of Events and Information	Remarks and references to Appendices
MERICOURT			
May 9th	12 noon	22. OR sick + 15 wounded admitted. 4 sick + 15 w.d. evacuated	
" 10th	12 noon	Visits A.D.S at BRAY. 33. OR sick + 5 wounded admitted. 10. sick + 7 w.d. evacuated	
" 11th	12 noon	29 " + 11 " " 23 " + 7 " "	
		Notified by A.D.M.S. that 7th Div? Rest Station to open at DAOURS. 20. Sept. B & OO No. 63 received	
" 12th	10 pm	Open at DAOURS	
	12 noon	27. OR sick + 5 wounded admitted – 13. OR sick + 6 w.d. evacuated	
" 13th	12 noon	27. OR " + 2. Off + 27. OR wounded admitted. 21. OR sick 6. O. Far. evacuated	
		10 " " + 2 " + 7 " " " "	
		Capt. Allan to the "CITADEL" A.D.S. in relief of Capt. Thornley who returns to M.D. Station.	
" 14th	12 noon	2. Off + 24. OR sick, + 7 wounded admitted. 20 sick to D.R.S	
		1 " 7 " " + 23 " " evacuated	
" 15th	12 noon	1 " 16 " " 1. Off + 3 " admitted 14 Sick to D.R.S	
		1 " 7 " " 7 " evacuated	
" 16th	12 noon	– " 44 OR " 1 Off + nil " admitted 19 sick to D.R.S	
		– " 21 " " + 1 " evacuated	
		Capt. READDIE, R.A.M.C. from Northumberland Hussars taken on the strength of this Ambulance from 15th for duty.	

Army Form C. 2118.

WAR DIARY
or
INTELLIGENCE SUMMARY

(Erase heading not required.)

Instructions regarding War Diaries and Intelligence Summaries are contained in F. S. Regs, Part II. and the Staff Manual respectively. Title pages will be prepared in manuscript.

Hour, Date, Place		Summary of Events and Information	Remarks and references to Appendices
MERICOURT			
May 17th	12 noon	1 Off + 35 O.R sick, 2 Off + 6 O.R w'd admitted 22 O.R to R.S	
		1 " 7 " - 2 " 2 " Evacuated	
	6 p.m.	Capt READDIE to Citadel A.D.S in relief of Lt DOWZER.	
	7 p.m.	20th Inf Bde O.O. 64 (received) -	
18th	12 noon	2 Off 41 O.R sick, 12 O.R w'd admitted 19 Sick + 2 Shell Shock to D.R.S.	
		1 " 10 " - 15 " 9 O.R - Evacuated to D.R.S.	
19th	12 noon	- 36 " - 4 " admitted 38 sick to D.R.S.	
		2 " 3 " - 7 " Evacuated	
20th	12 noon	1 " 28 " - 4 " admitted 22 w + 1 Shell Shock to D.R.S	
		1 " 68 " - 4 " Evacuated	
		Capt Hoat to BRAY A.D.S, in relief of Lieut Cooper	
		The town of BRAY was shelled by the enemy in the morning - No damage was done to the M.D.S.	
21st	12 noon	26 O.R sick, 4 Off 20 O.R wounded admitted 13 Sick to D.R.S.	
		3 " 4 " 10 " - " Evacuated	
	8 p.m.	Lieut Chisholm returned on completion of duty with 8th Devons -	

WAR DIARY
or
INTELLIGENCE SUMMARY

(Erase heading not required.)

Army Form C. 2118.

Hour, Date, Place		Summary of Events and Information	Remarks and references to Appendices
MERICOURT			
May 22nd	10.30 a.m.	Lieut Cooper to 20th Manchesters for temporary duty.	
	12 noon	2 Off. 3. O.R. sick, 4. O.R. wounded admitted. 28 sick+wd. to D.R.S.	
		— " 7 " 13 " " Evacuated	
		On 20th inst. under instructions received – the establishment was reduced as follows:–	
		Horses – 1 Riding + 1 light draught to 20th Bde. M.G. Coy.	
		1 Heavy draught – to 1/11th Div Train	
		M.T. Personnel – 1 Sergt A.S.C. + 1 Driver –	
		The Drivers were absorbed to complete establishment.	
	8 p.m.	Further orders received today to reduce the establishment of Motor Tricycles from 3 to 2. 1 N.C.O. A.S.C. (M.T.) to be sent to Base Depot + Establishment reduced to 2	
" 23rd	7 a.m.	26th Bde O.O. 65 received.	
	12 noon	4 O. OR sick, 6 OR wounded admitted, 33 sick to D.R.S.	
		2 Off. 7 OR sick 5 " " Evacuated	
" 24th	12 noon	2 " 28 " 6 " " admitted. 16 sick to D.R.S.	
		— " 9 " 6 " " Evacuated	

Army Form C. 2118.

WAR DIARY
or
INTELLIGENCE SUMMARY

(Erase heading not required.)

Instructions regarding War Diaries and Intelligence Summaries are contained in F.S. Regs., Part II. and the Staff Manual respectively. Title pages will be prepared in manuscript.

Hour, Date, Place		Summary of Events and Information	Remarks and references to Appendices
MERICOURT			
May 24th	12 noon	Lieut DOWZER Rame to 20th Manchesters for temporary duty in relief of Lieut. G. COOPER who has been sent back under arrest to await trial by Court Martial.	
	3.30 p.m.	Capt. T.S. WRIGHT- Rame (T.C) reports for duty from 37th Bde R.F.A. - on the brigade being broken up. The Medical Equipment of the brigade was taken over by the Ambulance for return to Store. The Medical Orderly (Rame) is attached to the Ambulance for duty	
" 25th		18 OR Sick, 5 wounded admitted 13 Sick to R.R.S. 1 Off + OR " 10 " Evacuated	
	12 noon	Instructions received from A.D.M.S. 7th Div. that the A.D.S. at BRAY is to be evacuated by the evening of the 26th inst. Laconsingly went up, + chose a spot on the BRAY- ALBERT ROAD about L.9.C.7.7. (1/40,000 ALBERT Sheet) as a car rendezvous for the two motor ambulances in waiting - Three Bell tents to be pitched alongside the road On the East side of the road are some old pun	

WAR DIARY
or
INTELLIGENCE SUMMARY
(Erase heading not required.)

Army Form C. 2118.

Hour, Date, Place		Summary of Events and Information	Remarks and references to Appendices
MERICOURT			
May 25th (Cont?)		Positions which can be enlarged to shelter the cars - Others when head cover has been provided, will protect the personnel. Gave instructions to Capt HART to carry out the necessary work at this spot. On completion he is to leave 1 NCO & 4 OR, 2 motor ambulances + 1 water cart at this spot, then return to the M.D.S. with the remaining personnel & equipment.	
" 26th	12 noon	2 Off. 32 OR sick 11. OR wounded admitted	13 sick to D.R.S.
		1 " 9 " nil " evacuated	
	4 pm	Capt Hart + detachment proceeded from A.D.S. BRAY. The building was handed over to a representative of the 18th Divn.	
" 27th	12 noon	34 OR sick + 13 wounded admitted. 20 sick to D.R.S.	
		1 Off, 11 " " , 1 Off 18 " evacuated	
" 28th	12 noon	26 OR " 4 OR " admitted 21 sick to D.R.S.	
		5 " " 3 " " evacuated	
" 29th	12 noon	10 Off, 2 Off, 6 OR " admitted	OR 12 sick to D.R.S.
		39 OR " " " admitted	1 OR wounded to D.R.S.

Army Form C. 2118.

WAR DIARY
or
INTELLIGENCE SUMMARY
(Erase heading not required.)

Instructions regarding War Diaries and Intelligence Summaries are contained in F. S. Regs., Part II. and the Staff Manual respectively. Title pages will be prepared in manuscript.

Hour, Date, Place	Summary of Events and Information	Remarks and references to Appendices
MERICOURT		
May. 29th (cont.)	6 OR. sick and 15 OR. wounded. evacuated.	
	1 off. wounded. evacuated.	
" 30th 12 noon.	34 OR. sick. 6 OR.2 wounded admitted	
	9 OR. sick. 7 OR wounded evacuated	34 OR sick to NP8
	1 off. sick. 1 off. wounded evacuated	2 OR wounded
" 31st 12 noon	22 OR sick. 8 OR. wounded admitted	
	1 off. sick. 1 off. wounded admitted	25 OR sick to RHO
	3 OR. sick. 6 OR. wounded evacuated	2 OR wounded
June. 1st.	1 off. sick. 1 off. wounded evacuated	

T. Mackie S.R.
Capt. Raine

4th Division

No 23. Field Ambulance

June 10th 1916

5/

WAR DIARY or INTELLIGENCE SUMMARY

Army Form C. 2118.

23rd Fd Amb

Hour, Date, Place	Summary of Events and Information	Remarks and references to Appendices
MERICOURT		
June 1st 9.a.m.	Lt J.S. CHISHOLM. RAMC. (T.C) proceeded to England on termination of contract.	
" 12 noon	36 OR. Sick and 19 OR wounded. Admitted	
	1 off " 2 off " "	16 OR Sick 6 ADS
	12 OR " 4 OR " Evacuated	2 OR wnded "
	1 off " 2 " " Evacuated	
2nd 12 noon	32 OR " 2 OR " Admitted	1st OR sick to DRS
	5 OR " 12 OR " Evacuated	6 OR wounded "
10 p.m.	Revd RAMC Rouzer reformed to complete tour of duty with 20th Manchesters	
3rd 12 noon	39 OR Sick and 38 OR wounded. admitted	
	2 off " 2 off " " admitted	32 OR Sick to DRS
	9 OR " 6 OR " Evacuated	
	2 off " 2 off " " Evacuated	
8 p.m.	Capt HART to CITADEL in relief of Capt ALLAN.	
11-30 p.m.	Capt ALLAN returned to MDS on being relieved by Capt HART.	

WAR DIARY
or
INTELLIGENCE SUMMARY

Army Form C. 2118.

Hour, Date, Place	Summary of Events and Information	Remarks and references to Appendices
MERICOURT		
June 4th 12 noon.	36 OR sick and 7 OR wounded admitted	
	2 off " 2 off " wounded	
	8 OR " " 31 OR wounded evacuated, 25 OR sick to DR?	
	2 off " 2 off " " 1 wounded to DR?	
5th 12 noon.	41 OR " 22 OR " admitted	
	2 off " 4 off " "	
	8 OR " 6 OR " evacuated, 19 OR sick to D.R.S.	
	1 off " 4 off " " 1 OR wdd to D.R.S.	
" 6 p.m.	Capt T.S. WRIGHT RAMC. (TC) returned from 14th Bde R.F.A. where he had been in relief of CAPT NELSON.	
6th 12 noon	34 OR sick and 17 OR wounded admitted	
	1 off - sick and 1 off " " admitted 17 OR sick to DR	
	7 OR " 22 OR " evacuated, 10 OR wounded	
	1 off " 1 off " "	
7th 12 noon.	1 off 22 OR sick, 1 off 4 OR wounded admitted. 20 sick to D.R.S.	
	1 " 4 " " 1 " 9 " " evacuated	

Army Form C. 2118.

WAR DIARY
or
INTELLIGENCE SUMMARY
(Erase heading not required.)

Instructions regarding War Diaries and Intelligence Summaries are contained in F.S. Regs., Part II. and the Staff Manual respectively. Title pages will be prepared in manuscript.

Hour, Date, Place	Summary of Events and Information	Remarks and references to Appendices
MERICOURT.		
June 8th 9 a.m.	Lieut Davidson to 2/Gordons for temporary duty.	
10 a.m.	Capt E. WORDLEY. RAINE (T.C.) reported for duty — from 2nd Indian Cavalry Division (13th Hussars)	
12 noon	1 Off. 14. O.R. sick, 6. O.R. wounded admitted 14. O.R. to D.R.S. 1 " 7 " " 2 " " Evacuated. The Advanced Dressing Station at the CITADEL has received considerable attention from the enemy of late. The shelling has been heavy at times and the dug-outs have been hit frequently by 4.2" shells. The overhead cover kept out these shells. The water-tank was destroyed by a shell, and one man N°. Pte Jones of the unit was severely wounded in the legs. In consequence the personnel at the A.D.S. has been reduced to 10 Officers & 14 men. The rest have been withdrawn to the Car Rendezvous at L.9.C.7.7. The A.D.S. party are relieved 2 to 3 times a week as the men are all showing signs of "nervousness" as the result of the constant shell-fire.	
9.15 p.m.	20th Bde. O.O. N° 66 received.	

Army Form C. 2118.

WAR DIARY
or
INTELLIGENCE SUMMARY

(Erase heading not required.)

Instructions regarding War Diaries and Intelligence Summaries are contained in F. S. Regs, Part II. and the Staff Manual respectively. Title pages will be prepared in manuscript.

Hour, Date, Place		Summary of Events and Information	Remarks and references to Appendices
MERICOURT			
June 9th	9 a.m.	Under instructions from ADMS 7th Divn, 2 Motor ambulance cars of 21st & 23rd Amb. will be attached to the 23rd F.A.- They will replace the 2 Motor ambulance cars now stationed at the Car rendezvous near BRAY. These cars reported at 9 a.m. & the 23rd F.A. Cars were withdrawn.	
	12 noon	41 O.R. sick, 2 wounded admitted. 24 sick, 2 wd. to D.R.	
		12 " 4 " " Evacuated	
	8 p.m.	Capt Mackie to CITADEL A.D.S. Capt Readdie to Rly. Rn. to Rn. D.S.	
" 10th	12 noon	36 O.R. sick, 3 wounded admitted. 14 sick to D.R.S.	
		NIL " 1 " 3 " " evacuated	
" 11th	12 noon	2 Off 44 O.R. sick, 8 " admitted 21 Sick to D.R."	
		1 " 6 " " 2 " " Evacuated	
	2.30 p.m.	Capt Wright for temporary duty to 2/Gordons in relief of Lieut Davidson, who proceeds to 7th Div Sanitary Section vice Capt Carson who is sick.	
" 12th	12 noon	1 Off 37 O.R. sick, 11 wounded admitted 17 sick 1 wd. to D.R.S	
		6 " 9 " " evacuated	
		Capt Wordley to A.D.S. for instruction.	

Army Form C. 2118.

WAR DIARY
or
INTELLIGENCE SUMMARY
(Erase heading not required.)

Instructions regarding War Diaries and Intelligence Summaries are contained in F.S. Regs., Part II. and the Staff Manual respectively. Title pages will be prepared in manuscript.

Hour, Date, Place		Summary of Events and Information	Remarks and references to Appendices
MERICOURT			
June 13th	12 noon	1. Off 29. OR sick, 3 wounded admitted 35 sick 1 w. to D.R.S. (Evacuated)	
" 14th	12 noon	1 " 6 " 1 " 3 " "	
		— 38 " 1 " Off, 3. OR " admitted 37 sick 6 D.R.S.	
		— 4 " " 1 " 4 " " evacuated	
		Under Army Instructions "Summer" time will be adopted from 11 p.m. tonight. At 11 p.m. all clocks will be advanced to 12 midnight – (i.e. by 60 minute).	
" 15th	11 a.m.	20 to Inf B.de J.70 R.O.! received	
	12 noon	45. OR sick + 4 wounded admitted 42 sick 6 D.R.S. 2 " " + 2 " Evacuated	
		Capt Hart returned to M.D.S last night on relief by Capt Worsley from Citadel A.D.S	
" 16th	12 noon	50 Off sick, 3 wounded admitted 31 Sick 6 D.R.S. 14 " " 4 " " Evacuated	
	2 p.m.	Under instructions from A.D.M.S 7th Div. L.T.T. Dowzer R.A.M.C reports to 21st F. Amt. for duty there on transfer from this unit	
" 17th	12 noon	2. Off 46. OR sick, 11 wounded admitted 26 sick + 2 w. to D.R.S. 1 " 11 " 6 " " Evacuated	
	8 p.m.	Capt Allan to CITADEL A.D.S in relief of Capt Mackie who returns to M.D.S.	

1247 W 3299 200,000 (E) 8/14 J.B.C. & A. Forms/C. 2118/11.

Army Form C. 2118.

WAR DIARY
or
INTELLIGENCE SUMMARY
(Erase heading not required.)

Instructions regarding War Diaries and Intelligence Summaries are contained in F. S. Regs., Part II. and the Staff Manual respectively. Title pages will be prepared in manuscript.

Hour, Date, Place		Summary of Events and Information	Remarks and references to Appendices
MERICOURT			
June 18th	12 noon	1. Off sick, 3 wounded admitted 27. Off sick 1w^d 6 R.A.S.	
		2 ~ 10 ~ 7 ~ evacuated	
	3 pm	Capt Wright returned on completion of temporary duty with 2/Gordons.	
	5 pm	20th Inf Bde O.O. 67 received.	
19th	10 am	20th " " 68 "	
	12 noon	50. Off sick, 1. Off 11. Off wounded admitted 46 sick 1w^d 6 R.A.S.	
		11. OR " 1 " 5 " evacuated	
		Sentence of G.C.M. on Lt Cooper promulgated today - Sentence:- "To be dismissed from His Majesty's Service" - Confirmed by G.O.C - in - Chief -	
20th	12 noon	2 Officers 28. OR sick, 11 wounded admitted 30 sick to R.A.	
		2 ~ 8 ~ 13 ~ evacuated	
	5.52 pm	Lieut Cooper left Mericourt Station for Boulogne en route for England - He is struck off the strength	
	11 pm	2.J.O. N° 2. of 20th Inf Bde received	

Army Form C. 2118.

WAR DIARY
or
INTELLIGENCE SUMMARY

(Erase heading not required.)

Instructions regarding War Diaries and Intelligence Summaries are contained in F.S. Regs., Part II. and the Staff Manual respectively. Title pages will be prepared in manuscript.

Hour, Date, Place		Summary of Events and Information	Remarks and references to Appendices
MERICOURT.			
June 21st	12 noon	42 O.R Sick, 1 Off/ 7 O.R admitted 27 Sick to D.R.S.	
	9 a.m.	1 " 10 " " " (Evacuated)	
		All the Officers of the Unit have now been issued with a steel helmet + a P.H.G. Smoke helmet.	
	10.20 pm	26 U.B & S.O.S. 0.0.6.9 received	
" 22nd	9 a.m.	26 U.B & S.O.S. J.30.3 received	
	12 noon	48 O.R Sick, 2 wounded admitted 26 Sick to D.R.S.	
		4 " 2 " " " (Evacuated)	
	3 pm.	Instructions from A.D.M.S. 7th Div. — From 23rd instant the Sick of the 7th Div. to be sent to 21st F.A. at MORLANCOURT instead of 23rd F.A. at Mericourt. On 24th the 23rd F.A. will hand over their present billets/buildings to a F.A. of the 21st Divn + move to MORLANCOURT.	
	8.30 pm.	26 (th) Inf. Bde. J.30.4 + O.O.70 received.	
" 23rd	7 a.m.	" " J.30.5 received.	
	9 a.m.	Advance party 1 N.C.O + 10 men sent on to MORLANCOURT.	
	12 noon.	Staff 28 O.R Sick, 1 Off/ 1 O.R wounded admitted	
		38 " " 1 " 2 O.R " " (Evacuated)	
	7 p.m.	26th U.B & S.O.S. J.30 R.2.7 received	

Army Form C. 2118.

WAR DIARY
or
INTELLIGENCE SUMMARY
(Erase heading not required.)

Hour, Date, Place		Summary of Events and Information	Remarks and references to Appendices
MORLANCOURT			
June 24th	9 a.m.	The unit marched from MERICOURT at 9 a.m., arriving at MORLANCOURT about 10.45 a.m., and established Main D.Stn in the old Church - VILLERS CHURCH - K9.a.4.4.	
	12 noon	NIL Admitted - 10.0R Sick, 2 wounded Evacuated	
	8.30 p.m.	20th Lnf Bde. J.O.8 & O.O. 71 received A.D.M.S 7th Div. Mes. Inst. F.O. No 1. received	Appendix I
" 25th	10 a.m.	25th Lnf Bde. 9.0.9 received Instructions from A.D.M.S that returns of wounded are to be rendered at 6 a.m., noon & 9 p.m. daily from today.	Omitted in 24th Entries
		Capt. WORDLEY proceeded to 9th Devons for duty at 11 a.m. on 24th inst	do -
		Capt. MACKIE to CITADEL A.D.S & Capt. HART. to Car Rendezvous. on 24th inst	do -
	12.10 p.m.	Wounded State - NIL	
		Daily State - NIL	
" 26th	8.30 p.m.	Capt BUCKLEY to CITADEL A.D.S. in relief of Capt ALLAN.	
	6 a.m.	Wounded State ; - NIL	
	9 a.m.	20th Bde. 9.90. 10 received.	
	12 noon	Daily State :- NIL	

Army Form C. 2118.

WAR DIARY
or
INTELLIGENCE SUMMARY

(Erase heading not required.)

Instructions regarding War Diaries and Intelligence Summaries are contained in F. S. Regs., Part II. and the Staff Manual respectively. Title pages will be prepared in manuscript.

Hour, Date, Place		Summary of Events and Information	Remarks and references to Appendices
MORLANCOURT			
June 26th (Cont.)	12 noon.	Wounded State - NIL.	
" 27-	9 a.m.	do NIL.	
	6 a.m.	do NIL.	
	12 noon	do NIL.	
		Daily State NIL.	
	2.30 p.m.	Lieut DAVIDSON RAMC to No 5. C.C.S. for duty - under instructions of D.D.M.S XVth Corps -	
	5. p.m.	61. OR proceeded to D.C.S. with 7 wheel-stretcher carriages. They remain at the D.C.S during the night, & proceed to the CITADEL A.D.S on the afternoon of the 28th inst -	
	9 p.m.	Wounded State :- NIL.	
" 28th	6 a.m.	Wounded State :- NIL Main Dressing Station opened for walking & sitting wounded.	
	12 noon	Daily State :- NIL Wounded State :- NIL.	
	6 p.m.	Instructions received for forming present arrangements. to Lieut orders to O.C. CITADEL A.D.S. to return 1 Officer & 47 O.R. to M.D.S.	
	7.45 p.m	20 th Inf Bn O.M. No 1. received	
	9 p.m	Wounded State :- 14 OR admitted - 8 evacuated 6 remaining.	

1247 W 3299 200,000 (E) 8/14 J.B.C. & A. Forms/C. 2118/11.

Army Form C. 2118.

WAR DIARY
or
INTELLIGENCE SUMMARY
(Erase heading not required.)

Instructions regarding War Diaries and Intelligence Summaries are contained in F.S. Regs., Part II. and the Staff Manual respectively. Title pages will be prepared in manuscript.

Hour, Date, Place		Summary of Events and Information	Remarks and references to Appendices
MORLANCOURT			
June 29th	6 a.m.	Wounded State :- 2 Wounded admitted, 6 evacuated, 2 remaining	
	12 noon	" " :- NIL " " 2 " NIL "	
		Daily State :- 16 wounded " 16 evacuated	
	9 p.m.	No wounded admitted during the day.	
		2 men of the Beaver Bn. reports wounded	
		Pte OWEN	
		Pte STUBBS	
" 30th	6 a.m.	Wounded State :- NIL	
	12 noon	" :- Been 1 wounded admitted remaining	
		Daily State :- 1 Wounded admitted - 2 evacuated	
	6 p.m.	47 O.R. of Beaver Bn. under Capt ALLAN to CITADEL A.D.S.	
	8 p.m.	Medical Arrangements 7th Div. received	
	8.45 p.m.	6 Mls to Ambe + 3 horse ambulances sent to O.C. 21st F.A.	
	9 p.m.	Wounded State :- 17 O.R. admitted 13 evacuated - 4 Rem 9.	
		An account of the distribution of the Ambulance prior to the advance will be found at the beginning of Part XIX (July)	

Jas A Brown
Lt Col RAMC
O.C. 23 F.A.

Secret.   Appendix I

Medical Instructions for forthcoming Operations,
No 1.
By Colonel A W Harper, CMG, D.SO
A.D.M.S. 7 Division

1. The area of the 7th Division is divided for purpose of collecting casualties by the ALBERT-PERONNE Road into A Right and Left Sector.

2. <u>Advanced Dressing Stations</u>
(A) Casualties from all aid posts Right of this road will be brought to the A.D.S at MINDEN POST. These include the aid posts at:-
    66th Street
    MANCHESTER AVENUE.
    FRANCIS AVENUE.

The <u>22nd</u> Field Ambulance will be in charge of MINDEN POST, and collect from the Battalions using the Aid Posts in front of it.

(B) Casualties from Aid Posts on Left of ALBERT-PERONNE Road will be brought to the A.D.S at the Citadel.
    These include the Aid Posts at:-
    CRAWLEY RIDGE.
    MAPLE REDOUBT.
    WELLINGTON REDOUBT.

The 23 Field Ambulance will be in charge of the Citadel & collect from the Battalions using Aid Posts in front of it.

3. <u>Divisional Collecting Station</u>
This will be allotted to 21st Field Ambulance.
This unit will collect casualties from the Advanced Dressing Stations and clear them to the Main Dressing Station at MORLANCOURT.

For this purpose the "FURBER" Wheeled Stretchers,

all motor and horse ambulance transport of the Field Ambulances and the Cars of the Sanitary Section will be temporarily handed over to the 21st Field Ambulance for the operation.

Main Dressing Station

(A) <u>Lying</u> cases will be conveyed to 21st Field Ambulance MORLANCOURT, and evacuated to Casualty Clearing Station by No 27 Motor Ambulance Convoy.

A loading party of 6 N.C.O.s & men will be provided by 6 Sanitary Section, for temporary duty at the Dressing Station.

(B) <u>Sitting up and Walking</u> cases will go to 23rd Field Ambulance at the Old Church MORLANCOURT, and will be evacuated to No 36 Casualty Clearing Station, as transport becomes available.

(C) <u>Ordinary light sick and very lightly wounded</u> will be sent to 22nd Field Ambulance at the Church Hut, MORLANCOURT.

The above arrangements will take place on 27th inst.

6.

5. Traffic Routes to MORLANCOURT from Collecting Stations

Motor Ambulance Cars

(a) Road from L.15.b.3.9. to L.14.d.5.8.
BRAY-CORBIE Road to K.20.b.3.9. MORLANCOURT
Return by road joining BRAY-CORBIE Road at K.21.b.7.9.

(b) If weather is fine, Motor Ambulance Cars may use the Blue and Red routes.

Horse Ambulance Waggons
    Red and Blue routes, or (c)

(c) Motor Busses & Lorries.
Same as (a) to BRAY-CORBIE Road and thence to K.17. Central and thence to MORLANCOURT, and return via K.21.b.7.9.

6. Office of A.D.M.S.
The office of A.D.M.S. will be established at MORLANCOURT on a date to be notified later.

7. Returns.
From the commencement of active operations, the following returns will be required in addition to those already rendered.

At 6 a.m., noon and 9 p.m.
    A return shewing:-

(a) Numbers (wounded only) admitted in the intervals between 6 a.m. and noon, noon and 9 p.m., and 9 p.m. and 6 a.m.
Officers, French troops, Indians, and Prisoners of War to be distinguished. The names and units of officers should be given and the greatest care should be taken that their rank, initials, names, etc. are given correctly.

(b) The number of wounded remaining in Field Ambulance, distinguishing between lying & sitting cases.

(Sd) H.S.Roche Lieut Colonel
D.A.D.M.S. 7 Division

24 June 1916

Copies to:- O.C. 21 Field Ambulance
    " 22 do
    23 Field Ambulance
    7 Division Sanitary Section

No 23 Field Ambulance

Army Form C. 2118

WAR DIARY
or
INTELLIGENCE SUMMARY
(Erase heading not required.)

Instructions regarding War Diaries and Intelligence Summaries are contained in F. S. Regs, Part II. and the Staff Manual respectively. Title Pages will be prepared in manuscript.

Place	Date	Hour	Summary of Events and Information	Remarks and references to Appendices
MORLANCOURT	1st July	7.30 a.m.	At the hour of the attack the 23rd Amb was distributed as follows. Reference 1/40,000 ALBERT Contours Sheet 1st Edition (tracing attached) Main Dressing Station at the Old Church (VILLERS Church) MORLANCOURT (K.q.a.7.3) for sitting + walking cases only. Accommodation for 300 wounded. Advanced Dressing Station at the CITADEL (F.21.b.3.8). It consists of 4 large dugouts - (a) "Hospital" for stretcher cases. (b) "Dressing" - 3 cubicles for 1 stretcher case each. (c) "Dressing" + "Store" - for sitting cases + for stores (d) "Staff" for personnel. This Adv. D.S. cleared the area F.11.c.5.4. to F.9.a.6.6. (ie the front of two battalions 20th Inf Bde. + the front of 22nd Inf. Bde) through the following Regt Aid Posts. (a) "CRAWLEY RIDGE" F.9.c.3.3 (b) "MAPLE REDOUBT" F.15.b.6 F.9.d.8.2 (c) "WELLINGTON REDOUBT" F.16.b.8.8 The post "7/NORTH" F.15.a.6.6. was intended to shelter personnel, to act as an auxiliary adv. dr. stn. in the event of the CITADEL being shelled. The Divisional Collecting Station (D.C.S) at about L.q.a.7.7 under control of the 21st ⚕ Amb - The motor + horse Ambulances of all three field Ambulances were collected here on the night of 30th June.	App. I

Army Form C. 2118

WAR DIARY
or
INTELLIGENCE SUMMARY
(Erase heading not required.)

Instructions regarding War Diaries and Intelligence Summaries are contained in F.S. Regs., Part II. and the Staff Manual respectively. Title Pages will be prepared in manuscript.

Place	Date	Hour	Summary of Events and Information	Remarks and references to Appendices
MORLANCOURT	10/6 July		Personnel. At the CITADEL A.D.S. the Bearer Division under command of Capt. D. MACKIE RAINE (SR) with Capts. C.D.M BUCKLEY (SR) J.E ALLAN (SR) & C.H. HART (T.C.) - Also 6 nursing orderlies to assist in dressing. 4 Bearer Squads were sent to each of the 3 R.A. posts. 11 Wheel stretcher carriages with the personnel to them remained at the CITADEL A.D.S. - All ranks are provided with steel helmets. Prior to the attack, the party of 4.7. O.R. under Capt ALLAN, who were at the D.C.S the previous night, moved up to the CITADEL. At the M.D.S. Tent Division less 6 nursing orderlies with 1 M.O. & myself (one of the two M.O's here) bore to assist at No 5 C.C.S- by D.D.M.S orders.) Dressings &c. A large reserve of dressings, splints &c. in addition to the light cart equipment was put at the CITADEL A.D.S. Also Oxygen tant gas material, dressings for burns &c. System of Clearing from R.A.P.s to CITADEL. (1) from CRAWLEY RIDGE - by trench & wheel stretcher carriage along the main road (2) - MAPLE REDOUBT } by trench or by W. St. Carriage in the open (3) - Wellington - }	

WAR DIARY
or
INTELLIGENCE SUMMARY
(Erase heading not required.)

Army Form C. 2118

Place	Date	Hour	Summary of Events and Information	Remarks and references to Appendices
MORLANCOURT			These arrangements were to be altered if by O.C. Bearer Div. of Cav. Div. necessitated alteration.	App II
			His report on the work of the Bearer Div. is attached.	
			From CITADEL to D.C.S. by trolley line, but Cars were to run right up as soon as the road was safe — (The Cars that ran up about 10 a.m.)	
			From D.C.S to M.D.S — walking & sitting cases were sent on in Horse ambulances & motor lorries — by the 21st F.A. personnel.	
			Food &c — All preparations at M.D.S. & M.D.S for feeding a large number of wounded. 20000 rations (Bovril & Biscuit) were on hand.	
			At the CITADEL A.D.S. a reserve dump of 150 stretchers & 250 blankets was made. (There was no shortage of either during the first part of the operations).	
	1-7-16	10.20 a.m.	The first two cases arrived at M.D.S. They has been hit near MAMETZ at about 8 a.m. & shortly after —	
		10.40 a.m.	Cases began to arrive in twos & twos on Motor Ambulances bringing stretcher cases. The first horse ambulance arrived shortly afterwards.	

Army Form C. 2118

WAR DIARY
or
INTELLIGENCE SUMMARY
(Erase heading not required.)

Instructions regarding War Diaries and Intelligence Summaries are contained in F. S. Regs., Part II. and the Staff Manual respectively. Title Pages will be prepared in manuscript.

Place	Date	Hour	Summary of Events and Information	Remarks and references to Appendices
MORLANCOURT	1/7/16	*	Cases came in steadily all the afternoon at about 100 an hour - 3 M.Os + 6 dressers tried to compete with the rush, but could not dress them as fast as they were coming in. About 35 Cases an hour were dressed. A number has been properly dressed at the A.D.S already, these were not touched. Every man was given 500 units T.A.T	
"		8pm	At 7.30 pm the numbers were so great that two parties were getting too full; + at 8pm the A.D.M.S directed me to send all further wounded (6.22 w. 73. Aus. till 9 cleared myself a bit.) With the help of the Divn Supply Col. lorries evacuation went on steadily to No 5 C.C.S at CORBIE	
"		9pm	Wounded State: — 6 Off + 813 O.R. British } admitted — 20 " Germans 6 " + 445 " Sick — 386 O.R. remaining.	
"		11 pm	Capt A. READDIE R.A.M.C. to 20f. Manchester Regt. to replace Capt. Smith R.A.M.C. (Killed in action)	

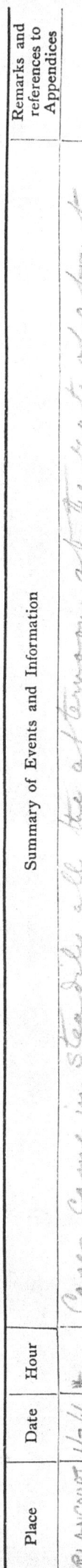

WAR DIARY or INTELLIGENCE SUMMARY

Army Form C. 2118

Place	Date	Hour	Summary of Events and Information	Remarks and references to Appendices
MORLANCOURT	2/7/16	1.AM	Instructions from ADMS 7th Div. that all C.C.S's were full & closed two more wounded were to be evacuated till further orders. The 22nd F.A. were full between 9.10 pm last night, so we had again started admitting wounded. — There were some 200 odd cases in the M.D.S. at 1 AM — In preparation of want of blockage, I had arranged for billetting 500 wounded, & as all cases were sent into billets & provided with blankets. Cases continued to come in till 4 AM after which there was a lull — The arrears of wounded had been caught up, at 5 am all cases had been relieved	
	"	6.30 am	Instructions from ADMS to evacuate 50 wounded to 36 C.C.S. This was done. Wounded State at 6 am showed	

Admitted — British — 1 Off / 141 O.R. — Remaining British 393 O.R.
Germans — — / 42 " — German 35 "

Only a few wounded came in during the forenoon, so some 60 to 70 of the cases were re-dressed, as they required it —

| | | 11 AM | Lt LOVELESS RAINE (T.C) joined for duty — from Stationary? ABBEVILLE | |
| | | 12 noon | Daily State. Admitted - British - 10 Off 953.OR - German prisoners - 6 / O.R - Remaining - 233.OR & 6 Germans & Nk - 13 Light w/d 62.2 w/d PH | |

WAR DIARY or INTELLIGENCE SUMMARY

Army Form C. 2118

Place	Date	Hour	Summary of Events and Information	Remarks and references to Appendices
MORLANCOURT	7/7/16	12 noon	Wounded State:- British – 4 ORs 3 admitted 297 ORs 01 in 3 remaining. German – –	
"		12.45pm	Wire received that evacuations could again be sent to 6 & 36 + 38 C.C.Ss – 12 Mo.to lorries were at once obtained from 7th Div. Sup. Col. + evacuation proceeded briskly.	
"		4pm	Visits CITADEL A.D.S. All were cheerful though tired – the trenches about MAMETZ & MAMETZ itself had been searched, & were reported to me as clean of all wounded. British & German. Only 6 sitting cases remaining at the A.D.S. + a car was on its way to remove them. Between 600 & 700 cases passed through the A.D.S. + its Collection + Evacuation + treatment of wounded & officers & men – Capt MACKIE in particular has done splendid work, & has been indefatigable in bringing in the wounded. Capt BUCKLEY is also deserving of great praise for his work.	

Army Form C. 2118

WAR DIARY
or
INTELLIGENCE SUMMARY
(Erase heading not required.)

Instructions regarding War Diaries and Intelligence Summaries are contained in F.S. Regs., Part II. and the Staff Manual respectively. Title Pages will be prepared in manuscript.

Place	Date	Hour	Summary of Events and Information	Remarks and references to Appendices
MORLANCOURT	2/7/16	5.15 pm	On returning found that the M.D.S. has been entirely cleared, & the station was empty for the first time since operations began.	
		7 pm	Instructions from A.D.M.S. 7th Divn that 36 & 38 C.C.S. are again closed. Evacuations to be sent to VECQUEMONT.	
		9 pm	64 OR British & 9 Germans admitted since noon. Remaining 11 OR British	
	3/7/16	6 am	During the night 1 Off & 34 OR British & 11 OR British prisoners were admitted. At 6 am 11 OR British remain.	
		10 am	The forenoon was quiet. O.C. A.D.S. reports at 10 am that his area was clear of all wounded.	
		12 noon	Only 3 OR wounded British admitted - none remaining - Station clear.	
			Daily State: Admitted - 1 Off + 98 OR wounded - 11 OR sick.	
			Evacuated :- 1 " 322 " " 11 " "	
			Total 6.22 = 7A :- — 8 " " 9 " "	
			Remaining :- — — 1 " " — " "	
	"	9 pm	1 Officer + 20 OR wounded (British) + 1 German OR. W. admitted since noon. The XV Corps Commander has, through the D.D.M.S., expressed his appreciation of the work done by the Medical Services of the Corps; & particularly with regard to its skillful way in which the wounded were drawn & the rapidity with which evacuation was carried out. He wishes this to be communicated to all ranks	

WAR DIARY
or
INTELLIGENCE SUMMARY

(Erase heading not required.)

Army Form C. 2118

Instructions regarding War Diaries and Intelligence Summaries are contained in F.S. Regs., Part II. and the Staff Manual respectively. Title Pages will be prepared in manuscript.

Place	Date	Hour	Summary of Events and Information	Remarks and references to Appendices
MORLANCOURT	4/7/16	6 a.m.	During the night 6.OR (British) were admitted - 4 remained at 6 a.m. A certain number of wounded came in during the forenoon, mostly slight wounds.	
"	"	12 noon	At noon 28.OR (British) has been admitted - 22 remain. Daily State:- Admitted :- 1.Off + 48.OR wounded, 1.OR sick. Evacuated :- 1 " + 15 " " , " " Transf. to 22nd FA — 3 " " , 1 " "	
"	"	8 p.m.	Shortly after 1 p.m. a very violent thunderstorm burst. The very heavy rain brought down such quantities of mud that the approach to the Church was blocked. (The road dips here to the main surface deviates) - A party had to be put on to dig out a passage for ambulance cars - Two hindered evacuation for nearly 2 hours, but by 3.30 p.m. the station was again clear. Under A.D.M.S. instructions 2.Off + 2 Sections of the Beaumont the CITADEL A.D.S. to the M.D.S. to rest.	
"	"	9 p.m.	Capt ALLAN will remain in command at the CITADEL	
"	"		Wounded State :- 27.OR (British) admitted - 3 Remaining	
"	5/7/16	6 a.m.	27.OR (British) during the night - 29 remaining at 6 a.m.	
"	"	12 noon	Wounded State :- Admitted 1.Off 68.OR (British) Remaining at noon. British - 3.OR 2 " (German) German - 2 "	

WAR DIARY or INTELLIGENCE SUMMARY

Army Form C. 2118

Place	Date	Hour	Summary of Events and Information	Remarks and references to Appendices
MORLANCOURT	5/7/16	12 noon	Daily State:- Admitted - 1 Off, 129 OR wounded + 1 Sick. Evacuated - 1 " 151 " "	
"	"	5 pm	Orders from H.Q. 38th Div. to hand over M.D.S. to 130 to 7.F.A. 38th Div. The Citadel A.D.S. to hand over at once to the M.D.S. tomorrow. After handing over the unit is to march to billets at MERICOURT. During the evening all Motor & Horse Ambulances rejoined from 21st C.C.S. The 130 th F.A. arrived about 6 p.m. + a party was sent up to relieve our bearers at the Citadel. The relief was carried out at 9.30, + the personnel returned at 11.30 pm to the M.D.S.	
"	"	9 pm	Since noon 1 Off + 16 OR wounded admitted + all were evacuated.	
"	6/7/16	6 am	7 OR wounded admitted during the night & evacuated. The unit cleared out of the Church & packed up.	
"	"	10 am	Handed over to 130 to 7 F.A. + the unit marched to MERICOURT.	
MERICOURT	"	11.30 am	Arrived at the new place & proceeded to establish a small dressing station in tents in a field at J.4.C.6.4. with accommodation for 50 sick. The personnel bivouaced near by.	

Remarks on the recent Operations

Prior to the Operations commencing a reserve of 150 stretchers & 250 blankets was stored at the A.D.S., + this was ample provision. At the main D.S. Pyjamas & suits were kept for wounded who needed clothing. 2,000 rations were laid in by orders of A.D.M.S. XV Corps.

Army Form C. 2118

WAR DIARY
or
INTELLIGENCE SUMMARY
(Erase heading not required.)

Place	Date	Hour	Summary of Events and Information	Remarks and references to Appendices
MERICOURT.			Remarks (could) - Bearer Bearers was excellent & quick - there was never any Confusion or blockage at the A.D.S. - Clearing of Sitting Cases by lorries of the Div. Supply Col. - Evacuation would have been impossible except for the assistance given by the O.C. 7th D.S.C. (Major Ricketts to A.S.C.) - (ases were cleared from the M.D.S almost faster than they could be dressed) - The only period of blockage was while the Column was rationing. The wounded were then collected for some 4 or 5 hours, when they were again cleared by the D.S.C. Seats were improvised with empty shell-boxes. These were arranged in the form of "E" - 3-ton lorries dealt 18 wounded, & 5-ton lorries 25 each.	
"	7/7/16	12 noon	4. Off sick admitted, & 4 evacuated.	
"	8/7/16	12 noon	14. Off " & 1 wounded admitted - 13. Off sick & 1 wounded evacuated.	
"	9/7/16	12 noon	14 " " admitted, 11 evacuated & 3 returned to duty.	
"	10/7/16	12 noon	1 Off, 12 O.R sick & 1 acc.d wounded admitted, all evacuated	
		9.15 pm	By order of D.D.M.S XV Corps, 2 officers (Capt Allan & Lt Loveless) were sent up to Minden Post A.D.S. to assist the 38th Div. F.A. there in dealing with the wounded	

Army Form C. 2118

WAR DIARY
or
INTELLIGENCE SUMMARY
(Erase heading not required.)

Instructions regarding War Diaries and Intelligence Summaries are contained in F.S. Regs., Part II. and the Staff Manual respectively. Title Pages will be prepared in manuscript.

Place	Date	Hour	Summary of Events and Information	Remarks and references to Appendices
MERICOURT	10/7/16		In the evening Quartermaster & Hon Lt. G.G. GREGSON R.A.M.C. reported for duty from 36th F.A. in relief of Q.M. & Hon Lt. Jackson, who is to proceed to Depôt R.D. 14 A. Dep. Med. Stores forthwith (D.M.S. Fourth Army N° P. 257 d/9th July 1916)	App III
"	11/7/16	1.30pm	Orders received from A.D.M.S that the unit should march to MORLANCOURT (47 Divn)	App III
"	"	5pm	The Unit marched to MORLANCOURT. On arrival there the 136th F.A. 38th Divn were not moving out + continued to receive wounded — The Unit therefore parked + bivouaced for the night	
MORLANCOURT	12/7/16	1 a.m.	Instructions to relieve forward A.D.Ss. of 38th Divn early. In the morning the Bearer Divn went forward under CAPT. D. MACKIE R.A.M.C. to take over in front. 2 Bearer Sub-divisions Established at the captured German dressing station in BRIGHT ALLEY. F.5.b.1.4. (MONTAUBAN Trench Map 1/20000) While one Sub-division Established a second M.D.S at MINDEN POST — 2 Motor Ambulances + 2 horse ambulances were sent to the proposed D.C.S at F.8.a.3.0. + 2 motor ambulances to MINDEN POST.	App IV
		9 a.m.	The old Church at MORLANCOURT was taken over from the 130th Fd Amb. + a M.D.S Established there. Some 60 odd wounded were taken over at the same time + dealt with — being evacuated by DI. Supt. of Lorries.	
		12 noon	A.D.M.S orders A 48 received — D.C.S handed over to 22nd F.A. The closing of MINDEN Post (Para 5 of above) was verbally cancelled later —	App V
		9 p.m.	A.D.M.S A 51 received + instructions in accordance sent to O.C. Bearer Divn. As this order also the arrangements for clearing, new routes for clearing has to be arranged.	App VI

Army Form C. 2118

WAR DIARY
or
INTELLIGENCE SUMMARY
(Erase heading not required.)

Place	Date	Hour	Summary of Events and Information	Remarks and references to Appendices
MORLANCOURT	13/7/16		Wounded continued to come in throughout the day in small numbers. The Bearer Div. is now established in MINDEN POST A.D.S. I visited the A.D.S. during the afternoon & completed the arrangements for the attack tomorrow. The orders for the attack are as follows:— The 7th Div. will attack on the front S.15.c.1.4 to S.14.a.6.4 (approximately) of the German 2nd line — with 13th Corps (3rd Div.) on the right & the 21st Div. on their left. The 20th Inf. Bde will lead, with 22nd Inf. Bde in Support; & 91st Inf. Bde in Div. Reserve. The objective of the 20th Inf. Bde is the whole of BAZENTIN-le-GRAND WOOD (S.14 + 15) — In the 20th Bde the 2/Border Regt. on the left & 8th Devons on the right lead the attack; with the 2/Gordons & 9th Devons in support. In the evening the 23rd F.A. was distributed as follows:— M.D.S. — At Old Church MORLANCOURT — for sitting & walking wounded only. A.D.S. — MINDEN POST. in a large dugout at F18.¢.4.4 (approx). Here the Bearer Div. under command of CAPT. D. MACKIE R.A.M.C. with three officers & 3 Bearer Squads were placed at the S. end of CATERPILLAR TRENCH (S.26.d.3.5) in communication with R.A.P. of 9/Devons in CATERPILLAR WOOD (S.20.d.1.3) and 1 Bearer Squad at R.A.P. of 2/Gordons in POMMIERS REDOUBT (A1.a.5.2.) Wounded to be brought down to MINDEN POST, by wheel stretcher carriage as much as possible — An account of the Bearer Div. operations will be found under 19/7/16. Report on work of Bearer Div by Capt MACKIE is attd.	MONTAUBAN Trench Map 1/20,000. Sheet 62 D.N.E. 1/20000 MONTAUBAN Sheet 1/20000 do do

Army Form C. 2118

WAR DIARY
or
INTELLIGENCE SUMMARY
(Erase heading not required.)

Place	Date	Hour	Summary of Events and Information	Remarks and references to Appendices
MORLANCOURT.	14/7/16		In the early morning, about 3.30 a.m. the attack began following an intense bombardment. It was entirely successful and the objective was quickly reached. About 7.30 a.m. the first walking cases arrived, & thereafter there was a small but steady flow of cases. The casualties in the first part of the operation were very light. The numbers increased markedly about 10 a.m., & the numbers began to run into hundreds by the afternoon. The work of the Bearer Division was made heavier by rain which fell during the forenoon. The advance of the line greatly increased the "carry" of each wounded man, & by the afternoon the work was so strenuous that the horse ambulance wagons were pushed up along the CARNOY ROAD to meet the wheel stretcher carriages in the subsequent. The line was still slowly advancing & at night Casualties from the 2nd Indian Cav. Div. came in. These apparently occurred during an attack in the vicinity of HIGH WOOD (S4.a.c.) By 6 a.m. 4 Officers 445 OR. British & 17 OR Germans had been admitted, & Casualties were still coming in. There was a lull in the forenoon. Daily State :- 3 Off. 495 OR. British admitted 3 " 487 " " evacuated	MARTINPUICH Trench Map.
"	15-7-16		Cases were evacuated by D.S.C. lorries to VECQUEMONT (some 20 miles E.W.). The 33rd Div. attacked during the forenoon in the direction of MARTINPUICH & there was an then influx of wounded in the afternoon. Between noon & 6 p.m. 3 Off. & 206 OR. were admitted, dressed & evacuated	

1875 Wt. W593/826 1,000,000 4/15 J.B.C. & A. A.D.S.S./Forms/C. 2118.

Army Form C. 2118

WAR DIARY
or
INTELLIGENCE SUMMARY
(Erase heading not required.)

Instructions regarding War Diaries and Intelligence Summaries are contained in F. S. Regs., Part II. and the Staff Manual respectively. Title Pages will be prepared in manuscript.

Place	Date	Hour	Summary of Events and Information	Remarks and references to Appendices
MORLANCOURT	16-7-16		During the day there were several light showers & it was cooler. On the night of the 14/15th the Enemy put a couple of shells into the A.D.S. at MINDEN POST. One was a "dud", the other demolished a bivouac in which Pte. TOLLERVEY was sleeping. He was flung into the air, but was not wounded. He was suffering from "shell-shock", was sent to 22 W J.A. for a rest.	
		12 noon	The Daily State since noon yesterday shows 5 Off. & 453 O.R. British wounded admitted — 22 O.R. were slight were sent to 22 W J.A. The rest were Sacraments.	
"	17/7/16		Heavy rain fell during the night, & the wounded coming in were wet & very muddy. Braziers were kept going to dry them.	
		12 noon.	2 Off. 52 O.R. wounded admitted) to 22 W J.A. 2 " 44 " " ") 8 light wounds Sacraments	
"	18/7/16		Driver BEAUCHAMP. (H.T.) A.S.C was accidentally wounded in the arm by the explosion of a Mills grenade which another man was meddling with. Showery weather continued, the sky being very overcast. Much colder today.	
		12 noon	88 O.R. wounded admitted since yesterday — 79 O.R Sac. & 9 sent to 22 W J.A. The Beaver Division has not had much to do for the last few days, & has been resting.	
"	19/7/16	12 noon	1 Off. & 119 O.R. wounded admitted since noon yesterday — all Sacraments.	

Army Form C. 2118

WAR DIARY
or
INTELLIGENCE SUMMARY
(Erase heading not required.)

Instructions regarding War Diaries and Intelligence Summaries are contained in F.S. Regs., Part II. and the Staff Manual respectively. Title Pages will be prepared in manuscript.

Place	Date	Hour	Summary of Events and Information	Remarks and references to Appendices
MORLANCOURT	19/7/16		To return to the Bearer Division - At the time of the attack on the 14th July 1916 the position was as follows A? D? Slater - at MINDEN POST A.D.S. F.18.c.4.4. (approx)	MONTAUBAN Trench Map 1/20,000 -
			Regt. Aid Posts. 20th Inf Bde. 2/ Border Regt. S.20.c.5.5.	
			9/ Devon " S.20.c.10.5	
			8/ " " S.20.d.5.0.	
			2/ Gordon High⁴? A.1.c.5.2 (in PONNIERS REDOUBT.)	
			Casualties from 2/Borders went to the A.D.S. 21st 2/ Amb at F.5.b.1.3 from 8th & 9th Devons by hand carriage along EAST TRENCH (S.26.b+d) & LOOP TRENCH (A2.a) to about A.2.C.8.5, from there they were taken by horse ambulance to MINDEN POST. - (The latter part was done by wheel - stretcher carriage during the earlier phase of the fighting.) This system of clearing remained in force till the 19th July. Orders were then issued for an attack by the 7th Div. (20 & 8 Bde) on the morning of the 20th with its object of securing HIGH WOOD. It had been apparent for some days that the MINDEN POST A.D.S. was much too far south - After a reconnaissance it was decided that the A.D.S. should be pushed up to where LOOP TRENCH cut the MAMETZ - MONTAUBAN ROAD at A.2.a.8.8 - & to this spot the Bearer Division moved at 10 p.m. - with an advanced Post in CATERPILLAR WOOD	
		10 pm		

WAR DIARY
or
INTELLIGENCE SUMMARY
(Erase heading not required.)

Army Form C. 2118.

Instructions regarding War Diaries and Intelligence Summaries are contained in F. S. Regs., Part II. and the Staff Manual respectively. Title pages will be prepared in manuscript.

Hour, Date, Place	Summary of Events and Information	Remarks and References to Appendices
MORLANCOURT 19/7/16 10pm	Orders were received from A.D.M.S. to the effect that (1) 23rd FA. will clear from R.A.P. to CATERPILLAR WOOD ADvPost (2) 22nd FA. " " " " CATERPILLAR WOOD to ADS at A.2.a.8.8. (3) Car Rendezvous at F.4.C. in NAMETZ under 22nd FA. to clear A.D.S at A.2.a.8.8. 10 motor busses were detailed to report at MORLANCOURT at 7. am on 20th. - 4 to be sent to D.C.S (22 wd FA) & Six to evacuate 23rd M.D.S.	MARTINPUICH Trench Map 1/25000 MONTAUBAN Trench Map 1/5000
20/7/16 3.30am.	At the time of the attack the situation was as follows. Regt Aid Posts. 8/Devons } in BAZENTIN-le-GRAND 2/Gordons } S.15.b.O.5. Evacuation by hand leaving one South, then bearing S. West along a track (not marked on map) to S.2.b.d.8.1, & thence West along MAMETZ - MONTAUBAN ROAD to ADS. (A.2.a.8.8) A.D.S - as described before - in a dug-out at A.2.a.8.8. From here by Motor Ambulance through MAMETZ (F5c) along the road through F4 Cd, thence by main road South of FRICOURT, through BECORDEL - MÉAULTE ROAD to M.D.S at old Church MORLANCOURT.	

Army Form C. 2118.

WAR DIARY
or
INTELLIGENCE SUMMARY

(Erase heading not required.)

Instructions regarding War Diaries and Intelligence Summaries are contained in F. S. Regs., Part II. and the Staff Manual respectively. Title pages will be prepared in manuscript.

Hour, Date, Place		Summary of Events and Information	Remarks and References to Appendices
MORLANCOURT 20/7/16			
	12 noon	The first walking & sitting cases arrived about 7 a.m. and a steady stream kept on thereafter. The Daily State showed - 3 Off + 182 OR wounded admitted + evacuated. During the day the following Casualties occurred in the unit 44866 Pte R. KAY. Killed in action. Shell in chest. 35243 Sgt W. JOHNSON. Shell Contusion. Left leg & Shell Shock. Evacuated 31381 Pte J. McKAY - Shell Shock - Returned to duty 9938 Pte F. BUDGE. Shrapnel W. Right ankle - Evacuated 52809 Pte R. PASQUILL " " " " R. Knee.	
	6.45pm	Under ADMS instructions, I withdrew the Bearer Div after 20th Div Bde had come out. They rejoined the HQrs at 3 a.m.	
	8.30pm	Orders received to hand over M.D.S. to 15th F.A. at 9 a.m on 21st & then march to bivouac near DERNANCOURT about E.19.C.	
" 21/7/16	9 a.m	Handed over M.D.S. to 15th F.A. Daily State:- 1 Off 288 OR wounded + evacuated. The unit marched after 10 a.m. arriving at the bivouac ground about noon.	
	4.15pm	The transport marched to join the 7th Divl Train en route by road to PICQUIGNY.	

Army Form C. 2118.

WAR DIARY
or
INTELLIGENCE SUMMARY
(Erase heading not required.)

Instructions regarding War Diaries and Intelligence Summaries are contained in F. S. Regs., Part II, and the Staff Manual respectively. Title pages will be prepared in manuscript.

Hour, Date, Place	Summary of Events and Information	Remarks and References to Appendices
22/7/16	At 8.30 a.m the unit marched to MERICOURT Ry. Stn to entrain there for PICQUIGNY. It arrived at HANGEST Station about 5 pm & then marched to billets at PICQUIGNY. — The motor Ambulances left in Convoy at 10 a.m arriving at PICQUIGNY about noon. The Horse transport reported in PICQUIGNY at 4 pm. Everyone was very tired, & glad of a rest.	
PICQUIGNY 23/7/16	A main Dressing Station for the Sick of the division was opened in the Chateau – the same place occupied by the unit when here in Dec 1915 & Jany 1916.	
24/7/16	Daily State:- 1 Off, 9 O.R. sick admitted – 1 Off. 8 O.R. sick evac. Also 1 O.R. wounded during the action	
25/7/16	— 26 " " — 7 " "	
26th to 29/7/16	The unit continued taking in & treating the Divisional Sick	
29th Mon	Lieut WEST R.A.M.C (T.C) temporarily attached for instruction.	
30th & 31st	A certain amount of Diarrhoea among the troops – probably the result of the very hot weather.	Geo. H. Brown Lt Col R.A.M.C O.C. 23rd FA

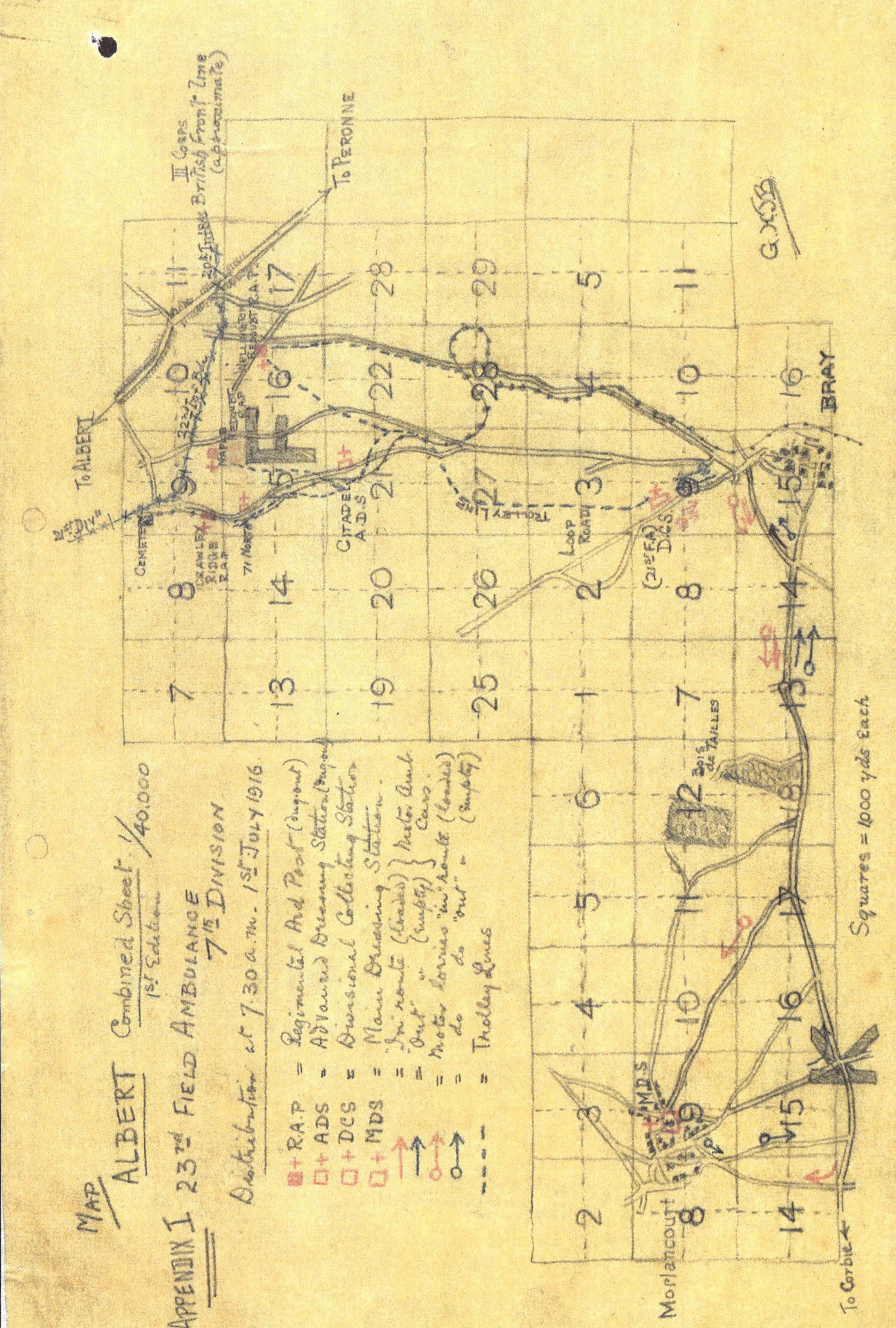

APPENDIX II

Report of Operations from 1st to 5th July 1916 of
Bearer Division. 23rd Field Ambulance.

On Saturday 24th June. arrived at Advanced Dressing Station (A.D.S.) F 21.b.2.10. and took over command from Capt Allan Raul. The advanced dressing station consisted of dugouts that had been built by us or altered to suit the requirements of the line. The main part consisted of one long dugout divided into an ante room, to hold 6 stretcher cases, leading immediately into a dressing room large enough to dress two stretcher cases at once, and this led immediately into a dugout ward which had bracket shelves on which thirty stretcher cases could be accommodated to wait for the cars or trolleys. The wounded came in at ante room end and went out to the cars from the far end of the ward. There was another dugout that had been the original advanced dressing station and in it the lighter sitting and walking cases were dressed. At the commencement of operations there were six Battalions depending on us to evacuate their wounded. and these were west of the PERONNE ROAD. This road was the line of demarkation for operations of the 22nd Field Ambulance Bearer Division and our own. All troops WEST of this road in our area were cleared by us. and all EAST of the road by the 22nd Fd. Amb. The Battalions that we were working with on our right from the Regimental Aid Posts (R.A.P.) at WELLINGTON REDOUBT. were all situated or conjoined round F.16.b. They were. 2nd BORDER REGIMENT. 8th and 9th DEVON REGIMENTS. and 2nd ROYAL WARICKSHIRE REGIMENT. In the Centre of our front at MAPLE REDOUBT. the 20th MANCHESTER REGIMENT. had their R.A.P. at about. F 9.d.8.2. On our left front was the ROYAL WELSH FUSILERS. who had their R.A.P. in a dugout West of CRAWLEY RIDGE. in RAILWAY AVENUE. at about. F.9.c.3.8. During the week of the bombardment. before the infantry went over the parapet on Saturday 1st July there were 2 officers and 49 men at the A.D.S. Two stretcher squads. of 4 men each. were kept at CRAWLEY RIDGE R.A.P. and one squad of 4 men at each of the other two aid posts. also a stretcher squad of 2 men at each of three Heavy Trench Mortar batteries. These squads brought down by wheel stretcher carriages or by trolleys what wounded came in during the enemy's counter bombardment, but as only few men were in the front line the wounded casualties were not many more than occurred. during an ordinary day of trench warfare. The remainder of the men were at the A.D.S. divided

2

into a day and night party to carry wounded, and attend to them at the Ward and load the cars and if no cars were available to run the wounded on a Trolley to the Divisional collecting station (D.C.S.) on the BRAY ALBERT ROAD. at L9a.5.5.

On Tuesday 27th June. Heavy thunder showers fell and made the ground very heavy for stretcher bearing. The rain continued to fall heavily all forenoon and the enemy heavily bombarded our trenches. Hitherto we had sustained no casualties but about 3.o'clock two bearers attached to one of the Heavy Trench Mortar Batteries were wounded by a shell exploding in the dugout in which they were living. Both these men. Ptes Stubbs and Owen R.A.M.C. were seriously enough wounded to be evacuated one being a stretcher case. These were replaced.

On the night of the 30th June. Capt Allan R.A.M.C. arrived at A.D.S. and reported for duty. And Capt Hart. R.A.M.C. with remainder of Bearer Division arrived at D.C.S. Sent down a message to Hart telling him to be ready but not to bring the bearers up until he received instructions. This was to avoid casualties among the bearers as the CITADEL had been frequently shelled lately.

The weather had been very showery up till this night but it cleared and a strong North West wind dried the ground and the morning of the 1st July was bright and dry.

The infantry on our right front between F10d.5.5 and the PERONNE ROAD. F11C.5.5. went over at 7.30 a.m. Message sent to Capt Hart. who arrived with remainder of Bearer Division. These were all sent up to clear the wounded from WELLINGTON REDOUBT. R.A.P. because all the wounded were coming from there. During the forenoon extra stretchers were sent up from time to time so that German Prisoners coming down could carry wounded with them and not interfere with the relay of stretchers that each bearer squad carries. Word was sent down to D.C.S. at about 10 am. that cars could come up, and from that time Ambulance Cars and the Trolleys worked steadily between the A.D.S. and D.C.S. and kept us fairly clear of wounded.

Towards the afternoon the cases that up till now had practically all been coming in from WELLINGTON REDOUBT began to be less numerous. Had reason to believe that the 20th Manchesters were going over. The wounded on our right front not being now so numerous and well in hand. Word was sent to O.C. D.C.S. that instead of sending all the trolleys to A.D.S. CITADEL half of them should be sent right up to WELLINGTON REDOUBT and clear the cases direct from there by trolley to D.C.S. At the same time all the bearers except C Subdivision with Capt Allan to supervise, were withdrawn. C Subdivision cleared the Aid post and loaded the trolleys for the D.C.S. men who were running them. A and B subdivisions now worked from MAPLE REDOUBT and CRAWLEY RIDGE Aid posts. Wheel stretcher carriers and trolleys were used from both these R.A.P.s. After the attack of the 22nd Infantry Brigade which started about 2-30 p.m. After dusk the wounded were all brought in over the open via CRAWLEY RIDGE R.A.P. where Capt FRY R.A.M.C. the M.O. i/c Royal Welsh Fusiliers was working and were wheeled by five wheel carriages to where the trolley line stopped at 71 North. 15 a. 6. 6. and there loaded on a trolley, or failing that brought right in on wheeled stretcher carriages to the D.C.S. At 9.15 p.m. received word from Capt Stewart R.A.M.C. M.O. i/c 2nd Border Regiment that all casualties from his regiment had been cleared. By midnight we had passed through the A.D.S. over five hundred seriously wounded lying and sitting cases. Not counting the walking cases who received attention and who were able to walk down to the D.C.S.

Sunday 2nd July was a very good day and the ground in good condition. The 1st Royal Welsh Fusiliers and 20th Manchesters, (the latter having lost heavily) having advanced, went up to see M.O. i/c R.W.Fs. and Capt Readdie R.A.M.C. M.O. now i/c 20th Manchesters. Found their aid posts in craters in German first line. Found several German wounded and marked their positions. On returning sent up some squads to bring in the German wounded. About 4 p.m. received word from Capt MILLER. M.O. i/c 8th Devons. that 8th and 9th Devons had advanced East of PERONNE ROAD and being now in the area of 22 Field Ambulance Bearer Division would be cleared by them through MINDEN POST. By midnight had passed over a hundred sitting and lying cases.

On monday morning 3rd July at 7 a.m. the 1st R.W.Fs and 20th Manchesters moved away from the Citadel in Carnoy direction. Saw both M.Ds. At 10 a.m. took Capt Allan and went to visit the M.Os in front of us. Border R.A.P. at WELLINGTON REDOUBT. Then visited the M.Os of 8th and 9th Devons who had a conjoined aid post in German dugout south of Mametz near the Halte at F10 b a 6. Saw the 2nd Gordon Highlanders working near Mametz. In afternoon had foot inspection and found bearers feet in fairly good condition. had them washed and dusted with powder. Up till midnight the number of wounded had not amounted to a dozen because the regiments we were working for were not now in action. Towards midnight the following regiments moved into our vicinity.

P.T.O.

2nd GORDON HIGHLANDERS   to 71 NORTH
2nd BORDER REGIMENT.   to 71 SOUTH (F.15.d.2.5).
9th DEVONS.   to CITADEL.

8th DEVONS remained at the Halte.

During the forenoon was visited by the M.Os of these three regiments who had come in.

About 8 p.m. received orders from Col. Brown DSO. Commanding officer 23rd Field Ambulance to return to Hd Qrs with the greater part of the bearers.

On 5th July in forenoon set out for headquarters at MORLANCOURT with B and C subdivisions and arrived there at 1 p.m. and reported arrival to Commanding officer.

D Mackie
Capt. RAMC. SR.

ALBERT Combined sheet 1/40,000
23rd Field Ambulance 14th July 1916
         + 20th July 1916

         A.D.S
         R.A.P
         Motor Amb. (full) in route
         do do (empty) "out"
         Approximate routes along
         which the wounded were
         brought to the A.D.S by
         hand and wheel stretcher
         carriage
The date of operations are marked
on A.D.S. R.A.P + routes
On 14.7.16 7th Divn S15.C.1.4 — S14.a.6.4.
On their Right — XIII Corps (3rd Divn)
  "   " Left — 21st Divn

SECRET.   Appendix III

C.O. 21 Field Ambce
        22   "
        23   "

1) 22ⁿᵈ Field Ambulance will march to MORLANCOURT at 5.P.M this evening and take over the Church tent Theatre & from 129 F. Amb there. They will also take over the Camp for wounded German Prisoners from 21ˢᵗ Field Amb.

2) 23ʳᵈ Field Ambᶜᵉ will march to MORLANCOURT at 5.P.M and take over "Old Church" & from 130. Field Ambᶜᵉ. They will also take over the Advanced Dressing Station in MAMETZ (Old German Dressing Station. F.5.b.1.3. relay post in MAMETZ and MINDEN POST.

3) 23. Field Ambᶜᵉ will be prepared to establish a Divisional Collecting Station & Car Rendezvous at F.8.a.3.0. at short notice.

4) Message for A.D.M.S. should be sent to MORLANCOURT (opp. rear prisoners Camp) from 6 P.M this evening.

11-7-16   H.S. Rock
1.30 P.M   A.D.M.S.
                                     7ᵗʰ Divⁿ

Urgent   Appendix IV

SECRET

O.C. 23. Field Amb^ce

The Field Ambulances of 36th Division must be packed ready to march at 1.0 cl. P.M. tomorrow 12th inst.

Please arrange to relieve their Advanced Dressing Station (MAMETZ – MINDEN POST &c in such time as to allow of this –

                              A.E. Roch
                              H/Lt Col
11/7/16   Mapmé. 7A
midnight.

Secret (A.M.) ~~Secret~~   OC 71 Field Amb^ce   Appendix V
                    " 72 "
                    " 73 "

(1) Para 3 of A.O. is cancelled.

(2) The Divisional Collecting Station will be established by 22 Field Amb^ce at F.8.c.2.9. in the open ground N. of MERCIER – CARNOY Road. Cars will be regulated here & will proceed to the MAMETZ – FRICOURT Road at F.4.d. & clear Advanced Dressing Station.

(3) All Cars of the Field Ambulances as well as Horse Ambulance Transport will be placed at Disposal of 22 Field Amb^ce for this Day, except Men as well as the Carts of Sanitary Section.

(4) 22 Field Ambulance will be responsible for the clearance of Casualties from the Advanced Dressing Station to MORLANCOURT.

(5) When the Divisional Collecting Station named in (2) is established the A.D.S. ~~MINDEN POST~~ will be closed equipment being moved to the A.D.S. at The Orchard F.4.d. 2.9. & at 5.b.1.3.

12.7.16.   H B Koch   ?? Rawe
                        ADMS 7 Div

A.51.

Secret

CC 21 Field Amb. Appendix VI
   23   "   "

Re my A.48 of this morning. The most direct line of clearance from the aid Post of our Battalion in the trenches is to MINDEN POST.

The only Battalion at present in the front line is the 9th Devons, aid Post in CATERPILLAR WOOD.

23rd Field Ambulance will therefore establish their Advance Dressing Station at MINDEN POST and clear 20th Bde, handing over the old German dressing Station at MAMETZ to 21st Field Amb.

Head Quarters 20. Bde. POMMIERS REDOUBT.
              22.   near HAP't Mametz wood
              91.   Citadel

July. 12. 1916
8. 30 P.M.

H S Rock
for A.D.M.S. 7 Div.

7th Division

No 22 Field Ambulance

Aug 1916

15

COMMITTEE FOR THE
MEDICAL HISTORY OF THE WAR
Date 26 OCT 1916

Army Form C. 2118.

Vol. III Part 20.

Vol 26

WAR DIARY
or
INTELLIGENCE SUMMARY
(Erase heading not required.)

Instructions regarding War Diaries and Intelligence Summaries are contained in F.S. Regs., Part II. and the Staff Manual respectively. Title pages will be prepared in manuscript.

Hour, Date, Place		Summary of Events and Information	Remarks and References to Appendices
AUGUST 1916. PICQUIGNY.		From 1st to 10th August the unit remained open at PICQUIGNY, taking in & treating the sick of the Division. The men were kept fit by route marching, swimming & sports.	Ref. Map Sheet 17 France (1/100,000 AMIENS Sheet)
10th August	12 noon.	On the 10th Orders were received that the Division would move to the forward area on the 12th	
	11 pm.	Detailed orders for the move received. The personnel is to go by rail, the Transport by road	
11th August.		The sick in the Main Dressing Station were Classified, all those requiring hospital treatment were Evacuated to No. 39 C.C.S at ALLONVILLE.	
August 12th.	2.30 am	The personnel under Capt Mackie Rame marched to HANGEST, Entrained there at 5.a.m. They Proceeded to MERICOURT, detrained there & marched to billets in BUIRE.	
	4.a.m.	1 Off & 32 OR sick left in motor ambulances to join the above train at HANGEST. On arrival at MERICOURT they were met by motor ambulances from 21 St D? Amb & taken as transfers to the IV Corps Rest Station at DERNANCOURT.	

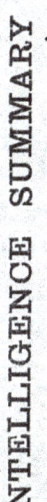

Army Form C. 2118.

WAR DIARY
or
INTELLIGENCE SUMMARY
(Erase heading not required.)

Instructions regarding War Diaries and Intelligence Summaries are contained in F.S. Regs, Part II. and the Staff Manual respectively. Title pages will be prepared in manuscript.

Hour, Date, Place	Summary of Events and Information	Remarks and References to Appendices
PICQUIGNY August 12th (Contd) 11 a.m.	The Transport marched under Capt Buckley Paine via ST-SAUVEUR — ALLONVILLE — QUERRIEUX — RIBEMONT to BUIRE. They bivouaced on the night of the 12th on the ST GRATIEN Road just North of QUERRIEUX, & arrived in BUIRE on the 13th at 12.30 p.m.	Ref 1/40000 ALBERT Combined Sheet.
12 noon.	The Motor Ambulances proceeded in convoy under myself, taking 21 O.R. sick for transfer to the XV Corps Rest Station. Arriving at BUIRE at 2 p.m.	
BUIRE. 13. 4 p.m.	Under orders of XV Corps "C" tent sub division of the unit under Capt BUCKLEY, with Capt WRIGHT, proceeded on duty at the XV Corps Main Dressing Station at DERNANCOURT. until further orders.	
	During the day under instructions from the M.O. i/c, all the tents of the Ambulance were pitched, arrangements made for the taking in & treatment of the sick of the 20th Infy Bde — in a field about D.30.a.3.3	

Army Form C. 2118.

WAR DIARY
or
INTELLIGENCE SUMMARY
(Erase heading not required.)

Instructions regarding War Diaries and Intelligence Summaries are contained in F.S. Regs., Part II. and the Staff Manual respectively. Title pages will be prepared in manuscript.

Hour, Date, Place	Summary of Events and Information	Remarks and References to Appendices
BUIRE August 15th	During the last two days additions have been made to the Camp M.D.S. A dining-hall has been made in a barn, tables & seats being made from empty ammunition boxes. A bath house has been made in a hypo, & every man bathes on admission. The soiled underclothing is sent to the Bath House to be exchanged for clean clothing. Shoes to be seen to by the O.C. Divn. Sanitary Section. Outer clothing to "crones" to get rid of lice + 29p.	Albert (Corbius) Sheet 1/40,000
Aug 20th 16th to 24th	All dirt are put into pyjamas after bathing. Lieut WEST to 21 Borders for tempy duty. The unit remained at BUIRE treating sick.	
August 25th 3pm	Orders received to take over the XVth Corps Main Dressing Station near DERNANCOURT (about E.19.a.) on 26th at 6 a.m.	
26th 7.45am	The unit marched to the Corps M.D.S. & took over from the 13th F. Amb. (5th Div). The Camp consists of 92 Marquees, two Brodes, into M.D.S. + Corps Rest Station	

Army Form C. 2118.

WAR DIARY
or
INTELLIGENCE SUMMARY
(Erase heading not required.)

Instructions regarding War Diaries and Intelligence Summaries are contained in F. S. Regs., Part II. and the Staff Manual respectively. Title pages will be prepared in manuscript.

Hour, Date, Place	Summary of Events and Information	Remarks and References to Appendices
XV Corps M.D.S (E 19.a) August 28th	The personnel is made up of the 23rd F.A. Plus a tent sub-division from each 3rd Amb. in the Corps. A tent sub-division from each of 72nd, 73rd & 74th F.A.	
2 pm	Amb. (24th Division) reported for duty	
3 pm	Lieut LOVELESS R.A.M.C. to 1/R. Irish Regt for temp duty Instructions received from D.D.M.S. that the site of the M.D.S. is to be taken over by a C.C.S about the end of the week; after which the M.D.S also will move to a new site which is being prepared near BÉCORDEL by 19th F.A. The Corps Rest Station will be separate from M.D.S. when it moves.	
29th to 31st	Heavy rain for two days – The unit remains at M.D.S.	
31st	Orders received that the personnel of Ambulances of the 33rd Div. (1st, 99th & 101st F.A's) are to rejoin their units on 3.9.16.	

Geo. H. Brown
Lt Col R.A.M.C.
O.C. 23rd F.A.

140/174

No. 23 F.A. - 7th Division

COMMITTEE FOR THE
MEDICAL HISTORY OF THE WAR
Date -2 DEC. 1916

War Diary
for September 1916
23 Field Ambulance.

PART XXI

Army Form C. 2118.

WAR DIARY
or
INTELLIGENCE SUMMARY
(Erase heading not required.)

Instructions regarding War Diaries and Intelligence Summaries are contained in F. S. Regs., Part II. and the Staff Manual respectively. Title pages will be prepared in manuscript.

XV th Corps M.D.S.
CAMP "EDGE HILL" (E19A)
September 1916

Hour, Date, Place		Summary of Events and Information	Remarks and References to Appendices
1st		The unit remained in charge of XVth Corps M.D.S & Rest Station.	
	8.30 p.m.	2 Offrs & 50 bearers of the unit sent, under orders of ADMS 7th Divn to establish a relay post near MONTAUBAN with the object of clearing wounded from 21st FA. A.D.S in BERNAFAY WOOD back to the Ambulance cars at the west end of MONTAUBAN. — the farthest point the cars could get to.	
2nd	6 a.m.	The tent subdivisions of 19th, 99th & 101st F.A's (33rd Divn) left to rejoin their units.	
	12 noon	Three tent subdivisions of 2/1st & 1/3 W.Lancs & 1/1 Wessex (55th & 8th Divns) reported for duty at M.D.S	
3rd		A party of men & two sets of equipment sent up to the BECORDEL M.D.S to open. The "Edgehill" M.D.S will close at 12 noon on 4th. The new M.D.S open at noon on 4th as the XVth Corps M.D.S. The Rest Station is to remain behind till its new Camp near BUIRE is ready, when it will be taken over by 21st FA. tmobile)	

WAR DIARY
or
INTELLIGENCE SUMMARY
(Erase heading not required.)

Army Form C. 2118.

Hour, Date, Place	Summary of Events and Information	Remarks and References to Appendices
XV Corps M.D.S. (E.19a). September 3rd	During the night two bearers were wounded & evacuated No. 34877 Pte (a/Cpl.) A.J. TAYLOR - Shell wound R.knee " T. LOCKIE - Shell wound L.axilla. 44893	
" 4th	The M.D.S. began to move up from 6 a.m. in heavy rain - in detachments. One Operating Marquee, with 4 tables working was ready by 11 a.m. & the M.D.S. open for wounded at noon. - By 5 p.m. the whole of the personnel & equipment was up, & 2 Operating Marquees were working. The Rest Station remained at Edgehill Camp, with its complete staff - till the morning of the 6th when it was taken over by 21st Fd. Amb., & moved to BORG.	
XV Corps M.D.S. (F.7.a). " 5th	A very wet day, & the Camp got very muddy. The new M.D.S. consists of 2 Operation tents (large R.Marquees) 4 small R. Marquees & 15 "Swiss Chalet" tents with accommodation for 600 wounded normally & 1000 close up. The Camp is divided into a Reception & Evacuation side, the two sides being divided by the Operation tents. The site of the Camp is on a Spring (known) N. of ALBERT - BÉCORDEL ROAD, in F.7.a (North-West quadrant)	

Army Form C. 2118.

WAR DIARY
or
INTELLIGENCE SUMMARY
(Erase heading not required.)

Instructions regarding War Diaries and Intelligence Summaries are contained in F. S. Regs., Part II. and the Staff Manual respectively. Title pages will be prepared in manuscript.

Hour, Date, Place		Summary of Events and Information	Remarks and References to Appendices
XV Corps MDS. (F7a.) September 5th			
" 7th	8 pm	During the morning No. 9410 Pte CURTIS. C.W. of the bearer Divn was killed by a shell, a fragment passing through his heart. His body was brought down, & buried in BÉCORDEL Cemetery.	
" 8th		Tent Sub division 2/1st W. Lancs F.A. ordered to rejoin its unit- by D.D.M.S. XV th Corps.	
		The relay post in MONTAUBAN having been taken over by 55th Divn, the bearers there rejoined H.Qrs of the unit-	
		Orders that the 23rd F.A. will accompany the 91st Bde 7th Divn to rest billets on 11th inst, & that the Corps MDS will be handed over to another F.A.	
		Tent subdivisions of 138th, 139th & 140th FA. (41st Divn) reports for duty	
" 9th		Tent subdivisions 72nd, 73rd & 74th FA. left at 6 a.m. entraining at ALBERT to rejoin the 24th Divn. FAs	
" 10th		The 63rd Fd Amb, which is to take over, not having arrived, the D.D.M.S. XV th Corps cancelled own orders to move on the 11th.	
		We now march on 13th inst with 21st Fd Amb	

Army Form C. 2118.

WAR DIARY
or
INTELLIGENCE SUMMARY

(Erase heading not required.)

Instructions regarding War Diaries and Intelligence Summaries are contained in F. S. Regs., Part II. and the Staff Manual respectively. Title pages will be prepared in manuscript.

Hour, Date, Place	Summary of Events and Information	Remarks and References to Appendices
XV Corps M.D.S. (E7a) September 11th	Tent subdivisions of 1st, 2nd & 3rd New Zealand F.As reported for duty - In the afternoon the O.C. 63rd F.A (Capt KAVANAGH RAmC) + 1 Section arrived.	
" 12th	Handed over the M.D.S. to 63rd F.A. & (packed) up	Ref Sheet 4. N.W. EUROPE 1/250,000
" 13th	The unit marched at 12 noon via MÉAULTE - DERNANCOURT - BUIRE - BONNAY - LANEUVILLE - to Camp near DAOURS; arriving between 6+7 p.m. The 21st F.A was picked up at BUIRE; the two Ambulances marched under my Command & bivouaced together for the night.	Ref Sheet 3. N.W. EUROPE 1/250,000.
" 14 to	March continued at 8 a.m via VECQUEMONT - AMIENS - PICQUIGNY - to CROUY, arriving about 5.30 p.m. - Both units went into billets for the night.	do.
" 15th	March continued to LIERCOURT arriving at 12.30 p.m. - FONTAINE - to HUCHENVILLE - Here the 21st F.A. was detached (to proceed) by itself to HUCHENVILLE - The Chateau to be used for the sick -	

Army Form C. 2118.

WAR DIARY
or
INTELLIGENCE SUMMARY
(Erase heading not required.)

Instructions regarding War Diaries and Intelligence Summaries are contained in F.S. Regs., Part II. and the Staff Manual respectively. Title pages will be prepared in manuscript.

Hour, Date, Place	Summary of Events and Information	Remarks and References to Appendices
LIERCOURT		
September 16th	While arrangements here being made to equip & open the chateau as a main Dressing Station, instructions were received from the A.D.M.S. to cancel all orders, to stand by to move with the Division at short notice.	
8 pm.	Orders for the move arrived. The unit is to entrain at LONGPRÉ in time to start at 7.45 a.m. on the 18th.	
" 17th	During the day Serjt.-Maj. CHAMBERS. A.S.C. from N° 3 Gen. 7th Div. Train reported for duty vice Serjt-Maj MIATT A.S.C. who proceeded to 21st F³ Amb. (A.D.M.S instructions)	
" 18th	Reveille at 1.30 a.m. In fairly heavy rain, the unit marched at 3.30 a.m to LONGPRÉ, arriving there at 5.25 a.m. The train did not arrive till 7.45 a.m. Loading began at 8 a.m., the train was ready by 9.15, & started at 9.45 a.m. — Following the coast route via ABBEVILLE - ETAPLES - BOULOGNE - CALAIS - ST OMER - HAZEBROUK - we reached BAILLEUL at 7.30 p.m.	

WAR DIARY
or
INTELLIGENCE SUMMARY
(Erase heading not required.)

Army Form C. 2118.

Instructions regarding War Diaries and Intelligence Summaries are contained in F. S. Regs., Part II. and the Staff Manual respectively. Title pages will be prepared in manuscript.

Hour, Date, Place	Summary of Events and Information	Remarks and References to Appendices
Sept 18th (Cont)	Unloading there, the unit marched at 8.30 pm via BAILLEUL & METEREN to billets — 3 farms — in X.1. b & d. (Sheet 27. 1/40000 Square map.) with the exception of a few men with blisters on feet, there has been no sickness in the unit since it began to march on the 13th inst. LT STORDY and LT MILLER — RAMC (TC) joined for duty. Instructions from HQrs to the effect that the unit will take over from 57th F.A. (19th Div.) The M.D.S. to be taken over on 20th & M.D.S. at PONT de NIEPPE on 21st.	
" 19th		
" 20th	On the morning of the 20th I proceeded forward with Capt ALLAN & one N.C.O & one man, as an advance party. Having gone over the ground, I left Capt Allan & the N.C.O at the M.D.S to learn the trenches & returned to the unit. At 2 pm I sent forward "C" Section under Capt BUCKLEY — the bearers to join at the M.D.S. & the tent subdivision to take over the M.D.S on the morning of the 21st, pending the arrival of the rest of the unit	

Army Form C. 2118.

WAR DIARY
or
INTELLIGENCE SUMMARY
(Erase heading not required.)

Instructions regarding War Diaries and Intelligence Summaries are contained in F. S. Regs., Part II. and the Staff Manual respectively. Title pages will be prepared in manuscript.

Hour, Date, Place	Summary of Events and Information	Remarks and References to Appendices
PONT de NIEPPE Sept 21st	The unit marched at 8 a.m. arriving in PONT de NIEPPE at 11.30 a.m.	Ref Sheet 36 Belgium & France 1/40,000 (green)
	The following places have been taken over:- M.D.S. in PONT de NIEPPE (B.23.6.2.2.) a School with accommodation for 60 cases normally. Can be expanded to 150 & communicated with good cellars.	
	A.D.S. - at the BREWERY. (C.1.d.4.4) - well sandbagged & communicates with good cellars. One bearer subdivision here - with 2 Officers.	
	The A.D.S collects from the following R.A.P.s (1) SURREY FARM. (C.9.d.4.2) (2) RESERVE FARM. (C.3.d.7.9) (3) LAWRENCE FARM (U.27.a.3.1) (Sheet 28. 1/40,000)	Sheet 28 - 1/40,000
	A stretcher squad (& stations in each of these - Nos 1 & 2 Posts are cleared by road, No. 3 by tramway which leads past the A.D.S	
5 p.m.	Capt BUCKLEY to Army Gas School for instruction.	
	Capt BUCKLEY rejoined from A. Gas School.	
	The new small bore respirator issued on the scale 1 per man & officer.	
6.30 p.m.	The village was shelled by the enemy - No Casualties in Unit - One man of the R.A. Sanitary Section brought in dead.	
" 25th		

WAR DIARY
or
INTELLIGENCE SUMMARY
(Erase heading not required.)

Army Form C. 2118.

Hour, Date, Place	Summary of Events and Information	Remarks and References to Appendices
PONT de NIEPPE		
September 26th & 27th	During the 26th & 27th all ranks were instructed in the use of the new Small box respirator, & tested them in a gas chamber.	
Sept 28th	Capt BUCKLEY with "A" bearer Subdivision proceeded to A.D.S. in relief of Capt ALLAN & "C" bearers —	
30th	In anticipation of a raid which takes place tonight 4 more squads of bearers were sent to the M.D.S. A second A.D.S was established at MOTOR CAR CORNER in a house at C.14.a.6.9. One NCO, 1 Nursing Orderly + 1 bearer squad will remain at this A.D.S. + a motor ambulance will also remain there in line. This is to facilitate the clearing of the Aid Post at C.9.d.4.2. SURREY FARM. Flies are still rather numerous, + all excreta & rubbish is being incinerated. New horse standings are being erected – brick standings with galvanized iron roofing.	(Trench Sheet France 36 N.W 1/20,000)

Geo N Horner
Lt Col Hawc
O.C. 23 F.A.

Army Form C. 2118.

23rd Field Ambulance

PART XXII

WAR DIARY
or
INTELLIGENCE SUMMARY
(Erase heading not required.)

Hour, Date, Place		Summary of Events and Information	Remarks and References to Appendices
1916. PONT DE NIEPPE			
October	1st	Lt STORDY to A.D.S in relief of Capt Hart Plane.	
"	2nd	S. Maj RIGBY (name proceeds), under instructions of D.D.M.S 7th Corps to report to D.M.S. First Army for duty.	
"	3rd	Lt DAVIDSON to Div. School for duty as M.O./Ch	
"	5th	Capt Allan with "B" bearer subdivision LADS in relief of Capt Buckley & "A" bearers.	
"	8th	Capt D. Mackie to 35th Bde R.F.A. for temporary duty. In the afternoon orders were received that from the 20 to 24th a Found-a-graph to meet emergencies, 2 squads bearer posted in Doct R.A.P. & the oxygen apparatus was got ready at A.D.S. A motor cyclist was stationed at the A.D.S (to bring down now) if assistance was required, & bearers were held in readiness at the M.D.S. There were no casualties from gas on our front.	

Army Form C. 2118.

WAR DIARY
or
INTELLIGENCE SUMMARY
(Erase heading not required.)

Hour, Date, Place	Summary of Events and Information	Remarks and References to Appendices
PONT de NIEPPE		
October 9th	Lt MILLER Rame to M.D.S in relief of Lt STORDY	
12th	"C" bearer subdivision to the A.D.S in relief of "B" bearer	
14th	Lt STORDY to 9th Devons for temporary duty.	
	Capt Buckley to M.D.S in relief of Capt Allan	
	I. R. To M.S. T. Corps inspected the Main D.S. also the A.D.S. at Mont Cat Corner.	
19th	"B" bearer subdivision to A.D.S. – usual weekly relief	
21st	Capts Allan & Wright to A.D.S in relief of Capts Buckley & Lt Miller.	
24th	Capt Mackie reported from 35th Bde R.F.A.	
25th	Capt Wright to 2/Gordons for temporary duty	
26th	Usual weekly relief of bearers at M.D.S.– Capt Hart to A.D.S	
27th	Handed over command temporarily to Capt Mackie as I am to proceed to Div H.Q. to act for the A.D.M.S during his absence	

WAR DIARY
or
INTELLIGENCE SUMMARY

(Erase heading not required.)

Army Form C. 2118.

Hour, Date, Place	Summary of Events and Information	Remarks and References to Appendices
Pont de Nieppe		
October 28th	Capt Buckley to A.D.M.S. in relief of Capt Allan who returned to Hqrs	
29th	Lieut Storey returned to Hqrs from relief of M.O. 9th Devons	
30th	Lieut Miller to 2nd Royal Warwickshire for temporary duty.	
	Reference Tk Bde O.O. No 97 concerning move received from ADMS VII D-n	
31st	8.30 a.m. 20th Bde O.O. received (O.O. No 95)	

Mackie
Capt RAMC

140/1849

COMMITTEE FOR THE
MEDICAL HISTORY OF THE WAR
Date -3 JAN 1917

7th Div.

23rd Field Ambulance

PART XXIII

War Diary 23 Field Ambulance
November 1916

23rd FIELD AMBULANCE
No.
Date 2-4-16
7th DIVISION

Army Form C. 2118.

Vol 23

WAR DIARY
or
INTELLIGENCE SUMMARY
(Erase heading not required.)

Instructions regarding War Diaries and Intelligence Summaries are contained in F. S. Regs., Part II. and the Staff Manual respectively. Title pages will be prepared in manuscript.

Hour, Date, Place	Summary of Events and Information	Remarks and References to Appendices

Pont de Nieppe

November 1st

6 a.m. — On the previous afternoon I went with Capt Buckley & inspected the advanced dressing station and regimental aid posts in the line with Col. Kelly C.O. 77th Field Ambulance. A and D. book closed and billets and hospital finally handed over to 77th F.A.

10-30 a.m. — Unit left Pont de Nieppe in accordance with Bde O.Os. and moved to La Creche where we remained over night.

10-30 a.m. — Subdivision (bearer) at ADS under Capt. C.D. Buckley handed over A.R.S. to Bearer Subdivision of 77th Field Ambulance and under orders moved to rejoin the Hqrs of 25th F.A. at La Creche at which place they arrived at 12-30 a.m.

November 2nd

10-30 a.m. — Went forward in advance under instructions of O.R.M.S. to take over Chateau at Caestre which had been allotted to 25th Field Ambulance to use as a Main Rest Station for the 91st and 20th Bdes.

10 a.m. — 25th F.A. in accordance with 90th Bde. O.Os. No 95 moved off, under command of Capt. Buckley and annexing the town of Bailleul and arrived at Caestre at 2 p.m. One room prepared as ward so cleared of over remainder of Chateau cleaned troops equipped with stretchers and blankets, and arrangements for bathing patients set down.

Caestre.

November 3rd

9 a.m. — Chateau equipped with stretchers and necessaries to take six 160 cases if necessary.

November 7th

9 p.m. — Received orders from O.R.M.S. to be ready to move off any time within next two days.

10-15 p.m. — Received instructions for line of march. (VII Div)

November 8th

10-37 a.m. — Received orders from 90th Bde. to be in readiness to move off at an early hour on the morning of the 9th.

WAR DIARY
or
INTELLIGENCE SUMMARY
(Erase heading not required.)

Army Form C. 2118.

Hour, Date, Place	Summary of Events and Information	Remarks and References to Appendices
1916 Nov. 8th	Rejoined the Unit during the afternoon (Flanders Convoy)	
Nov. 9th	The Unit marched at 9 a.m., arriving at RENESCURE about 1.30 p.m. Here a M.D.S. was opened in the school, the men's billets being some two Kilometres away, in a farm.	Ref Sheet 5A HAZEBROUCK 1/100,000.
Nov. 10th	March Continued at 9.30 a.m. via ST OMER to TIQUES, where the unit billeted for the night. M.D.S. established in the Chateau.	do.
Nov. 11th	March continued at 9 a.m. to NORDAUSQUES where the unit went into very poor billets which were insufficient for all the personnel. The M.D.S. was established in a glass-roofed factory. Ventilation had, but it was the best place available. Accommodation for 60 Cases. The weather throughout the march was bright + cold. 2 men fell out with sore feet on the first march; none afterwards.

Army Form C. 2118.

WAR DIARY
or
INTELLIGENCE SUMMARY
(Erase heading not required.)

Instructions regarding War Diaries and Intelligence Summaries are contained in F. S. Regs., Part II. and the Staff Manual respectively. Title pages will be prepared in manuscript.

Hour, Date, Place	Summary of Events and Information	Remarks and References to Appendices
1916 NORDAUSQUES —		
Nov 14th Nov 15th	The unit remained at NORDAUSQUES taking in the list of the 20th Inf. Bde Group. till Nov 14th & taking part in the Brigade training. Lieut STORDY to 8th Devons for temporary duty. The unit continued the march at 9.20 a.m to reach the starting point at MENTQUE CHURCH at 10.35 a.m. in accordance with 20th I.B.G. Order No 4. proceeding via road junction S. of the second E in LES ÉPERLECQUES — M — NORTLEULINGHEM to LUMBRES where it billeted for the night. 30 men of the Brigade who were unfit to march were sent ahead by rail from WATTEN.	Ref Sheet 5.A HAZEBROUCK 1/100,000 —
Nov 16th	In accordance with 20th I.B.G. O. N°5 the unit marched via AVROULT — AUDINCTHUM — DONNEBROUCK to RECLINGHEM to billets. This was a long & trying march. The Division rested for the day.	
Nov 17th — 18th	The march was continued to AMBRICOURT, in bitterly cold weather.	Ref Sheet 11 LENS 1/100,000

Army Form C. 2118.

WAR DIARY
or
INTELLIGENCE SUMMARY
(Erase heading not required.)

Instructions regarding War Diaries and Intelligence Summaries are contained in F. S. Regs., Part II. and the Staff Manual respectively. Title pages will be prepared in manuscript.

Hour, Date, Place	Summary of Events and Information	Remarks and References to Appendices
1916 November 19th - 20th -	The march continued to BEAUVOIS in heavy rain On the 20th the unit marched to BOUBERS-SUR-CANCHE. Here the billets were exceptionally good & a welcome change from the open barns used as billets previously.	Ref Sheet 11 LENS 1/100,000
" 21st -	Marched to HEM (West of DOULLENS), & billeted there for the night. The men who had been sent on from WATTEN by rail rejoined here. A certain number of cases of sore feet & colds had been carried in the ambulance wagons thus far; but under instructions from the A.D.M.S these were now sent to the 19 CCS in DOULLENS — there being no room for cases at our destination	
" 22nd -	The unit marched to its destination in BERT-RANCOURT. The 90th F.A. which we were to relieve, had received no orders to hand over, to the unit remained parked	

Army Form C. 2118.

WAR DIARY
or
INTELLIGENCE SUMMARY
(*Erase heading not required.*)

Instructions regarding War Diaries and Intelligence Summaries are contained in F. S. Regs., Part II. and the Staff Manual respectively. Title pages will be prepared in manuscript.

Hour, Date, Place	Summary of Events and Information	Remarks and References to Appendices
1916 BERTRANCOURT		
Nov. 22nd	Lieut MILLER rejoined from temporary duty	
Nov 23rd	Took over the M.D.S at BERTRANCOURT from 92nd F.A. (32nd Div.) During the afternoon a considerable number of wounded of the 32nd Div passed through – The rush continued throughout the night & following morning. All wounded were cleared by 3.30 p.m. Also over ± 100 sick that came in during the day. The Relief Div under Capt ALLAN RAWE proceeded forward to take over the A.D.S & other medical stations from 92nd F.A.	
" 24th	The 7th Division began, on 23rd, the relief of 32nd 37th & 51st Divisions in the line from R.I.C.7.0. 16 K.34.b.9.1. – the former being junction with 11th Div. II Corps & the latter junction with 3rd Div. XIII Corps The 20th Inf Bde. Relief from WAGGON ROAD at Q5.6.6.5.6 K34.b.9.1.	Reference Sheet 57D 1/40,000

Army Form C. 2118.

WAR DIARY
or
INTELLIGENCE SUMMARY
(Erase heading not required.)

Instructions regarding War Diaries and Intelligence Summaries are contained in F. S. Regs., Part II. and the Staff Manual respectively. Title pages will be prepared in manuscript.

Hour, Date, Place	Summary of Events and Information	Remarks and References to Appendices
1916 BERTRANCOURT Nov. 25th	The Ambulance is now disposed as follows:— **M.D.S.** In trams & Canvas huts at BERTRANCOURT about J.33.a.4.1. **A.D.S** at the Sucrerie — K.33.c.15. with some leavers also at RED HOUSE Q.1.d.1.2. (holding par 4) Relay Bearer Post — in dug-out on the Roman Road at K.34.a.1.0 Ambulance Cars — 2 Cars at K.33.C.1.5, & one at Q.9.a.8.7. **R.A.P.s** K.35.c.5.2.3/4 & Q.5.5.7.*2 for the line K.30.c.4.7 for [illegible] The R.A.P.s on the left of the line are cleared to the A.D.S. that on the right to the A.D.S. at 215.32 Post in MAILLY, the Cave being carried to Q.4.c.5.2 where a Car meets the bearers All sick evacuated from the line held by the 7th Div. are sent in to the D.S. BERTRANCOURT. From there, light cases are sent to the Corps Rest Station at CLAIR FAYE, & others evacuated to CCS 3	Reference Sheet 57 D 1/40,000

WAR DIARY
or
INTELLIGENCE SUMMARY
(*Erase heading not required.*)

Army Form C. 2118.

Hour, Date, Place	Summary of Events and Information	Remarks and References to Appendices
1916 BERTRANCOURT		
Nov. 26th	Very heavy rain all day, making the conditions in front very bad. The A.D.S at the Sucrerie was shelled, & the latrine demolished.	
" 28th	Weather conditions very bad. A dense wet mist all day, very cold. The trenches are waist deep in mud in places; the work of the bearer squads is very arduous. From the left of the line it takes 1½ to 2 hours to carry a man down to A.D.S. On the Right, 1½ hours from Aid Post to Car. Several bearers have stuck in the mud, & have to be dug out.	
" 29th	Wet fog, with frost at night continues. Numbers of men with trench feet are coming in. The conditions in front are still very bad; but the laying of "duck boards" has somewhat improved matters. Men coming back are suffering chiefly from the effects of exposure - 2/3 of the sick are either P.U.O or Trench feet. The rest are chest complaints & myalgias.	

Army Form C. 2118.

WAR DIARY
or
INTELLIGENCE SUMMARY
(Erase heading not required.)

Instructions regarding War Diaries and Intelligence
Summaries are contained in F. S. Regs., Part II.
and the Staff Manual respectively. Title pages
will be prepared in manuscript.

Hour, Date, Place	Summary of Events and Information	Remarks and References to Appendices
1916 BERTRANCOURT		
Nov. 29th (Con td)	Lt STORDY reported from duty with 8/Devons Lt Miller to 2/Borders vice Lt West (Sick) Capt HART to A.D.S. vice Lt Miller	
„ 30th	Cold foggy weather continues, large numbers of sick continue. Much trouble has been experienced caused by the shortage of tyres for the Motor Ambulances, & by the cars breaking down on the bad roads. Today there are 2 large & 1 Ford car in Service the other 4 have broken down.	Geo N Brown Lt Col RAMC O.C. 23rd W. Amb.

140/1902.

23rd Field Ambulance.

COMMITTEE FOR THE
MEDICAL HISTORY OF THE WAR
Date 31 JAN 1917

23 Field Ambulance

War Diary.
        xXIV
December 1916

23rd FIELD AMBULANCE
7th DIVISION

Army Form C. 2118.

WAR DIARY
or
INTELLIGENCE SUMMARY
(Erase heading not required.)

PART XXIV   December 1916

1916 Hour, Date, Place	Summary of Events and Information	Remarks and References to Appendices
BERTRANCOURT		
December 1st	Capt Buckley to A.D.S in relief of Capt Allan -	
„ 3rd	Capt ALLAN to Border Regt. for duty. Lt Miller remains attached for further instruction -	
„ 6th	Capt Mackie to A.D.S vice Capt Hart to M.D.S. Lt Miller rejoined from 2/Borders, reported sick with pleurisy.	
	G.O.C 7th Div inspected M.D.S - Lt Miller evacuated to C.C.S with pleurisy. Dr West to Divisional School for duty vice Dr Davidson who went sick while on leave in England, two granted an extension to 19th Dec. Capt Hart reports sick with P.U.O. & admitted.	
„ 7th	This leaves 2 Officers at A.D.S & 2 at M.D.S The weather continues are not improving. Fog & rain are constant, but it is not so cold. Large numbers of sick are still coming in daily - principally "P.U.O." Chest complaints & myalgia - Trench foot cases are on the wane.	

WAR DIARY
or
INTELLIGENCE SUMMARY

(Erase heading not required.)

Army Form C. 2118.

Hour, Date, Place	Summary of Events and Information	Remarks and References to Appendices
1916 - BERTRANCOURT		
Dec 9th	Capt Hart Rawe Evacuated to CCS at PUCHVILLERS with "P.U.O (? Enteric Group)	
" 11th	Capt Fox - RAMC(T) Joined for duty	
" 12th	Lt. Storby to Div Sanitary Section for temporary duty Capt Wright to A.D.S vice Capt Buckley to 7.1.6.3.	
" 13th to 18th	Unit remained as before. The weather has been bad but fogs return with frost at night. A keen frost set in on the 18th afternoon.	
" 19th	Capt Gov to A.D.S. vice Capt Mashe to M.D.S. Two Daimler Cars joined in place of 2 Sunbeam Cars Evacuated to the Base.	
" 21st	Thaw set in again, & it no warmer. Heavy rain followed & conditions returned to their previous muddiness.	
" 22nd	Orders received from A.D.M.S to the effect that the SUCRERIE A.D.S is to be handed over to a F.A. of the 3rd Div. on the 24th inst. After handing over the 23rd 9.A will take over Clearing of the Right Sector of the 7th Divst line.	

WAR DIARY
or
INTELLIGENCE SUMMARY

Army Form C. 2118.

Hour, Date, Place	Summary of Events and Information	Remarks and References to Appendices
1916. BERTRANCOURT Dec. 23rd	Capt Buckley & ADS in relief of Capt Wright (6 M.D.S) After a reconnaissance of the right sector of our line, it was decided to make the following dispositions A.D.S. In cellars of a ruined farm in AUCHONVILLERS (about Q.9.a.1.1) — 2 Medical Officers & bearers here Another ADS in "Y RAVINE" an old German dug-out at Q.11.c.4.4. This is to deal with men hit going to/from the trenches; fourth walking cases in the event of active operations The R.A.P. is at Q.12.c.2.4 — junction of STATION ROAD & "STATION ALLEY" trench — As there is no water at either ADS storage in petrol tins was arranged for —	Sheet 57 D S.E. 1/20,000
" 24th	Suxerne A.D.S. handed over to 3rd Div. & the Bearer Division of 23rd F.A. moved to AUCHONVILLERS, & proceeded to establish the new ADSs. "Y"Ravine is an extremely unpleasant locality as it is shelled every day — the dug-out is deep & good, but the approaches are much harried in the open	

Army Form C. 2118.

WAR DIARY
or
INTELLIGENCE SUMMARY
(Erase heading not required.)

Instructions regarding War Diaries and Intelligence Summaries are contained in F. S. Regs., Part II. and the Staff Manual respectively. Title pages will be prepared in manuscript.

Hour, Date, Place	Summary of Events and Information	Remarks and References to Appendices
1916 BERTRANCOURT		
Dec. 25th	Capt. D. GARDINER came (one) for duty from No. C.C.S. (T.C)	
" 26th	The A.D.Ss are now ready. The one at MICHONVILLERS will hold 12 stretcher cases. 2 Motor Ambulances are also kept there. The rest of the "Sunbeam" Moto Ambulances (2) sent to 30 D.S. Col. for exchange with 31st Div. Daimlers replacing them. They gave us 5 Daimlers + 2 Ford Cars.	
" 30th	Lt. Storby to A.D.S. in relief of Capt. Fox - to M.D.S. Capt T.S. Wright to 8/Devons as M O 4th vice Capt Mills transferring to No. 4. C.C.S.	
" 31st	Capt Mackie to A.D.S. vice Capt Buckley - to M.D.S. Capt H.E. Fox to 7th QAC as M.O 4th vice Capt B. WRIGHT who takes his place in the Ambulance. The weather conditions during the month have been very bad.	

Geo H Brown
Lt Col RAMC
OC 2/3 SM

140/9+1

7th Div

No. 23. Field Ambulance

COMMITTEE FOR THE
MEDICAL HISTORY OF THE WAR
Date 13 MAR. 1917

Recd. x_ray ? 31 January 99

Recd. x_ray 9

2/6

93rd FIELD AMBULANCE

Army Form C. 2118

23 [?] Army
PART XXV
Vol 25

WAR DIARY
or
INTELLIGENCE SUMMARY
(Erase heading not required.)

JANY. 1917

Place	Date	Hour	Summary of Events and Information	Remarks and references to Appendices
BERTRAN-COURT	2/1/17		Capt Gardiner to M.D.S in relief of Lieut Storby. Capt A.H. Pollock. RAMC (T.C.) reported from Englans for duty	
	4th		Lieut F.F. Carr-Harris. RAMC (T.C.) " " to No 44 CCS	
	6th		Lieut Storby to 2/ Gordons for temporary duty	
	7th		Capt Pollock to A.D.S in relief of Capt Gardine to M.D.S	
	8th		Capt W.H. Godby. RAMC (T.C.) joined for duty from No 4 CCS	
	9th		Orders for operations on our own front received. These have been on orders cancelled several times - the weather being unfavourable. The water has been consistantly wet for some time - the operations will now take place wet or fine, & under (1) Capture of LEAVE AVENUE and MUCK Trench by 2nd Borden Reg t. (20th & 4/05) Zero = 2 A.M. on 10th January 1917 (2) Capture of MUNICH TRENCH - by units of 91st Inf. B te. Zero = 6.40 a.m. 11th January.	
	10th		A.D.S of the Ambulance at AUCHONVILLERS, with a second A.D.S at Y. RAVINE - for the Right Sector. The left sector for operations of the 11th is to be cleared by 21st Fd Amb ce. The attack was successful. The wounded some 30 & 40 - were in the M.D.S by 10. a.m. All cases came via Y. RAVINE, as the roads through	

Army Form C. 2118

WAR DIARY
or
INTELLIGENCE SUMMARY
(Erase heading not required.)

Instructions regarding War Diaries and Intelligence Summaries are contained in F. S. Regs, Part II. and the Staff Manual respectively. Title Pages will be prepared in manuscript.

Place	Date	Hour	Summary of Events and Information	Remarks and references to Appendices
BERTRAN-COURT	10/1/17		BEAUMONT HAMEL was Constantly shelled by the Enemy. There were no casualties in the Bearer B.S.	
	11/1/17		The decoy operations here also Successful. Some 120 wounded were in the M.D.S. by noon — No. 21762 Pte R. TAYLOR RAMC 23rd SA was wounded at AUCHONVILLERS A.D.S. – Shell wound of abdomen. He died the same day in No. 4 C.C.S VARENNES.	
	12/1/17.		Some 50 casualties in on night 12/13 – the reliefs having been caught by shell fire.	
	13/1/17		The weather has been very bad for the last two days – very cold with sleet & snow.	
	16/1/17		Lieut Car Harris to A.D.S vice Capt Pollock to M.D.S. Heavy snow, some 4" or 5" fell during the night.	
	18/1/17		Capt Pollock Evacuated to No. 4 C.C.S with P.U.O	
	19/1/17		Received orders from A.D.M.S re handing over.	
	20/1/17		Took over "Tenderloin" A.D.S & R.A.P in Wagon Road from 2nd SA.	

Army Form C. 2118

WAR DIARY
or
INTELLIGENCE SUMMARY
(Erase heading not required.)

Instructions regarding War Diaries and Intelligence Summaries are contained in F.S. Regs., Part II. and the Staff Manual respectively. Title Pages will be prepared in manuscript.

Place	Date	Hour	Summary of Events and Information	Remarks and references to Appendices
BERTRAN-COURT.	22/7		Handed over all the front line stations to 92nd F.A. (32nd Div.) Bearer Divn. returned to M.D.S.	
	23/7	9.30am.	Having handed over the M.D.S. to 90th F.A. (32nd Div.) the unit marches to Pitts in BEAUVAL via ACHEUX – ARQUEVES – BEAUQU- –ESNES – A very keen frost has prevailed of late in spite of which the transport had but difficulty in getting along – A M.D.S. establishes in a factory at G.21.a.6.2 with accommodation for 40 sick. Capt Pollock Rame rejoined from No. 4 C.C.S.	Sheet 57D 1/40,000
BEAUVAL	24/7		Capt GODBY Rame to H. Gordon vice Lt. STORDY sick – Lt. STORDY sent to C.R.S. & thence evacuated to No. 29 C.C.S	
	25/7		Lieut WEST. Rame rejoined from Divisional School.	
	26/7		The keen frost continues, this being the 13th day of unbroken frost.	
	27/7		Several cases of frostbite of the hands admitted today.	
	29/7	11 pm	20 A.B.O. received – The unit marches to HALLOY. On the 31st Advance party sent to HALLOY to take over 2nd Aubee Ville 16	
	30th			

Army Form C. 2118

WAR DIARY
or
INTELLIGENCE SUMMARY

(Erase heading not required.)

Instructions regarding War Diaries and Intelligence Summaries are contained in F. S. Regs., Part II. and the Staff Manual respectively. Title Pages will be prepared in manuscript.

Place	Date	Hour	Summary of Events and Information	Remarks and references to Appendices
HALLOY.	31st		The unit marched to HALLOY - via MONTRELET - CANAPLES - & establish there - "Nilsen Hut" capable of holding 40 sick formed the M.D.S. Lieut STORDY Rame rejoined from 29 C.C.S. A very keen frost has prevailed continuously since 15th Jan'y The temperature has averaged about 18°F. falling at times to 25° of frost. Fuel has been scarce & the cold has been very severe on the men - whose billets have been none too good.	

Geo A Brown
Lt Col RAMC
O.C. 23rd 20 Feb 19

1875 Wt. W593/826 1,000,000 4/15 J.B.C. & A. A.D.S.S./Forms/C. 2118.

140/1994

Items

23rd Field Ambulance

COMMITTEE FOR THE
MEDICAL HISTORY OF THE WAR
Date 4.- APR.1917

War Diary for Period 1/2/17 to 28/2/17

Part XXVI

Army Form C. 2118

WAR DIARY
or
INTELLIGENCE SUMMARY
(Erase heading not required.)

PART XXVI

FEBRUARY 1917

Place	Date	Hour	Summary of Events and Information	Remarks and references to Appendices
HALLOY.	Mon 5.2.17	9.a.m	Lieut. HARRIS RAMC (TC) to 8th Devons for Remunerant duty in place of Capt T.S. Wright RAMC who proceeded to Boulogne for duty at Hospital there.	
	Mon 12.2.17		Capt W.H. Godby RAMC (TS) sick to Corps Rest Station at Beauval.	
	Tues 13.2.17		Capt D.G. Gardiner RAMC (TC) to 2/Royal Warwickshire Regiment to replace Capt Hurst RAMC on leave.	
	Wed 14.2.17 9-30 p.m		2015 Infantry Brigade Group Order No. 118 received fixing for three days the unit was at Halloy we had hand training consisting of Squad and Company drill, Stretcher drill, Route Marches and lectures.	
	Thurs 15.2.17 10 p.m		Amend ments to 30th Infantry Brigade Group Orders No 118 received	
	Frid 16.2.17 9 a.m		Received orders from ODMS VII Division to keep patients already in NISSEN hut. leaving behind enough personnel to carry on with Lieut Stordy with Corpl Smith and two Orderlies.	
		11-45	Marched from Halloy via CANAPLES MONTRELET BONNEVILLE to BEAUVAL.	
BEAUVAL		2 p.m	Arrived at BEAUVAL. Remained closed sending cases directly to Corps Rest Station	
	Sat 17.2.17 10-30 a.m		Review by GENERAL NIVELLE Commander in Chief FRENCH ARMY held half a mile N.E. of VAL DE MAISON. The unit was represented by three officers on W.D. 5 NCOs and 50 Men	
		2 p.m	Orders from ODMS to evacuate the cases at HALLOY to R/1st Field Ambulance and hand over NISSEN hut and Stores belonging to Unit to Town Major	
		11 p.m	Received Movement Order 20/BM/10/39/1. from ROT Brigade.	
	Sunday 18.2.17	9 a.m	Marched from BEAUVAL to RUBEMPRÉ. Roads in very bad condition due to thaw starting.	
RUBEMPRÉ		12.30 p.m	Arrived at RUBEMPRÉ. Remaining closed for present. Cases going to R/1st Field Ambulance.	

Army Form C. 2118

WAR DIARY
or
INTELLIGENCE SUMMARY
(Erase heading not required.)

Instructions regarding War Diaries and Intelligence Summaries are contained in F. S. Regs, Part II and the Staff Manual respectively. Title Pages will be prepared in manuscript.

Place	Date	Hour	Summary of Events and Information	Remarks and references to Appendices
RUBEMPRE	Monday 19.3.17	3 pm	Received 20th Brigade Group orders No.120. LIEUTS STORDY and BALL to 21st Fd Amb for temporary duty	
	Tuesday 20.3.17	9 am	Received y/r Cpls Medical arrangements No.15. together with R.A.M.C. VIII Division Operation Orders No.16.	
	Wednesday 21.3.17	12 pm	Addm to 20th Bde Order No.121.	
	Thursday 22.3.17	10.15am	Moved from RUBEMPRE via PUCHEVILLERS. RAINCHEVAL. ARQUEVES. LOUVENCOURT to BERTRANCOURT. Roads in very bad condition owing to thaw and held up by wagons in front. No difficulty whatever without our transport	
		5.30pm	Arrived at BERTRANCOURT. Capt GOODBY R.A.M.C. Rejoined from C.C.S.	
BERTRANCOURT	Friday 23.3.17	9 am	Took over from 2/1 WEST RIDING FIELD AMBULANCE	
		2.30 pm	Went up to look at an old GERMAN DUGOUT in WAGON ROAD at Q.5.d.0.4. to see if possible to use it for an ADS. Found it suitable and marked out a best route up WAGON ROAD for site of New Dugout that we had orders from ADMS to make for a Regimental Aid Post. to Regimental Medical Officer	
		9 pm	Routine Orders from ADMS regarding move to and taking over ADS at Q.5.d.0.4 with 2/1st Field Ambulance. LIEUTS. STORDY and BALL returned from temporary duty	
	Saturday 24.3.17	9.30 pm	Capt. BUCKLEY R.A.M.C. with Lieut BALL and B and C section bearers to establish ADS at Q.5.d.0.4 and to build dugout for use of Regimental Medical Officer	
	Sunday 25.3.17		Enemy fell back and our troops advanced. During our stretcher bearers Ptes CLAYTON and RUSSELL wounded (CLAYTON shell wound back, RUSSELL shell wound ankle fracture tibia) and were evacuated. Pte GWYNNE also slightly wounded in forearm but not sent down	
	Monday 26.3.17	12 noon	Capt. FOX. R.A.M.C. (T) reported at Hqrs. for duty from D.A.C.	

Army Form C. 2118.

WAR DIARY
or
INTELLIGENCE SUMMARY

(Erase heading not required.)

Place	Date	Hour	Summary of Events and Information	Remarks and references to Appendices
BERTRANCOURT	Tuesday 27/3/16	2 p.m.	Capt Godby RAMC to ADS Wagon Road, in relief of Lieut Ball who returned to Hqrs.	
	Wednes. 28/3/16	9.30 p.m.	RAMC VII division Operation orders by Col. Hooper. CMG. DSO. ADMS VII div.	

F Mackie
Capt RAMC SR
Capt 23rd Field Ambulance
for O.C.

Manual S

4th Div.

No. 23. Field Ambulance.

14/2042

COMMITTEE FOR THE
MEDICAL HISTORY OF THE WAR
Date 11 MAY. 1917

WAR DIARY
or
INTELLIGENCE SUMMARY

Army Form C. 2118.

PART XXVII   March 1917

Vol 27

Place	Date	Hour	Summary of Events and Information	Remarks and references to Appendices
BERTRANCOURT	1st March 6/17		The Unit remained at BERTRANCOURT looking after sick only.	
	7/3/17		Orders received from ADMS 7th Div'n to send two tent subdivisions to V Corps M.D.S for duty.	
	8/3/17	10a.m.	Capt BURNLEY + 20 O.R. proceeded to V Corps M.D.S as advance party.	
	9/3/17	11a.m.	Capt MACKIE with the remainder of B+C tent subdivisions proceeded to V Corps M.D.S for duty.	
	11/3/17		7th Div. Route O.O. No 18 received	
	12/3/17		do do No 19 "	
	13/3/17	8 a.m.	Capt Gardiner R.A.M.C with 50 O.R. 3 horsed ambulances 2 B.S. ambulances + 50 stretcher bearers proceeded forward to report to O.C. 22 W.F.A. We take over the following Relay Bearer Posts.	SHEET 57D
			SUCRERIE - K 33.c.1.4.	
			"Sioe Bridge" Post - L 34.A.o.o.	
			SKUNK POST - L 35 a 77	
			SERRE POST - In the village of SERRE	
			MIDWAY POINT - L 19 c.6.1	
			The tramway will be used if available from Midway Point. The rest of the "carry" will be by hand and wheel stretcher carriage	

Army Form C. 2118.

WAR DIARY
or
INTELLIGENCE SUMMARY
(Erase heading not required.)

Instructions regarding War Diaries and Intelligence Summaries are contained in F. S. Regs., Part II. and the Staff Manual respectively. Title Pages will be prepared in manuscript. March 1917

Place	Date	Hour	Summary of Events and Information	Remarks and references to Appendices
BERTRAN COURT			On the night 16/17 March, the enemy retired from his line, & on 17-3-17 BUCQUOY was occupied.	Sheet 57D 1/40,000
	18th	7 a.m.	Received orders to take over the V th Corps MDS (P.17 Sheet 57D 1/40,000) at to move my headquarters to RED HOUSE (N.1.d.2.3) Took over the V C.M.D.S. at 10 a.m. and moved up to RED HOUSE in the afternoon — the 22nd F.A. less its H.Q. O.P. was there, & someone in charge of the place.	
RED HOUSE	19th		The 22nd F.A. moved forward, do I brought up the rear to part of A tent subdivision from BERTRAN COURT — leaving some personnel there to look after local sick — I was detailed by the A.D.M.S. to supervise & work the line of evacuation from the 22nd F.A. M.D.S. backward — during the afternoon I visited the area & found as follows :— Roads — from RED HOUSE to SKUNK POST (L.35.a.7.7) fair, but passable to motor ambulances. From SKUNK POST to PUISIEUX - extremely bad — impossible for motor, barely possible for horse ambulances with 4-horse teams. PUISIEUX to BUCQUOY impassable — full of shell holes, & in BUCQUOY were 3 huge craters about 20 feet deep, across the road.	

Army Form C. 2118.

WAR DIARY
or
INTELLIGENCE SUMMARY
(Erase heading not required.)

March 1917

Place	Date	Hour	Summary of Events and Information	Remarks and references to Appendices
BERTRANCOURT RED HOUSE			BUCQUOY to ABLAINZEVILLE. Surface fair, but road again cut by mine craters at F.28.a. central F.29.a.3.9 & F.23.d. central – ABLAINZEVILLE & COURCELLES — Surface bad — but road floored by trees blown across it by the enemy. (These were being removed) Filling up the craters was in progress — also the repair of the SKUNK POST – PUISIEUX ROAD. Personnel — The 23rd F.A. Beaver Division was not sufficient to carry on the long line of evacuation — in view of the amount of hand carriage necessary. I sent up the Beaver Divn of 21st F.A. + 3 horse-ambulances under Capt JARDINE, to take over all posts held by the 23rd F.A. from SKUNK POST to PUISIEUX inclusive. The 23rd F.A. Beaver divn to move forward to BUCQUOY taking over from 22nd F.A. which moved on to COURCELLES retained a post in BUCQUOY in a ruined house at F.28.c.3.9 The line of evacuation was now in 3 stages:- COURCELLES to BUCQUOY — 22nd F.A. with 4 horse ambulances BUCQUOY to PUISIEUX — 23rd " " 2 " " PUISIEUX to SKUNK POST — 21st " " 3 " "	Sheet 57D 1/40,000
	20th			

WAR DIARY or INTELLIGENCE SUMMARY

Army Form C. 2118.

March 1917

Place	Date	Hour	Summary of Events and Information	Remarks and references to Appendices
RED HOUSE	20th (Cont'd)		At SKUNK POST cases were broken up by Motor Ambulances & wounded were taken to V Corps M.D.S. & sick to RED HOUSE. The roads were still too bad to permit anything but a limited use of horse-ambulances. The first wounded man, a stretcher case, arrived at 7.30 p.m. He had been hand-carried to SKUNK POST, and took 7 hours to come from COURCELLES. The distribution of the 23rd JA on the evening of the 20th was thus:- V Corps M.D.S. (P17) — B+C Tent Subdivisions. BERTRANCOURT — 1 Off + 60 R of A Tent Subdivision. RED HOUSE — OC, HQ & remainder of A Tent Subdivision. BUCQUOY — Bearer Divn in dugouts about F.3.a.6.3. This gave one an extremely long line to control in view of the difficulty of getting over the roads. CAPT GODBY. R.A.M.C. proceeded to Englebelmer on 3 weeks Course.	Vide 57 D Mobilisation
	21st		The 21st JA took over at BERTRANCOURT, & the 23rd JA removed from there & rejoined at RED HOUSE.	
	22nd		Again visited my area. Evacuation proceeding smoothly, but slowly. The rain, heavy during the night, turned the roads (Kew Carriage Way) again between BUCQUOY & SKUNK POST	

WAR DIARY or INTELLIGENCE SUMMARY

Army Form C. 2118.

March 1917

Place	Date	Hour	Summary of Events and Information	Remarks and references to Appendices
RED HOUSE	23rd		Took four (4) 2 Large + 1 Ford) motor ambulances to 2.nd 2A. COURCELLES owing to the condition of the roads (Icy) to go from RED HOUSE via BERTRANCOURT - BUS - AUTHIE - COUIN - SOUASTRE - BIENVILLERS - HANNESCAMPS - ESSARTS - BUCQUOY - ABLAINZEVILLE. This was a very long round, but justified by the better roads. The roads from MAILLY-MAILLET through HEBUTERNE + PUISIEUX were impassable to motors. These cars worked from Courcelles to PUISIEUX - the roads behind BUCQUOY having been repaired - from PUISIEUX cases went on by horse-ambulance or hand-carriage as before. This arrangement greatly expedited the removal of cases to the rear. A medical officer was stationed at SKUNK Post with cars to see to the loading of cases during transfer to motor ambulances.	
BUCQUOY	24th		Took over the Post at F.28.c.3.9. in BUCQUOY from 22.nd DFA. and moved that 57D up there myself to be better able to look after things - bringing down 2 Large + 1 Ford motor ambulances - the road to PUISIEUX has improved greatly - Cars now have right through to there, + replace full cars at COURCELLES with empty cars from BUCQUOY. Orders received from ADMS that all sick (wounded) are to be sent to the CCS at COUIN CAMPS (K25C) from morning of 25th.	

Army Form C. 2118.

WAR DIARY
or
INTELLIGENCE SUMMARY
(Erase heading not required.)

Instructions regarding War Diaries and Intelligence Summaries are contained in F. S. Regs., Part II. and the Staff Manual respectively. Title Pages will be prepared in manuscript.

March 1917

Place	Date	Hour	Summary of Events and Information	Remarks and references to Appendices
BUCQUOY	24th (con't)		Proceeded to examine all the roads to COLIN CAMPS, found that the only good road was BUCQUOY — HANNESCAMPS — FONQUEVILLERS — SAILLY-au-BOIS — COURCELLES-au-BOIS — COLIN CAMPS. The last part to Colin camps was very bad, but under repair. Reported accordingly to the A.D.M.S. & D.D.M.S. (V Corps) and asked that the repairs might be made on	
	25th		Handed over V.C. M.D.S. (P.17) — which now becomes the Divn Rest Station — to 21st F.A. RED HOUSE also handed over to 21st F.A. aux) A tent sub-division moved from there to BUCQUOY, to establish the M.D.S. at F28.c.3.9. — A.D.M.S. O.O. 21 here — B&C heavier sub-divisions (2 horse amb wagons O.O. 22nd F.A. at 5.30 p.m. The unit was situated thus on evening 25th:— Divn Rest Station (P.17) — B&C. tent sub-divns BUCQUOY — H.Q. & A " " COURCELLES-le-Comte — B&C heaven sub div — (atta 22nd F.A.) 10 M.A.C cars reported for duty at BUCQUOY	

2449 Wt. W14957/M90 750,000 1/16 J.B.C. & A. Forms/C.2118/12.

WAR DIARY or INTELLIGENCE SUMMARY

Army Form C. 2118.

March 1917

Place	Date	Hour	Summary of Events and Information	Remarks and references to Appendices
BUCQUOY	27th		Evacuations are now as follows:— C.C.S cases (wounded & sick) by M.A.C cars to COLINCAMPS Rest Station, by car to PUISIEUX, thence by horse ambulance to SKUNK POST, thence by motor ambulance to D.R.S (P17). At there is room for only 6 cases in the return of the Lorries at F28.C.3.9., Tents are being pitched in the adjoining field to a road leading to them is in progress. During the day both Ford & large motor ambulances ran from BUCQUOY to RED HOUSE via PUISIEUX and SERRE — Another stay or two is really required before the road is safe for motors.	Ref of 57th /4 opos
		3 pm	Under instructions of A.D.M.S., O.C. 21st S.A. armoured change of the evacuation line from behind PUISIEUX (Guerbine) A.D.M.S O.O. 23 received. Arrangements were also made for a special gas tent at the M.D.S BUCQUOY for treatment of (gassed) cases.	
	28th		The attack fails in its object. M.A.C cars sent up to COURCELLES to evacuate wounded direct from 22nd F.A. M.D.S to C.C.S at COLINCAMPS. 10 more M.A.C cars were ordered up by D.D.M.S V Corps to BUCQUOY. These were not required & were returned in the evening.	

2449 Wt. W14957/M90 750,000 1/16 J.B.C. & A. Forms/C.2118/12.

WAR DIARY
or
INTELLIGENCE SUMMARY

Army Form C. 2118.

(Erase heading not required.)

March 1917

Place	Date	Hour	Summary of Events and Information	Remarks and references to Appendices
BUCQUOY.	29th		A day of heavy rain, which made the ground very sodden – The roads too bare suffering – Work in the camp continued – Roads & paths making & tent-staking. The distance that marquees & other things have to be transported over bad roads – (from the camp at P.17?) – greatly delays the work at BUCQUOY. *which is the nearest P.line*	
	30th		Rain & some snow – A temporary canvas water tank holding 130 galls. has been erected in the camp, & has to filled daily by motor lorries tank –	
	31st	9 pm	Another day of heavy rain & hail. Continued work in the camp. T Cope has had arrangements N° 24 recovery. The health of the unit during the month has been so great amount of work it has been called on to do, & the very inclement weather with inadequate shelter	

Geo. H. Brown
M.C. Rowe
O.C. 23rd 3rd Mob.

140/2086

1st Div.

No. 23. F.A.

COMMITTEE FOR THE
MEDICAL HISTORY OF THE WAR
Date 6 JUN. 1917

WAR DIARY or INTELLIGENCE SUMMARY

Army Form C. 2118.

23 3rd Aust
PART XXVIII
Vol 28

April 1917

Place	Date	Hour	Summary of Events and Information	Remarks and references to Appendices
BUCQUOY	1st	3 p.m.	A.D.M.S. O.O. No 23 received.	
		6 p.m.	Bearer Divn. with stretchers under Capt Fox Rowe, proceeded to COURCELLES to report to O.C. 22nd F.A.	
	2nd		The attack by the division attained its objectives.	
	"	1.30 p.m.	Received orders to proceed personally, with one officer, to the A.D.S. at ERVILLERS (B.13.C.9.7 Sheet 57C 1/40,000) – Leaving there with CAPT GARDINER R.A.M.C. at 3.30 p.m. Learned command of all the Bearers of 23rd + 22nd F.A's – according to instructions – The situation was a 3 Cdn. Advanced A.D.S's had been formed at MORY L'ABBAYE (B.22.c.4.7). under Capt MEAGHER + 1 Officer (22nd F.A); + at near ST LEDGER in B.3.C. under Capt McKINNON (22nd F.A). The Bearer Divn of 22nd F.A were clearing from the line to these two A.A.D.S while the Bearers Divn of 23rd F.A + horse ambulances were clearing them to the A.D.S ERVILLERS. Avery heavy fall of snow began shortly after our making the A.D.S from MORY as the road (most of the A.D's posts were well nigh impassable for wheeled) was very heavy + no ? the heavy snow. Sheet 57C 1/40,000	
		5 p.m.	There being no risk of casualties, Cpl. Fox was allowed to Bucquoy to rest.–	
		11.30 p.m.	Capt JARDINE Rowe with one Bearer Subdivision + 2 Horse ambulances reported at the A.D.S – under A.D.M.S instruction.	

Army Form C. 2118.

WAR DIARY
or
INTELLIGENCE SUMMARY

(Erase heading not required.)

April 1917

Instructions regarding War Diaries and Intelligence Summaries are contained in F.S. Regs., Part II. and the Staff Manual respectively. Title Pages will be prepared in manuscript.

Place	Date	Hour	Summary of Events and Information	Remarks and references to Appendices
BUCQUOY	3rd		The Bearer Divn 23rd R.A. having come in over-night & being tired, one bearer subdivn was sent to A.D.S. ST LEDGER to relieve bearers of 22nd R.A. there – The bearer subdivn 21st R.A. were sent to MORY A.D.S. to relieve bearers of 22nd R.A. – The 2 horse ambulances of 21st R.A. were also sent up to relieve 2 others – A certain number of casualties came in during the day – but on the whole it was a quiet day.	
	4th		1 Bearer Subdivision 22nd R.A. proceeded to ST LEDGER in relief of 23rd R.A. bearers – several wounded who had been lying out in shell holes in "no man's land" were brought in.	
		6 p.m.	Orders of A.D.M.S – O.O. No 24 received – Advanced party of 2/2nd West Riding F.A. (62nd Divn) arrived about 11 p.m.	
	5th	9 a.m.	Remainder of 2/2nd W.R. F.Amb arrived – I handed over the A.D.S to them, leaving Capts Meagher & McKinnon there for the day to show the new men the line – At the A.D.S. I left Capts etc. 1 Bearer Subdivn to carry on in the meantime – & I rejoined M.I unit at BUCQUOY at 1 p.m.	
		6 p.m.	The M.D.S at BUCQUOY opened as the Divn Rest Station	
	6th		Instructions from A.D.M.S to withdraw B+C tent subdivisions from the Rest Station at P.17 (Sheet 57D 4/40,000)	

WAR DIARY
or
INTELLIGENCE SUMMARY

(Erase heading not required.)

Army Form C. 2118.

April 1917

Place	Date	Hour	Summary of Events and Information	Remarks and references to Appendices
BUCQUOY	7th	1.30pm	2 Officers and 1 tent subdiv. reported from Rest Stn. (P.17)	
		3 pm	Capt Foy + 1 bearer sub div'n in A.D.S. ERVILLERS.	
		8 pm	1 NCO + 3 Stretcher Squads proceeded under A.D.M.S orders to Rejoin 1st F.A. at L'HOMME MORT (B.10.c.5.3 sheet 57.3) to 22nd Bde R.F.A.	
	8th		1 Officer + 1 tent subdivision rejoined from Rest Station (P.17) - The personnel of the Ambulance is now together again. R.A.M.C. reported for duty from England.	
	9th		Capt JARDINE R.A.M.C. with 2 bearer subdivisions of 2/1 F.A. 62 Divn. are attached under A.D.M.S instructions.	
	10th	9 pm	B.O. received - from 4.30 a.m. on 11th the 2nd B Bde F.A. will be prepared to move at 2 hours notice.	
	11th	9.30pm	Lt. Col. Brown D.S.O. R.A.M.C. O.O. 2/3rd Field Ambulance left for MORY (57.c. Sheet. B.21) to take temporary command of Main Dressing Station of 2nd/3rd WEST RIDING FIELD AMBULANCE. 62nd DIVISION.	
		11 pm	Received orders from Col Brown that Capt C.R. Busby with Capt's Foy and Gardiner and BEARER DIVISION were to proceed to MORY to be there by 6 a.m. next morning	

Army Form C. 2118.

WAR DIARY
or
INTELLIGENCE SUMMARY

(Erase heading not required.)

Instructions regarding War Diaries and Intelligence Summaries are contained in F. S. Regs., Part II and the Staff Manual respectively. Title Pages will be prepared in manuscript.

Place	Date	Hour	Summary of Events and Information	Remarks and references to Appendices
BUCQUOY	12th	3.30am	Beaver Division 25th Field Ambulance. Sudden command of Capt. Brierley handed to MORY.	
		9.p.m	LIEUT. MacAphee. RAMC. to 9th Devons for Temporary duty in absence from illness of M.O. Capt. REYNOLDS.	
	13th		LIEUT. McAphee. returned from duty with 9th DEVONS S.	
	20th		CAPT. H. H. GODBY. RAMC reported to 25th FIELD AMBULANCE for duty	
	29th		LIEUT. MCAPHEE RAMC to MAIN DRESSing Station MORI in relief of Capt. Fox Rowe. who reported at HQrs here.	

M MacIntire
Capt. Rowe RAMC

COMMITTEE FOR THE
MEDICAL HISTORY OF THE WAR
Date   10 JUL.1917

WAR DIARY
or
INTELLIGENCE SUMMARY

Army Form C. 2118.

23 M Amb
PART XXIX

MAY 1917

Place	Date	Hour	Summary of Events and Information	Remarks and references to Appendices
MORY	1st		Two tent subdivisions still at BUCQUOY; the Bearer Division under Capt BUCKLEY is distributed between the ADS in ECOUST, & the relay posts along the ECOUST - SUCRERIE ROAD. The following were the arrangements for clearing the line. M.D.S at MORY L'ABBAYE B.12.a.9.7. A.D.S - ECOUST - C.2.c.4.6. Relay Posts at B24.b.8.6, C13.b.3.4, & C8.a.2.3 -. These also collected from the batteries in the vicinity. A post was established at C7.a.3.8 to collect the wounded of the batteries in the neighbourhood. 2 Horse Ambulance wagons were between B24.b.8.6 & SUCRERIE. (rounds) were brought down to them on wheel stretcher carriage. A Motor Ambulance (Ford) went up to about B12.d.4.6. to collect from the post at C7.a.3.8.	Sheet 57 C 1/40000
	2nd		In the evening all personnel was sent up to the various posts in readiness for the attack next morning.	
	3rd		Attack on BULLECOURT by 62nd Divn took place at dawn. There were heavy casualties - The R.A. Bearers placed in R.A. posts soon cleared all casualties through it & these were passed rapidly through the A.D.S relay posts to be taken to M.D.S by 5 Motor Amb: Cars which had been sent to B24.b.8.6.	

Army Form C. 2118.

WAR DIARY
or
INTELLIGENCE SUMMARY

MAY 1917 (*Erase heading not required.*)

Place	Date	Hour	Summary of Events and Information	Remarks and references to Appendices
MORY	3rd	7AM	Beaver Division (& 21st F.A. and 3 Officers reported for duty. These 3 kept in reserve at the M.D.S. A considerable number of both walking & stretcher cases passed through during the day - There was never any congestion at either A.D.S. or M.D.S.	
	4th		The previous days operations having partially failed, attack to-day's attack - all producing heavy casualties. By the evening of the 4th roughly 800 cases had passed through the M.D.S. - Evacuation was quick & no hitch occurred - About 50% of the 800 were stretcher cases -	
	5th		A very sultry day, followed by a heavy thunderstorm. The fighting has been almost continuous & very intense. Many lightly wounded (and in during the night. There has been in shell holes since the morning of the 3rd) were unable to get back by reason of the heavy fire - machine gun & shell.	
	6th		A cold day - Received A.D.M.S. O.O. No. 27. Handed over the night flank line to Lt.Col. W.G. WRIGHT. D.S.O. R.A.M.C. O.C. 21st F.A. Amb.	
	7th		Handed over M.D.S. & took clearance to O.C. 21st F.A. by orders of A.D.M.S. 7th Div. returned to BUCQUOY for rest.	
	8th		Capt BALL to M.D.S. MORY for duty. Capt GODBY to R.q.E Devon vice Capt REYNOLDS wounded.	

Army Form C. 2118.

WAR DIARY
or
INTELLIGENCE SUMMARY

(Erase heading not required.)

MAY 1917

Place	Date	Hour	Summary of Events and Information	Remarks and references to Appendices
BUCQUOY			During the operations around BUCQUOY the shell fire on all the back area was very intense at times. The A.D.S. was shelled heavily every day, & once was subject to 16 hours bombardment - (at times 4 cookhouses were destroyed.) 5 times by direct hits on different occasions. - The strain on the M.D.S was intense that relief is due to Capt. C.D. BUCKLEY R.A.M.C. who was in charge for 3½ weeks for his coolness & fine organization during these trying & dangerous times. - The ELOUST - SUCRERIE ROAD was shelled daily Many casualties occurred there - The bearers showed great gallantry in their disregard of danger along this road The M.D.S. was shelled frequently, but fortunately none of the personnel were hit. One day it was shelled every 2 hours from morning to evening - 60 HE shells fell round the M.D.S. within 10 minutes during one of these episodes	
	8th 9th		Capt BUCKLEY reported to rest - LT MACAFEE R.A.M.C. 23rd admitted sick - P.U.O. - He was evacuated to No. 49 C.C.S. on 12.5.17 -	
	10th		Capt GARDINER reported on completion of duty with 2/6th Manchester Regt Orders received to take over Corps Rest Station at Q.9.C.6.2. on 12th, handing over the camp at BUCQUOY to 2/3 West Riding F.A. (62nd Divn)	

Army Form C. 2118.

WAR DIARY
or
INTELLIGENCE SUMMARY

(Erase heading not required.)

MAY 1917

Place	Date	Hour	Summary of Events and Information	Remarks and references to Appendices
V Corps Rest Station (G.9.c.2.6.)	12th		Marches from Bucquoy and took over site of Corps Rest Station from 2/3 West Riding F.A. There were some 25 marquees & 150 patients at in hospital	
	15th		The tents & patients were not suitable for a Rest Station, so they were all shifted - A cook-house & Expense-counter arrangements were started, with a view to taking in 800 patients. In the afternoon No. P.G. SMITH - A. Rawe attempted to commit suicide by cutting his throat with a razor. He was sent early to No. 61. C.C.S. as "SI" (wound). After observation as a mental case. C. of. I. on P.G. SMITH held - (more info forward S to A.D.M.S.V Corps)	
	16th		Bearer Div returned from the line -	
	7th		During operations following here wounded in action	
			56142 P.G. ADAMS - G. - Shell Wd. R. leg. 17/4/17 Evacuated	
			1305 " CALLIS. F.G. - Acc. S. Nose + neck. 20/4/17 D. to B. 3/5/17 - {Gone to collapse of better from fire concussion}	
			5225 Sgt. YOUNG W.F. Shrap Wd. face. 26/4/17	
			57943 Pte. DRAGE H. " R. arm. 26. 27/4/17	
			90729 " GILES A.S. Shell " R. leg. 1-5-17 do. 1-5-17	
			89103 " LYNAS W. " " R. leg. 6-5-17 Evacuated	
			7075 " JENKINS H. " R. Shoulder 6-5-17 do.	
			88539 " THEOBALD W - Shrap + R. Arm. 6-5-17 do.	
			→ Shell Wd. Arm + leg. 12-5-17 do.	
			40773 " HUNT S. Shell Wd. L. Arm. 7-5-17 Seb. 7/5/17	

Army Form C. 2118.

WAR DIARY
or
INTELLIGENCE SUMMARY

(Erase heading not required.)

MAY 1917

Place	Date	Hour	Summary of Events and Information	Remarks and references to Appendices
A.G.C.b.2 "C.b.6s Post Station	20th		Lt. McAPHEE rejoined from hospital at Rouen	
	18th to 31st		Carried on with the work of improving the V.C.R.S. A cookhouse, latrine, bath-house with spray bath, laundry, this to clarifying soap, w.c. were built, the accommodation was increased to 800, with 8 beds for Officers. Dining tents were also provided.	
	30.		Capt E.T. GAUNT RAMC. joined from No.6 M.A.C. for duty. During the past week the following honours have been awarded for gallantry:- 9007 Cpl. TREGLOWN. R. RAMC. D.C.M. 8659 Pte STURGESS. H.A. " M.M. 47495 " GWYNNE. S. " Medaille Militaire	

Geo. H. Brown
Lt. Col RAMC
O.C. 23rd F.A.

140/2230

No. 93. J. C.

June, 1917.

COMMITTEE FOR THE
MEDICAL HISTORY OF THE WAR
Date —7 AUG. 1917

Army Form C. 2118.

WAR DIARY
or
INTELLIGENCE SUMMARY

23 /1 Amb
PART XX

JUNE 1917

(Erase heading not required.)

Instructions regarding War Diaries and Intelligence Summaries are contained in F.S. Regs., Part II. and the Staff Manual respectively. Title Pages will be prepared in manuscript.

Place	Date	Hour	Summary of Events and Information	Remarks and references to Appendices
G.Q.C.6.2. V Corps Rest Station	1st 6 15th		The unit remained at the V Corps Rest Station breathing seat. The numbers have risen steadily to about 500 under treatment - these are principally Pyrexia Chr & Minor Septics - Results have been good so far - the discharges to duty keeping the evacuation s.	Sheet 57 C 40,0.0.0
	10th		1 NCO + 6 bearers to 22nd B.E. R.G.A. (in action) in relief of the 21st F.A's men - these were relieved on 17th by 21st F.A.	
	13th		Capt BALL Rawe to 2/Gordons for temporary duty	
	18th		Capt McAFEE Rawe to 3/Queens " " "	
	19th		V Corps Rest Station inspected by D.M.S. 3rd Army. On the 16th the Convalescent Camp in Connection with the C.R.S. was opened - under orders of V.D.M.S. - It is a separate camp (in G 15.a.) of bell tents to accommodate up to 300 - Convalescent men from the C.R.S. are sent there; are utilized on fatigues till well enough to return to their units - this camp is under the administration of O.C. V CRS.	
	21st		A.D.M.S. 7th Div. O.O. N° 28 received.	
	26th		Capt BALL reported on completion of temporary duty.	
	30th		The unit remaining in charge of V Corps Rest Station - About 40% of admissions return to duty -	

Geo. H. Brown
Lt. Col. R.A.M.C
O.C. 23 F.A

COMMITTEE FOR THE
MEDICAL HISTORY OF THE WAR
Date 10 SEP. 1917

140/2298

7th Div.

No 23. F.A.

Sept 1917

Army Form C. 2118.

WAR DIARY
or
INTELLIGENCE SUMMARY
(Erase heading not required.)

JULY 1917

Part II

Instructions regarding War Diaries and Intelligence Summaries are contained in F.S. Regs., Part II. and the Staff Manual respectively. Title Pages will be prepared in manuscript.

Place	Date	Hour	Summary of Events and Information	Remarks and references to Appendices
49.C.6.2 V Corps Rest Station	2nd		Lt. McAFEE RAMC rejoined on completion of duty with 7/Queens Regt.	
	7th		From noon today the designation of the Rest Station is changed from "V Corps R.S." to "VI Corps Rest Station" — the VI Corps having taken over the area from the V Corps.	
VI CRS	9th		Capt. C.D. BUCKLEY RAMC to 7/HAC for temporary duty - rejoined on 24th.	
	31st		During the month the unit remains in charge of the Corps Rest Station is working well. Up to the present 42% of cases have returned to duty. 45% have been evacuated. The evacuations are mainly for Trench Fever kits degrees &c. The health of the unit has been good.	

Geo. A. Brown
Lt. D. B. Raine
O.C. 23rd — 22 Amb.

140/2264

No. 23. T.A.

Aug. 1917

COMMITTEE FOR THE
MEDICAL HISTORY OF THE WAR
Date -1 OCT. 1917

WAR DIARY

*23rd FIELD AMBULANCE
7th DIVISION*

PART XXXII

Month ending August 1918

Army Form C. 2118.

WAR DIARY
or
INTELLIGENCE SUMMARY

(Erase heading not required.)

PART XXXIV

AUGUST 1917

Vol 3

Place	Date	Hour	Summary of Events and Information	Remarks and references to Appendices
VI.Corps C.R.S. G9C.c (57)	1st		The unit remains in charge of VI Corps Rest Station.	
	5th		Capt D. MACKIE RAMC to 2/Border Regt. Lt W.G. McAFEE RAMC to 2/Queens Regt. as M.O. i/c - temporary duty. Orders received that the establishment of riding horses will be reduced from 11 to 5 ie 6 are to be withdrawn -	GAB
	7th		Handed over command of the unit to Capt E.T. GAUNT RAMC during my absence as a/ADMS 7th Div. Took over command from Lt.Col. G.H. BROWN D.S.O. RAMC during his alone as a/ADMS 7th Div.	GAB
	7th		Handed over VI C.R.S. to 2/2 W.R.F.A. 62nd Div.	
BELLACOURT	9th 10th		Marched under Brigade arrangements to BELLACOURT. Under no sanction by A.D.M.S left that Subaltern & two officers a/temporary duty with VI C.R.S from 10th to 11th inclusive & count 2/2 W.R.F.A.	Kent + McBain
	12		To 7th cav div. with two officers & men deponed for VIERS	I.T.

2449 Wt. W14957/M90 750,000 1/16 J.B.C. & A. Forms/C.2118/12.

Army Form C. 2118.

WAR DIARY
or
INTELLIGENCE SUMMARY
(Erase heading not required.)

Instructions regarding War Diaries and Intelligence Summaries are contained in F. S. Regs., Part II. and the Staff Manual respectively. Title Pages will be prepared in manuscript.

Place	Date	Hour	Summary of Events and Information	Remarks and references to Appendices
BELACOURT	13th		The unit is collecting and [?] from the Bgde + obn from as follows:- Diarrhoea cases to C.C.S. 20 & 43 (Hitching) BOISLEUX au MONT Scabies cases to scabies station ACHIET LE GRAND Cases of Arrhythmia + minor illness to 22nd F.A, ADINFER WOOD Other cases to C.C.S. as above.	8.T
	15th		Training in "gas masks" is being carried out. His unit Advanced dressing station are formed, communications established with regimental aid posts, stretcher bfr organised, specialist instruction is given to N.C.O's in Map Reading.	P.T.S. P.T.S. P.T.S.
	23rd		Capt. STORDY proceeded on leave.	P.T.S.
	24th		Capt. FOX returned from leave.	P.T.S.
	26th		Capt. FOX proceeded to infirmary duty with 21st Newhole Regt.	P.T.S.
	27th		Proceeded on 5 days leave to PARIS & handed over command of unit to C/H. MACKIE R.A.M.C	P.T.S.

Army Form C. 2118.

WAR DIARY
or
INTELLIGENCE SUMMARY

(Erase heading not required.)

Instructions regarding War Diaries and Intelligence Summaries are contained in F. S. Regs., Part II. and the Staff Manual respectively. Title Pages will be prepared in manuscript.

Place	Date	Hour	Summary of Events and Information	Remarks and references to Appendices
BELLACOURT	AUGUST 1917 29th	2 p.m.	Route Administrative Orders for VIIth Divis. wn received	AM
		3 p.m.	LIEUT PETTIT USAM, MRC USA attached to Unit for instruction	
		7 p.m.	20th Infantry Bde Order No. 155 received regarding move	
	30th	9.30 am	Transport marched to SAULTY to entrain	
		11.30 am	Unit less transport marched to SAULTY, where with transport un entrained	
		8.30 pm	Left SAULTY for PROVEN.	
	31st	1.30 am	Arrived at PROVEN Station F.7.b (Sheet 27) where received 20th Bde March Orders	
		2.30 am	Marched to Billets in Camps at R.3.a.55 (Sheet 28) arriving at 5.30 a.m. being sick of 30th Bde	
			During day received and treated sick of 30th Bde	
			Evacuation "Cases to VII Div Rest Station Q.15.a.30. (Sheet 28)	

N Mackie
Col R.A.M.C

140/2438

COMMITTEE FOR THE
MEDICAL HISTORY OF THE WAR
Date -5 NOV. 1917

S No. 23. 7. a.

July 1917.

WAR DIARY or INTELLIGENCE SUMMARY

Army Form C. 2118.

23 Jnf Aust

Vol 33

PART XXXIII

SEPTEMBER 1917

Place	Date	Hour	Summary of Events and Information	Remarks and references to Appendices
G.23.a.7.6. (Sheet 28)	SEPTEMBER 1917 1st	10.58am	Received 70th Bde Warning Orders No 156	
	2nd	12.45pm	Received 70th Bde Orders No 156	
		1.15pm	Received 70/BM/10/186	
		4pm	23rd Field Ambulance marched from G.23.a.7.6. to STEENVOORDE to take over sick	
STEENVOORDE O.R.a.55. (Sheet 27)		7pm	Arrived at billets in O.R.a.55 where we prepared to feed troops in sick during march	
	3rd		Received acc: Treated sick of 70th Bde. Some Australians, Army Pioneers and other troops in vicinity. Evacuation Cases to Nos 11 and 17 CCS at GODEWAERZVALD	
		3-4 pm	70th Infantry Group Warning Orders No 157 received	
	4th	10am	Capt BALL RAMC to 65 Army Bde RFA G 36.a.6.8. (Sheet 28) for temporary duty	
		12 noon	Capt Gaunt RAMC returned command	
	4th		Returned from leave, 7pm. M.S. from Captain Machie RAMC First Lorraine	

Army Form C. 2118.

WAR DIARY
or
INTELLIGENCE SUMMARY

(Erase heading not required.)

Instructions regarding War Diaries and Intelligence Summaries are contained in F. S. Regs., Part II. and the Staff Manual respectively. Title Pages will be prepared in manuscript.

Place	Date	Hour	Summary of Events and Information	Remarks and references to Appendices
HONDEGHEM	4th		Unit marched from STEENVORDE to HONDEGHEM at 5 p.m.	
	5th		Arrived HONDEGHEM at 6.45 p.m.	
			A.D.M.S. visited Ambulance. Informed me that we should probably remain here a week or ten days. Pitched ourselves 12 bell tents & 3 privates.	
			Unit accommodated for about 50 cases.	
	7th		Captain CAIRDINER R.A.M.C. returned from temporary duty with 1/1 S. Staff.	2.T.
	8th		Lt. Col. B. Nixon D.S.O. R.A.M.C. returned	
			Resumed command of unit on completion of duty as a/A.D.M.S. of the Div.	G.H.B
	10th		Capt. Fox rejoins on completion of temporary duty with 2/1st Manchester Regt.	
	11th		20th Inf. Bde Order 158 received.	
	12th		Capt. E.T. GAUNT R.A.M.C. to permanent duty as M.O. i/c 2/1 H.A.C. under instructions of A.D.M.S. 7th Div. - He is struck off the strength of the unit from 14th inst.	G.H.B
	13th		The 2nd Border Regt + 20th M.G.C. being in isolation for diphtheria to remain behind when the 20th Bde Group marches today - To deal with them one tent sub-division under Capt. D. Mackie, with 2 M. Amb. Cars will remain in HONDEGHEM - 6 bell & 1 operating tent to be left for accommodating sick contacts.	G.H.B

Army Form C. 2118.

WAR DIARY
or
INTELLIGENCE SUMMARY
(Erase heading not required.)

Instructions regarding War Diaries and Intelligence Summaries are contained in F.S. Regs., Part II. and the Staff Manual respectively. Title Pages will be prepared in manuscript.

Place	Date	Hour	Summary of Events and Information	Remarks and references to Appendices
RENESCURE	13/9/17	11.55 a.m.	The Unit – less one tent subdivision – marched to RENESCURE, arriving there at 3 p.m. Billets for the men in farms – tents being erected for the sick	G.4.B
	14th		The Brigade rested for the day – Capt Gaunt left to join 2/1 M.A.C. – 20th Inf Bde Order 159 received	G.4.B
LONGUENESSE	15th	11.30 a.m.	The Unit – less one tent subdivision – marched to LONGUENESSE (S.E. of St OMER) arriving in billets at 2.30 p.m. Field Amb. tentage pitched for the sick there being no other accommodation	G.4.B
	16th	6.15 p.m.	Capts MACKIE & B. tent subdivision rejoined the Unit, under A.D.M.S. orders They marched straight through from HONDEGHEM – no one fell out during the march	G.4.B
			Field Training & lectures for the unit commenced	G.4.B
	19th		Under A.D.M.S. orders 4 Off + 38 O.R. proceeds to C.C.Ss. – Capt FOX, 1/Lt PETIT M.O.R.C. U.S.A. with 38 O.R. reports to H.Q.K.S. – for transport to C.C.S. at REMY SIDING Capts Buckley & Gardiner Raine by Car to GODEWAERSVELDE C.C.S.	G.4.B

Army Form C. 2118.

WAR DIARY
or
INTELLIGENCE SUMMARY
(Erase heading not required.)

Place	Date	Hour	Summary of Events and Information	Remarks and references to Appendices
LONGUENESSE	24th		Since arrival in this area Field Training of the Unit has been in progress - Instruction is also given by lectures to the men.	G.448
	26th		CAPT MOIR RAWE reports for duty from England. The unit took part in a practice attack carried out by the 22nd & 91st Inf. Brigades. Removal of wounded was practised, with evacuation to A.D.S. & M.D.S. (the latter being a skeleton station only).	G.448
			20th Inf. B.O. training order rec'd.	
	27th		20th Inf. B.O. rec'd - to move by road on 28th inst - Orders cancelling the preceding received at 1 p.m.	G.448
			20 Bde O - 161 received - The Group marches to the LUMBRES Area on 28th inst. CAPT STORDY RAWE to No 2 Can. C.C.S. in relief of CAPT H.E. FOX RAWE(T). Transferred to 11 E.Lancs F.A. 66th Div. - Capt Fox proceeded to his new unit. He struck off the strength.	
LUMBRES	28th	2.30 p.m	Unit marched from LONGUENESSE at noon. Arriving in billets at LUMBRES at 2.30 p.m.	
		11.30 p.m	20th Inf. B.O. 162 received.	
	29th	10.30 a.m	The unit, as part of the Column under my command marched at 10.30 a.m. to billets near at O.34.6.7.7. (Sheet 27) arriving there at 6.30 p.m. A very long march but not by fell out.	

Army Form C. 2118.

WAR DIARY
or
INTELLIGENCE SUMMARY
(Erase heading not required.)

Place	Date	Hour	Summary of Events and Information	Remarks and references to Appendices
BAVINCHOVE Area.	29th	7.30 pm	Received 2nd Inf Bde wire to march tomorrow to RENINGHELST. Issued the necessary orders to the Column.	G.H.B.
METEREN	30th	10 am	The Column continued its march. While on the line of march instructions received from A.D.M.S. 7th Div. that the 23rd F.A. is to take over the D.P.S. at METEREN — so I handed over the Column to Capt MacDonald - A.S.C. Comdg No. 2 Coy 7 Div Train, with instructions to proceed to RENINGHELST. I report to H.Q. 20th Inf Bde. The 23rd F.A. then proceeded to bivouac at X.16 d 7.4 (Sheet 27) went to see the A.D.M.S., received verbal instructions to send the Bearer Divs to 22nd F.A. on Oct 1st. Received 7th Div R.A.M.C. O.O. No 30.	G.H.B.

Geo. H. Brown
Lt Col R.A.M.C.
O.C. 23rd F.A.

No. 23. 7. C.

COMMITTEE FOR THE
MEDICAL HISTORY OF THE WAR
Date 8 DEC. 1917

Capt 1917
Capt Staley, M.O.
went to

WAR DIARY
or
INTELLIGENCE SUMMARY

Army Form C. 2118.

2 3 JA Aml
Vol. 54
PART XXXIV

OCTOBER 1917

Place	Date	Hour	Summary of Events and Information	Remarks and references to Appendices
METEREN	1st	10.30am	The bearer division under Capt D. Mackie Raine with 7 wheel-stretcher carriage, 3 horse ambulance waggons, light Cart, water cart, + 2 motor ambulances left to report to O.C. 22nd F.A.	A.H.B
		1pm	Took over the B.R.S at the HOSPICE, METEREN.	
	2nd		During last night several air-bombs were dropped near the village 4 dead + 8 wounded of 1st OXR were brought into the Rest Station	A.H.B
	3rd	5pm	Capts BUCKLEY & GARDINER reported from 41 CCS.	
		7pm	Capt STORDY with a tent-subdivision reported from 2 Au. CCS.	A.H.B
		9pm	Received orders from ADMS to march to M 6.a.8.8. (Sheet 28) on relief there by a holding party of a F.A. of 23rd Divn.	
	4th		Capt MOIR Raine to 21st F.A. for temporary duty at M.D.S. at EOLE BIENFAISANCE on YPRES-MENIN ROAD Handed over to holding party of 71st F.A. during late afternoon.	A.H.B
CHIPPEWA CAMP	5th	10am	The Unit marched to CHIPPEWA CAMP (M6.a.8.8) doubling up there with 32nd F.A. Capts BUCKLEY + GARDINER to 21st FA. M.D.S for temporary duty Capt MACKIE reported in evening for rest + sleep.	A.H.B

Army Form C. 2118.

WAR DIARY
or
INTELLIGENCE SUMMARY
(Erase heading not required.)

Instructions regarding War Diaries and Intelligence Summaries are contained in F. S. Regs., Part II. and the Staff Manual respectively. Title Pages will be prepared in manuscript.

Place	Date	Hour	Summary of Events and Information	Remarks and references to Appendices
CHIPPEWA CAMP.	6/10/17	11 A.M.	Having been asked by the A.D.M.S. if I could find more men as stretcher bearers, I sent up 32 men of the Tent Division to act as stretcher-bearers.	
		1 p.m.	Received orders to proceed myself to the ECOLE BIENFAISANCE, & to take over the forward area evacuation. Leaving there about 4 p.m., having been to see the A.D.M.S. for instructions — I gathered that a certain amount of reorganization was necessary. The unit was handed over to Capt. MACKIE R.A.M.C. The unit now consists of the remnant of the Tent Division & the transport. At dawn I proceeded forward to see what was wanted. Having gone over the evacuation line from the R.A.P.s at "THE BUTTE" to the M.D.S. (reorganizing the posts). The bearers were done up with want of rest. I submitted my scheme to the A.D.M.S. who approved of it. During the day I brought back all men who could be spared to rest. The condition of the bearers necessitates acceptance, so I asked for 200 Infantry as bearers. These relieved the bearers who were sent to rest for a night.	G.H.B
	7th			
	8th			
	9th		An attack was made by the 7th Div. which was successful. Every available man was sent up to act as a bearer, being so far back I transferred my H.Q. to the CRATER at HOOGE. The enemy was very liberal in barrages during the day, serious hampered own evacuation.	G. H. Brown

2449 Wt. W14957/M90 750,000 1/16 J.B.C. & A. Forms/C.2118/12.

Army Form C. 2118.

WAR DIARY
or
INTELLIGENCE SUMMARY
(Erase heading not required.)

Place	Date	Hour	Summary of Events and Information	Remarks and references to Appendices
HOOGE CRATER.	10/5		The Infantry were Splinters with the work, to I applied through 22nd Bay N.Q. for a fresh 200 - These arrived in the afternoon. A block in the traffic on the main road stopped all Carts for 3½ hours in the forenoon & the CRATER became very congested for a time. At 1.30 p.m. a violent shelling of all roads began & then knots till 3 p.m. This further hampered the clearing, but by 4 p.m. all Cases had been got rid of. At 5 p.m. heavy shelling began again & the CRATER was hit repeatedly. Evacuation at night has now become impossible, on account of the darkness & the mud — Cases were therefore collected at the R.A.Ps. & Relay posts. At dawn, all cases were brought down & the R.A.Ps left clear. The Division has been relieved by the 23rd Divn., but I remained on to make sure that all our Cases were cleared. Owing to a hitch, part of the Infantry were not relieved & Carnally continues to come in. By 6 p.m. bearers of the 70th & 71st (23rd Div) went up the line & part of my men were relieved — the Infantry were stamming to their units.	[635 A.O.]
	11/5			
	12/5		At dawn, the relief of all posts has been completed & the line being clear, I returned to my unit, which had been moved near HESKIN.	

WAR DIARY
or
INTELLIGENCE SUMMARY

Army Form C. 2118.

Place	Date	Hour	Summary of Events and Information	Remarks and references to Appendices
CONQUEROR CAMP. M.2.d.8.2 (Sh 28)	13th		The unit is under canvas on a very wet & muddy site 4 O.R. + 2 motor ambulances sent to GODEWAERSVELDE by order of ADMS	A/HB
	14th to 20th		Capt STORDY to m/c of D.H.Q. at BERTHEN. GARDINER to 2/Border vice Capt ALLAN - sick. MOIR to 9/Gordons " Paulthorpe on leave " Gordons " " The unit remained in rest. The weather has been cold & wet. On 20th I received orders to take over from ADMS as a temporary measure & become A/DMS of the Division	A/HB
	20th	2pm	Handed over the unit to CAPT BUCKLEY RAMC & proceeded to Div. H.Q. Casualties during recent operations have been Killed 9, wounded 24. Missing believed killed 2.	Lieut. Col. A/HB
	21st		9hr in Longues Camp. Capt T.P. COLE R.A.M.C. reported to the ambulance for duty from the base	Col. B
	22nd		Received R.A.M.C. operation orders No 33 & 34. In the afternoon visited and dined round to M.B.S. ambulances	Col. B

WAR DIARY
or
INTELLIGENCE SUMMARY

(Erase heading not required.)

Army Form C. 2118.

Place	Date	Hour	Summary of Events and Information	Remarks and references to Appendices
	23rd		Completed arrangements for moving the following day.	C.W.S.
	24th		Moved at 8.15 a.m. from Engineers Camp and took over the M.D.S. at Vermezeele. He advance station consisted of three cellars. Three cellars for stretcher cases and two for remaining wounded. Three dressing tables were set up at the same time, and there was accommodation for twenty stretcher cases in the waiting room. Capt. MARR R.A.M.C., 1st LIEUT WILLIAMS and 1st LIEUT VANCE M.O.R.C. U.S.A. reported for duty being temporarily attached from 21st & 22nd Amb. CAPT CAMERON R.A.M.C. and 20 O.R. reported from 22nd F. Amb.	
	25th		At M.D.S. Vermezeele. Received orders that the 7th Div. were going to attack at 5.30 a.m. on the following morning.	
	26th		The attack by the 7th Division started about 6.45 a.m. At first a large number of walking wounded but practically no wounded lying cases were received.	

WAR DIARY
or
INTELLIGENCE SUMMARY

Army Form C. 2118.

Place	Date	Hour	Summary of Events and Information	Remarks and references to Appendices
			At the commencement I had at my disposal in the evacuation of the M.D.S. 15 M.A.C. motor ambulances and 3 lorries. At 10 O'Clock these were increased to 3 lorries and 28 M.A.C. cars. There was no congestion at the M.D.S. the lorries and M.A.C. cars being easily able to cope with the numbers. By 5 p.m. about 700 cases had passed through the M.D.S.	
	27		Shell at Vormezeele caused one case in at evacuating intermed.	C913
	28		CAPT. MOLT RAMC returned to the unit CAPT PALTHORPE leaving returned from leave. Received orders that the M.D.S. was being taken over on the following day by the 132nd Field Ambulance 39th Division and that the 28th Oct took Great Ops. Warner — to proceed to Scottish Wood.	C933
	29		We are relieved by the M.D.S. by 132 = T.O. front and proceeded with the unit to billets in Scottish Wood.	

Army Form C. 2118.

WAR DIARY
or
INTELLIGENCE SUMMARY
(Erase heading not required.)

Instructions regarding War Diaries and Intelligence Summaries are contained in F. S. Regs., Part II. and the Staff Manual respectively. Title Pages will be prepared in manuscript.

Place	Date	Hour	Summary of Events and Information	Remarks and references to Appendices
	30th		CAPT STOTT of RAMC read a certificate lent ambulance proceeded by motor lorry to the VAN RESTANT to take over the OO.T.P.'s & officers' rear station. Received orders for move the remainder of the unit with the following day. The transport marched at 7 A.M. proceeding to the new area. At 1.30 PM 2nd Lieut DUDLEY BROWN & 9 O.R. moved on cycles to ETREUX & ETREUX also assumed CAPT MOIR RAMC He remained in charge of the unit at 5.10 p.m. Arrived at ETREUILLINGHEM at 9 P.M. and marched to new billets area C.20 & 9.3 (Sheet 36 A) 2nd LIEUT BROWN who took over charge of the unit. Resumed Command of unit	Corps 113
	31st		CAPT H.W. MOIR RAMC to 2/ R. Welsh Fusiliers for temporary duty	

Geo. H. Boisier Lt Col RAMC
O.C. 23rd FA

ITALY

COMMITTEE FOR THE
MEDICAL HISTORY OF THE WAR
Date   17 JAN.1918

No. 23. 7. a.

Army Form C. 2118.

WAR DIARY
or
INTELLIGENCE SUMMARY.
(Erase heading not required.)

NOVEMBER 1917

PART XXXV

Place	Date	Hour	Summary of Events and Information	Remarks and references to Appendices
MOULIN FONTAINE	2nd	10 pm	Recd. 20th Bde. orders directing the unit to move to RACQUINGHEM on 3rd inst.	
RACQUINGHEM	3rd	11 am	Marched at 11 a.m. reaching RACQUINGHEM. (B13.d Sh 36A) at 1 pm. A scattered billeting area with no hospital accommodation - One section billetted at B20.a.o.9 + 2 sections + Transport around REAUMONT (B19.a.) - Capt COLE RAMC to 23rd Div for duty vice Capt CRAIG RAMC to 7th Div from 23rd Div Capt GARDINER rejoined on completion of duty with 2/Border Regt Capt MACKIE with 4 OR + 2 Motor Ambulances rejoined from duty with Div Arty at DICKEBUSCH	G.H.Q
	4th		Went round the area with the Atons looking for a suitable place in which to keep sick - but could find nothing. All sick are evacuated to C.C.S	G.H.Q
	5th		1/Lt C.D. McKINNEY M.O.R.C. U.S.A reports for duty.	G.H.Q
	7th		Capt VAUGHAN RAMC reports for duty from a C.C.S. of 2nd Cav. Div.	G.H.Q
	8th		Capt C.D. Brakley to 8/Devons for temporary duty The unit took part today in a Divisional Parade which was inspected by H.M. The King of the Belgians - Received RA we O.O. No. 37. + 20 Inf Bde O.O. for move on 12th	G.H.Q

Army Form C. 2118.

WAR DIARY
or
INTELLIGENCE SUMMARY.
(Erase heading not required.)

Instructions regarding War Diaries and Intelligence Summaries are contained in F. S. Regs., Part II. and the Staff Manual respectively. Title pages will be prepared in manuscript.

Place	Date	Hour	Summary of Events and Information	Remarks and references to Appendices
RACQUINGHEM	11th		1/Lt. McKINNEY. M.O.R.C. U.S.A. to 33rd Div. - Relieves by Capt HARWOOD R.A.M.C. from 33rd Div. - 20/B.O. N° 170 received - for march on 13th, 14th & 15th.	GWB
OUVE WIRQUIN	12th	10.25 a.m.	The unit marched to OUVE WIRQUIN to billets arriving at 4 p.m.	
		6 p.m.	Under instructions from A.D.M.S. Capt D.G.GARDINER R.A.M.C. proceeds to 9th Devons for duty in relief of 1/Lt. PETIT. M.O.R.C. U.S.A. who reports to the Ambulance.	
		8 p.m.	Capt STORDY R.A.M.C. & Lieut. sub/Division rejoins from X Corps Officers Rest Station on relief by an ambulance of the 5th Div.	
			1/Lt. LLEWLLYN. R.A.M.C. reports for duty from 33rd Div. ¾ in relief of Lt. ¾ Q'M'r. GREGSON R.A.M.C. - The latter is to be sent sick - he has recently had all his teeth extracted, is not considered fit to proceed to Italy.	LytB
		10 p.m.	20/B.O. N° 170 - Cancelled. The unit will not move now on 13th inst.	
	13th		Capt MILLER R.A.M.C. reported to me at 1.15 a.m. from 24th F.A. (6th Div.) & is now posted to 23rd F.A. for duty.	
		2 p.m.	1/Lt. PETIT M.O.R.C. U.S.A. proceeds to 19th Div. for duty.	
			Received Administrative & Strategic Instructions for move of 7th Div. by Rail.	
		3 p.m.	Capt DOW R.A.M.C. reported for duty from 32nd Div.	
		6 p.m.	March table of B.O.170 for march tomorrow received.	

Army Form C. 2118.

WAR DIARY
or
INTELLIGENCE SUMMARY.
(Erase heading not required.)

Instructions regarding War Diaries and Intelligence Summaries are contained in F. S. Regs., Part II. and the Staff Manual respectively. Title pages will be prepared in manuscript.

Place	Date	Hour	Summary of Events and Information	Remarks and references to Appendices
FRUGES	14th	10.15 a.m.	The unit marched to billets in FRUGES arriving there at 2.15 p.m.	
			Lt. & M. G.G. GREGSON R.A.M.C. 23rd J.A. evacuated sick to CCS with "loss of teeth".	Appx 3
			Capt PATON R.A.M.C. attached temporarily to 23rd J.A. on 13th inst. evacuated sick to CCS " Chronic gastritis".	
ANVIN	15th	11.15 a.m.	The unit marched to billets in ANVIN arriving at 2.15 p.m.	
			Capt MILLER R.A.M.C. to 23rd J.A. Buckley — to 23rd J.A.	
			Capt MOIR R.A.M.C. rejoined from 1/R. Welsh Fus. on completion of duty.	Appx 8
	18th		"C Section" 23rd J.A. proceeded under Capt BUCKLEY R.A.M.C. to ARQUES to join 7th Div Art. The Transport proceeded by road, the personnel by train.	
			Under instructions from D.M.S. 2nd Army I handed over Command of 23rd J.A. this day to Capt E.W. VAUGHAN R.A.M.C. & report to 3rd ETAPLES (Cavalry) Squadron for duty.	Appx

Geo H Browne
Lt Col R.A.M.C.
O.C. 23rd Fd Amb.

Army Form C. 2118.

WAR DIARY
or
INTELLIGENCE SUMMARY.
(Erase heading not required.)

Instructions regarding War Diaries and Intelligence Summaries are contained in F. S. Regs., Part II. and the Staff Manual respectively. Title pages will be prepared in manuscript.

Place	Date	Hour	Summary of Events and Information	Remarks and references to Appendices
ANVIN	17th		STUDY TRAINING 2nd Bde Brigade commenced to entrain Capt Fraser R.A.M.C. with an N.C.O. and nursing orderly equipped with two hammocks, medical comforts and blankets accompany to HONIGCAMP SKETLEW and thence with Brigade H.Q.	
[of] [of] LENS 1/100,000			A.D.M.S. instructions, proceeded to the first drawn with Brigade H.Q. to act as veterinary officer Rev MacKenzie C.F. reported from leave. The new Brunch C.O. arrived too late the place of [Rev] Thomas went of medical who Controls M Matthews established at entraining station where Capt MOIR R.A.M.C. — Capt C. FISCHER R.A.M.C. returned to duty from the Base[?]-HOURS) IK. Reserve took tropical leave and was relieved by Entrained Comforts NCO, the Nursing orderly and team in what this was medical comforts & Netaria Capt MACKEY [accompanies] each team is [Netaria] medical officer — Capt MOIR-R.A.M.C. proceeded with I Netaria Capt MOIR-R.A.M.C. proceeded with I Netaria R.A.M.C. returned from leave The new part was arrived to relieve [his] re-sal with the Rainbow cake arrived on train carrying ½ Battalion Capt FISCHER took a sub veterinary officer. Entraining continued.	cat cat
	18th			E.D
	19th			cat
	20th	11.12am	A & B sector's entrained today in train no 260 at 11:12am all brought has a [entraining] station 3 hours before them and personal 1 hour [trainway] took place just afterwards — 2 Company's practice gun toys entrained with us, including also 4 officers of 16 B.R. Devon Regt returning from leave. Received instructions for O. train & rations necessary orders, also received list of halts.	FDD EntQ(?)

A5834 Wt.W4973/M687 750,000 8/16 D. D. & L. Ltd. Forms/C.2118/13.

Army Form C. 2118.

WAR DIARY
or
INTELLIGENCE SUMMARY.
(Erase heading not required.)

Instructions regarding War Diaries and Intelligence Summaries are contained in F. S. Regs., Part II. and the Staff Manual respectively. Title pages will be prepared in manuscript.

Place	Date	Hour	Summary of Events and Information	Remarks and references to Appendices
In the train	21st		Passed through TROYES and DIJON. Train already behind time with the second part	
			Halts were never more than 30 minutes	
	22nd		Passed LYONS.	
	23rd		Arrived MARSEILLE, left at 6 p.m.	
	24th		Pass through NICE & MONACO and arrived at VINTIMILLE midday.	
	25th		Arrived PIACENZA & received instructions to detrain at CEREA.	
	26th		Reached MANTOVA after many long halts and left for [? the evening].	
	27th	4 a.m.	Reached CEREA and commenced detraining, detraining officer gave no instructions to proceed to LEGNAGO. Marched there and obtained billets after some delay. At midday communication with a.D.T.S. and received orders to march to NOVENTA the following day and billet there.	
LEGNAGO				
Col near FERRARA 200,000				
NOVENTA	28th	9 a.m.	Started off at 9 a.m. and arrived at NOVENTA 4 p.m. Good billets — orders to march to	
			following day to BOSCO DI NANTI.	
FERRARA?				
70,000				
BUSCO DI NANTI	29th	9.30 p.m.	Left NOVENTA 9.30 a.m. arrived BOSCO DI NANTI at 3 p.m. — 21 Kilometres. Here we join up again with the 20th Brigade whose headquarters were in the village. Visited by G.O.C.	
61 Inf.				
PADOVA				CAMPO SANMARTINO
10,000				
CAMPO	30th		Marched with Brigade from BOSCO DI NANTI to billets at CAMPO, left at 9.30 a.m. arrived at 5.30 p.m. — Length of march 21 Kilometres.	
Inf. Divl. PADOVA				
100,000				

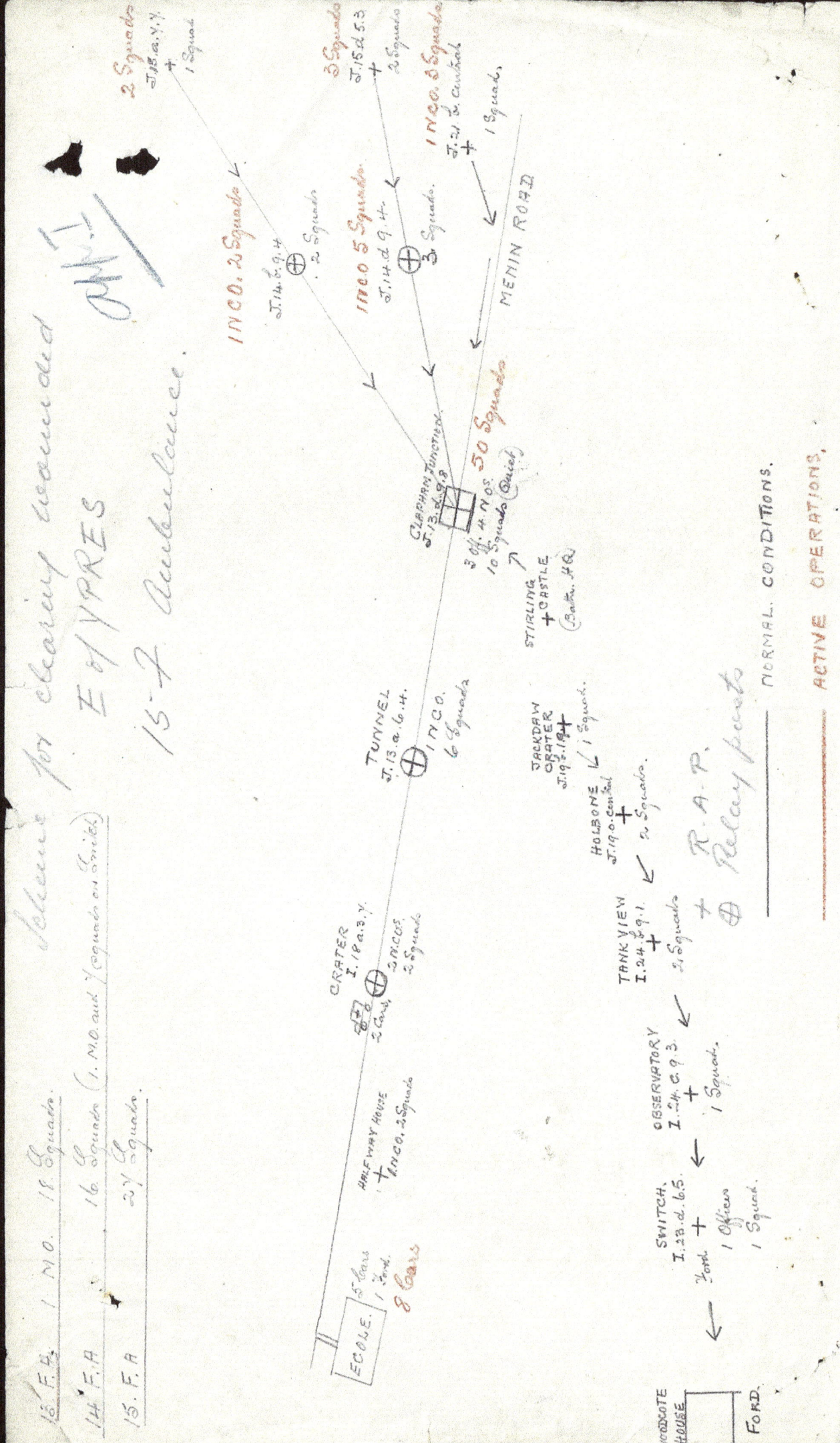